Rethinking university teaching

Teachers in higher education are slowly accepting the fact that they have to become more professional in their approach to teaching, matching their professionalism in research. The notions of quality audit and teacher appraisal are new, and in their existing forms ill-founded, but they represent a challenge that teachers will have to face. The book aims to prepare them for this: both to contribute towards a well-founded implementation of quality audits and appraisal, and to achieve their personal aims of improving their teaching and students' learning. There is also a growing recognition that the technological media have the potential to improve student learning, or at least teaching efficiency, and university teachers are looking for ways of increasing their understanding of what can be done with the new media, and how to do it. This book will inform them about what has been done and what is already known, helping them to think constructively and critically, and building towards a practical methodology for the design, development and implementation of educational technologies. Part I explores students' learning, and what it is that they need from educational technology; Part II looks at individual teaching methods and media, including non-interactive media (lectures, print, audio), hypermedia (CD-ROM), and interactive media (simulations, modelling programs); and Part III discusses design methodology, designing learning activities, setting up the learning context and maintaining quality.

Diana Laurillard is Senior Lecturer at the Institute of Educational Technology at the Open University.

Rethinking university teaching

A framework for the effective use of educational technology

Diana Laurillard

London and New York

First published 1993
by Routledge
11 New Fetter Lane, London EC4P 4EE

Simultaneously published in the USA and Canada
by Routledge
29 West 35th Street, New York, NY 10001

Reprinted 1994 and 1995

Typeset in Baskerville by
NWL Editorial Services, Langport, Somerset
Printed and bound in Great Britain by
TJ Press (Padstow) Ltd, Padstow, Cornwall

British Library Cataloguing in Publication Data
A catalogue record for this book is available from the British Library

Library of Congress Cataloguing in Publication Data
A catalogue record for this book is available from the
Library of Congress

ISBN 0-415-09288-4 (hbk)
ISBN 0-415-09289-2 (pbk)

Contents

Figures

Tables

Acknowledgements

The book was planned and written during study leave from the Open University, while I held a Visiting Fellowship at the Institute of Education, University of London. I am grateful to both organisations for their support.

I would like to thank the following people for their helpful and insightful comments on early versions of chapters: Lorraine Baric, John Brennan, David Clark, Ben du Boulay, Nicola Durbridge, Noel Entwistle, Simon French, Roger Hartley, David Hawkridge, Elaine Martin, Rod Moyse, Dagmar Neuman, Paul Ramsden, Royston Sellman, John Self, Josie Taylor, David Warren Piper. I have drawn many times on the work of my colleagues at the Institute of Educational Technology, in the faculties and in the OU/BBC Production Centre, and have returned again and again to the works of both Ference Marton and Gordon Pask as the original inspiration for the ideas developed here. Of course, none of these people can be held responsible for any infelicities in the book.

Finally, my affectionate thanks to Brian Butterworth for his constant support, and to our children, Amy and Anna, for their philosophical acceptance of the occasional lapses in my total and immediate obedience to their wishes.

Introduction

My first lecture as a student was a wretched experience. With 199 other students I counted myself lucky that I was in the main lecture theatre and not in the overspill room receiving closed circuit television. The lecturer was talking formulae as he came in, and for fifty minutes he scribbled them on the board as he talked and we all scribbled more in a desperate attempt to keep up with his dictation.

My first lecture as a teacher was no better. For this group I had been given a syllabus listing thirty or so topics, and a timetable of three lectures a week. Fresh from finals and desperate not to bore the seventy-odd engineering students with the trivia of introductory complex analysis I prepared reams of notes from several textbooks and my own scribbled lecture notes, entered the room talking formulae, and scribbled them on the board as I went.

One lucky thing happened. At the end of the lecture I asked if there were any questions, and one brave student asked a question of such breathtaking 'stupidity' that it was clear he could not have understood anything beyond my first sentence. Did anyone else have that problem? Yes, they all had that problem. I learned a lot more than they did from that lecture. Their stupidity or mine? Who has the greater responsibility for that situation?

This book starts from the premise that university teachers must take the main responsibility for what and how their students learn. Students have only limited choices in how they learn: they can attend lectures or not; they can work hard or not; they can seek truth or better marks – but teachers create the choices open to them. The students in my lecture could only choose to concentrate hard, they could not choose to understand. It is the teacher's responsibility to create the conditions in which understanding is possible, and the student's responsibility is to take advantage of that. Students have little control over their access to knowledge. The university operates a complex system of departments, curricula, teaching methods, support facilities, timetables, assessment – all of which determine the possible ways in which students may learn. Our responsibility as teachers is commensurate with the degree of control we exert on the learners.

It would be quite possible to argue that students should take responsibility for their own learning, where they use the university as a set of resources largely under their control. This is the most attractive vision of academic learning – that of a community of scholars pursuing their own course towards knowledge and enlightenment, inspired but not directed by their teachers. Universities still aspire to this at post-graduate level, and at its best this model is indeed attractive and highly productive. It is essentially a minority provision, however. To support students properly in their own exploration of what is known in a field, where its frontiers are, and how they might be extended, is extremely costly in staff time. Guidance is a labour intensive process, which means that any one academic can only service a small number of students. Assessment is also labour intensive, as each case must be judged on its own merit, not in terms of a pre-defined 'model answer'. And working at the frontiers of knowledge is essentially a lonely task done by individuals and very small groups, not amenable to any form of mass education or support. That is the proper model of post-graduate education, but that is where it must be confined. At undergraduate level, students are exploring an already known field of knowledge; they are explicitly not breaking new ground, except at a personal level. Although it is often argued that in university education we should encourage students to develop their own point of view within a subject, to be critical and not accept spoon-feeding, we none the less expect right answers. It is perfectly permissible to criticise an authority's argument, but students must give an accurate account of it, and their critique must be well-argued. No matter how democratic we are about respecting the student's point of view, there is always a pre-defined standard of answer. That is why our model of education at undergraduate level is more often didactic than negotiated, teaching methods are many–one rather than one–one, and we control rather than offer resources. And that is why as teachers we have the major responsibility for what and how our students learn.

So are students just puppets, dancing to the tunes of their various teachers, helplessly buffeted by the forces around them? This is a model that university teachers strongly resist, remembering, perhaps their own heightened sense of personal responsibility for what they learned, and anxious to preserve the joy of exploration and discovery for their own students. We particularly value those students who, in Bruner's phrase, go 'beyond the information given'. Yet the individual learner's sense of breaking new ground makes learning something personal, peculiar to that individual, and therefore not so amenable to the mass treatment that a didactic education system tends to adopt. This is the paradox that challenges the teaching profession: we want all our students to learn the same thing, yet we want each to make it their own.

As teachers relating to individual students it is possible to adopt and live by the values of a community of scholars, and that can be a common experience of post-graduate teaching. But at undergraduate level, while teaching and assessing *en masse*, teachers are as embedded in a system they cannot fully control as their students. My first lecture may have been worse than most – it does not have to be that bad – but it brought home to me the farcical nature of the system I was caught up in. Consider what the lecturer, meeting a class for the first time, has to do: the lecturer must guide this collection of individuals through territory the students are unfamiliar with, towards a common meeting point, but without knowing where they are starting from, how much baggage they are carrying, and what kind of vehicle they are using. This is insanity. It is truly a miracle, and a tribute to human ingenuity, that any student ever learns anything worthwhile in such a system.

The academic system must change. It works to some extent, but not well enough. And as higher education expands we cannot always rely on human ingenuity to overcome its inadequacies. It is always possible to defend the inspirational lecturer, the importance of academic individuality, the value of pressurising students to work independently, but we cannot defend a mode of operation that actively undermines a professional approach to teaching. Teachers need to know more than just their subject. They need to know the ways it can come to be understood, the ways it can be misunderstood, what counts as understanding: they need to know how individuals experience the subject. But they are neither required nor enabled to know these things. Moreover, our system of mass lectures and examinations ensures that they will never find them out.

Higher education cannot change easily. Traditions, values, infrastructure all create the conditions for a natural inertia. It is being forced to change, and the pressures being brought to bear have nothing to do with traditions and values. Instead, the pressure is for financial input to go down, and some measurable output to go up. This means that academics are facing an unprecedented challenge to the traditions and values of the profession. There is an appetite for reform from within higher education in many countries now, but it moves slowly as we all scurry about in response to the increasing external pressures which exercise their own peculiar forms of change. Academics are going on courses on management training and marketing methods. Reform of an education system might be better served if they went on courses on how to teach better.

Higher education should be reformed through pressure from within. Academics share some important traditions, some of which should be preserved: the pursuit of research and scholarship (OECD 1987), the advancement of learning (Robbins 1963), the freedom to conduct a radical critique of knowledge claims (Barnett 1990). Academic values, not accountancy, should guide the direction of reform, albeit within the requirements of financial probity. We need to rebuild the infrastructure that will find the fit between the academic values we wish to preserve and the new conditions of educating larger numbers.

I see the solution as being found in a new organisational infrastructure, not in guidelines on how to teach, in spite of my caustic comment above. It is not as though there is a body of knowledge out there on how to teach thermodynamics, as there is on how to cure headaches. Given that the human mind is probably at least as complicated as the human body, it will be a long time before we understand the many ways in which it can fail. The time, energy and money spent on medical science will never be spent on instructional science, so the outlook for knowing very much about how to teach is bleak. But we can at least take the right approach to the task. The organisational infrastructure will be a series of mechanisms, tasks, responsibilities that together ensure a benign process, one that will be progressive, in much the same way as research methodology aims to ensure that knowledge progresses. Methodology is generative and ultimately more productive than prescriptive guidelines. We may have only limited knowledge of how to teach well, but at least we can use a productive methodology that helps us build our knowledge.

This book discusses how to think about teaching. It works towards an analysis in the final chapter of what the infrastructure of higher education should be if the effectiveness of teaching and therefore the quality of student learning is to improve and go on improving. This final chapter attempts to describe the structures and mechanisms constituting a system that would not have the farcical effects we experience as students and later as teachers, but would support both sides in an approach to teaching and learning that fits the academic values we proclaim. The idea is to find an infrastructure that enables university teachers to be as professional in their teaching as they try to be in their research.

The chapters in Part I build up to this. Each one takes an aspect of teaching and learning that the professional teacher needs to know about, and gives a critical account of the key studies in the research literature to establish both what we know and how it comes to be known. Methodology plays a part all the way through, therefore, as this will inform our approach to the task of teaching. The argument begins in Chapter 1 with an exploration of the nature of academic learning. University teachers have a rich but largely unarticulated experience of what it means to learn their subject. In this first chapter I attempt to tap that experience and develop a description of it that will provide the basis for motivating the rest of the book. The central idea is that academic learning is different from other kinds of learning in everyday life because it is not directly experienced, and is necessarily mediated by the teacher. Undergraduates are not learning about the world directly, but about others' descriptions of the world, hence the term 'mediated'. This view is developed from and contrasted with other prominent views on the nature of learning in the current literature, and raises the question of how teachers are to perform this mediating role.

Chapters 2 and 3 address the issues I referred to in my partial analogy of teacher as travel guide, as needing to know what students bring to their learning and how they do it. Here, the sum total of what we know is negligible in comparison with what there is to know. This is not because every student is individual and infinitely variable, but because there is so much for them to know, and so many ways it can be known. The research literature tells us enough about a few key concepts in certain subject areas that it becomes clear that the ways a concept can be understood is an empirical question, not a logical one. As we shall see in Chapter 2, we cannot deduce from the definition of a concept the range of misconceptions and partial conceptions students will exhibit. The research methodologies that produce these results are generalisable, however, and that will enable us in later chapters to look at how this kind of knowledge base can be extended. Chapter 3 moves away from students' epistemology into the even more uncertain area of trying to understand how they come by what they know. Here we are trying to see the learning process from their point of view, to see their ways of understanding not as wilful perversity but as something explicable and rational. These studies provide the basis we need for thinking about how to teach.

By Chapter 4, we return to more familiar territory for the teacher, but having looked in some detail at the inner life of the learner, we should be in a better position to see the implications of this for how we might generate teaching strategies. There is a long tradition of instructional design, particularly in the USA, and there are current contrasting theories of instruction; Chapter 4 will critically analyse and draw on some of the principal ones. At this stage of the book the problem is still being treated analytically. I do not wish to suggest that teaching is a science that can determine precisely how a topic should be taught, and in later chapters I will come to the creative side of designing teaching. But first I think it is possible, given the grounding from Chapters 2 and 3, to take an analytical approach to the relationship between the curriculum-defined goals of teaching, the specification of the learning activities students must therefore carry out, and the forms of assessment appropriate to these goals and activities.

So far there is nothing in the argument that implicates the use of any particular teaching method or medium. Chapter 4 led us towards thinking about how to specify appropriate learning activities for students, which raises the question of how these are to be facilitated. Up to this point the idea of teaching as mediating between the world and the learner has been used to define a particular way of viewing the teaching–learning process, which opens up access to some interesting research findings, and a more elaborated description of the role of the teacher. Now we come to the practicalities of what it means to mediate, and the ways it can be accomplished via educational media. Teachers are familiar with the particular kinds of teaching method that constitute their contact hours – lectures, seminars, tutorials, etc. – and they will be aware of a range of educational media – print, audio-visual, computer-assisted learning, teleconferencing. Part II begins by describing an analytical framework for classifying these media. It is based on the specification developed at the end of Part I for the kinds of activities the media must foster if all aspects of the learning process are to be supported. In Chapters 5 to 9, we look at the complexity of defining these various educational media, not from the point of view of their apparent characteristics, which is the standard approach of books on educational media, but through research and evaluation studies which have investigated how students use them. Studies of this type, together with the analytical framework, allow us to develop a comparative description of what the various media can contribute to learning.

Part III is more practical. It is the task of Chapter 10 to create the link between the media and methods described in Part II and the analysis of learning activities arrived at in Part I. The relationship is a complex one. It is a sad fact of research and development funding in educational technology that the focus is always on a particular medium or method. Vast sums are made available to investigate the best way of using computers, where the subject matter taught is incidental. The more rational approach, seldom adopted, is to offer vast sums to investigate the best way of teaching a particular topic, and through that to fund the use of computers as an incidental part of the strategy. As a result of irrational funding we have studies that tell us that computers, video, etc. can be effective and can also fail utterly, but we have very little idea of how they might work in combination, or how design relates to the content being taught. The best we can do in this chapter, therefore, is to use the analysis of the learning activities students will need for a given topic, as developed in Part I, and use the strengths and limitations of the educational media defined in Part II, and from this deduce how they might be selected and combined to facilitate the learning activities needed. The details of this analysis are different for every topic, of course, so the aim is to describe the design process in general terms, and illustrate its application to specific content.

The most brilliantly designed educational materials can fail completely if the same care is not given to the way they are used.

Research and development projects on educational media pay quantities of hard cash for development, lip-service to evaluation, and no attention to implementation. There is never enough cash to equip a decent programme of piloting, dissemination, and staff training that would be needed properly to establish an innovation. Development projects of this kind trust to luck and the dedication of enthusiasts to carry them through. That is how educational technology has progressed as far as it has done, but it cannot achieve its potential this way. In Chapter 11 we look at what it means to use educational technology as a fully integrated part of everyday academic life. It is important from the students' point of view, because they respond primarily to the institutional context and its demands, so these must be congruent with the demands of the technology. It is also important for the teachers, who are no less subject to the institution's demands. And it is important for making the best use of what investment there is in educational technology. We can draw on evaluation studies of the implementation of new media, although they are few in number, and on studies of institutional contexts, and use these to define the aspects of institutional life that will tend to influence the success or failure of new technologies in use.

Implementation of a new medium or method cannot be expected to work perfectly, but probably provides some benefits along with its disadvantages. We need to learn the lessons of each implementation, and then use those lessons learned. In this way we slowly build a body of knowledge of how best to use educational media, and a teaching profession that knows what it is doing and why. Chapter 12 discusses how this might be done in practice, focusing on the organisation, and how teachers and students operate within it. The book does not offer 'how to do it' advice in the other chapters because I do not believe that teaching is a normative science. It is not possible to specify the pre-conditions that would make prescriptive advice, other than of the most bland and general sort, likely to be effective. My strategy, therefore, is to offer a way of thinking about teaching and the introduction of media that is informed by a more elaborated understanding of what students do when they learn. The assumption here is that when teachers think differently, they can act differently. Thinking differently is not a sufficient condition for acting differently, however. It is half the battle, but only half – we must also be enabled to act differently. That depends on the institutional context in which we operate being constructed so that it affords and encourages the actions prompted by analysis. For that reason, the final chapter turns to 'how to do it', not at the level of teaching, but at the level of defining a 'blueprint' for an organisational infrastructure that enables good teaching to be done.

Each individual has a certain locus of control within their own institution, ranging from students, who can control little more than their own actions, to vice chancellors who can aspire to control the actions of most staff and students, and, more importantly, committees. In this chapter we have to address the full context within which the professional teacher is operating if we are to make the best attempt at an effective infrastructure. The analysis does not stop at the level of institution, of course. Academic institutions are no longer autonomous. They are highly dependent on government, and they exist as part of a national and international network. The individual has little control, it is true, beyond the institution, but as professional teachers we all have a responsibility to understand and improve the system we operate within, and our responsibility goes beyond the institution we work for. In any case, to create change for improvement within an institution requires an understanding of its role in relation to others, and that is why I believe it is worth attempting to take the argument to this very wide context.

The book ends, then, with a suggestion for how higher education should operate – a prescription for enabling the effective use of media in teaching. Institutions operate within national boundaries, so it is right to consider the national contexts within which these changes are to be made. But education as an ideal does not recognise national boundaries. A sense of nation has no place in the sense of vocation that an academic feels in wanting others to experience the delight of a true under-standing of their subject. We have to recognise national and cultural differences for the part they play in the logistics of imple-mentation but, at the level of affording understanding of a subject, all academics come together in a common purpose, and that is why finally the international context seems the only suitable place to stop the analysis.

There is a boundary to all this, however. This is not a blueprint for government. It is the task of professional educators to change education, not politicians. The book ends with a blueprint for an

academic system as the logical conclusion from its premise that
university teachers must take responsibility for what and how
their students learn.

Part I

What students need from educational technology

Chapter 1

Teaching as mediating learning

INTRODUCTION

What we believe to be of practical help to lecturers depends upon what we think the aim of teaching is, so the greater part of this chapter is concerned with clarifying this basic issue. If you believe that teaching is about imparting knowledge, then the main requirement of the lecturer is that they should possess that knowledge in the first place. This used to be the prevailing view of university teaching, which is why academics are appointed on the basis of qualifications in subject matter knowledge. There is probably also an implicit requirement that they should be capable of imparting the knowledge as well as knowing it, but since this is done through lectures, and they can all talk, the requirement has not been dignified with any sort of qualification. For this model of the nature of teaching the practical help would consist entirely of increasing subject matter knowledge.

Of course, 'imparting knowledge' does not succeed as a teaching aim, as many essays and examination papers testify. Academics have always been well aware of this, but while higher education was an élitist enterprise it was possible to make this failure the responsibility of the student, reified in the 'fail' grade. This is not now the prevailing view – 'The aim of teaching is simple: it is to make student learning possible' (Ramsden 1992: 5). As higher education has become less élitist, and has taken on the task of educating anyone who wishes to pursue their studies, many institutions of higher education have developed an approach to teaching that comes much closer to this more ambitious aim. However, although changes in approach are important, changes in practice will make the real difference to students, and we are still a long way from defining and requiring professional practice for university teachers (Warren Piper 1992).

What might that professional practice be? If it is not simply imparting knowledge, what is it? 'Making student learning possible' places much more responsibility with the teacher. It implies that the teacher must know something about student learning, and about what makes it possible. This is what I have characterised as 'mediating learning', and since this is the idea that motivates the approach taken in the remainder of the book, I should begin by explaining it. An analysis of the nature of academic learning of the kind done by students at university level should reveal what 'making student learning possible' means.

THE CHARACTER OF ACADEMIC LEARNING

There is no professional training requirement for university teachers as far as their teaching is concerned and, possibly for this reason, there is comparatively little research on student learning at university level. Of the many books and journals concerned with teaching, the ratio of those at university level to those at school level is way below the ratio of teachers or the ratio of students at the two levels. Advice to university teachers has to draw on other fields to supplement the meagre information we have from direct research. The research that underpins any such advice could be based on school students, or even non-academic learning, so as this book is directed specifically at university teaching it is worth deciding what kind of transformation has to be wrought on this data to make it applicable in a different context. Is learning at university different from learning at school, or learning outside formal education?

Academics have ambitious definitions for student learning. When asked to define the nature of learning in their subject area they produce descriptions of high-level thinking, such as 'critically assessing the arguments', 'compiling patterns to integrate their knowledge', 'becoming aware of the limitations of theoretical knowledge in the transfer of theory to practice', 'coming to accept relativism as a positive position'.[1] Course descriptions and syllabuses inevitably tend to focus on the subject content that students will be learning, but clearly, in reflecting on what it is really about, academics are fascinated by the process itself. They see learning not simply as a product, but as a series of activities.

How students approach their subject is as important to them as what they end up knowing. If you listen to the way academics talk in an examiners' meeting, this becomes clear. Missing out some key points will be forgiven if the argument is good; high praise is offered not just for accuracy, but more often for evidence of integrating lectures with background reading; accuracy is the *sine qua non*, perhaps, but more is needed. So student learning is not just about acquiring high level knowledge. The way students handle that knowledge is what really concerns academics, as the above quotes imply.

If academic learning is not just about acquiring knowledge, is it really different from the acquisition of everyday knowledge? We learn a great deal about the world very successfully outside academic institutions, with no help from any didactic process. The tradition of pedagogy that stretches back to Dewey's rejection of the classical tradition of passing on knowledge in the form of unchangeable ideas, has always argued for the active engagement of the learner in the formation of their ideas. More recent exponents of the latter tradition are Vygotsky, Piaget, Bruner, all of whom argue for the active engagement of the learner rather than the passive reception of given knowledge. These psychologists have had an effect in schools, especially at primary level, but in universities, with their continued reliance on lectures and textbooks, the classical tradition of 'imparting knowledge' still flourishes.

The idea of academic knowledge as an abstract Platonic form is not yet dead; it has had a new impetus from the development of information processing models of cognition, which use the metaphor of knowledge structures, or conceptual structures to describe mentalistic entities that can be changed through instruction, or even represented in a computer program. Computational models of cognition now form the mainstream of cognitive psychology. Lecturers are likely to be attracted by the idea of a conceptual structure as a stable and well-defined entity abstracted from the contexts in which the concept was experienced. The notion sits well with the ideal of classical knowledge, or the modern 'discipline' knowledge. However, it does not address the reality that all teachers surely recognise – that students do not transfer their knowledge across different settings, that there is a problem in relating theory to practice, i.e. that knowledge does seem to be context-related. Perhaps some ideal final product could be represented as a knowledge structure, but learning is more realistically seen as an activity and knowledge as an aspect of that activity, and therefore not easily abstracted from it. Academics need a description of academic knowledge that goes beyond the stable mental model.

The next section presents a recent critique of the classical tradition and its emphasis on decontextualising knowledge. This is followed by a critique of the critique, and the chapter ends with a synthesis of what I take to be the essential character of academic learning that provides the basis for discussion in the rest of the book.

A CRITIQUE OF ACADEMIC LEARNING AS IMPARTED KNOWLEDGE

The current interest in the idea of 'situated learning' expresses dissatisfaction with the computational models of mainstream cognitive psychology. The origins of this approach are completely different as they lie in ethnographic studies and the Vygotskyan theory of the social character of learning. The idea is to recognise that learning must be situated, in the sense that the learner is located in a situation and what is known from that experience is known in relation to the particular context:

> Situations might be said to co-produce knowledge through activity. Learning and cognition, it is now argued, are fundamentally situated.
>
> (Brown, Collins and Duguid 1989a: 32)

This is a rather surprising idea in the context of academic knowledge, the whole point of which is normally seen as being to transcend the particular, and thereby abstract from the physical and social context, precisely in order that the knowledge may be transformed into something more generalisable. The supposition is that this process empowers the individual to do more with this knowledge than they could if it remained situated. The revolt against the purely mentalistic computational models of learning has brought us to another extreme that appears equally far away from what academics feel they need. Interestingly, some of the key people in this field were formerly at the forefront of the computational paradigm (for example, James Greeno, Allan Collins and John Seely Brown). They have spent a long time thinking hard and doing a prodigious amount of research on learning, so this axial turn in their conceptualisation of learning is interesting. The article published in *Educational Researcher* by Brown, Collins and Duguid (1989a) provides a well-articulated statement of the position, and bases it on several research studies of learning. The article also has the benefit of further discussion through critiques from others and a reply by the authors, making it a good focus for our analysis. We need to go through the arguments in some detail rather than as a general summary, as that is the best way to see how the perspective defines learning, and what these ideas mean for the practising teacher. It is the detail that makes it easier for the lecturer to relate the broad generalities to their own subject.

The argument begins with a demonstration that knowledge has a contextualised character, which means that we cannot separate knowledge to be learned from the situations in which it is used. The idea of 'situated knowledge' invites the analogy of knowledge as tools:

> We should abandon once and for all any notion that a concept is some sort of abstract, self-contained substance. Instead, it may be more useful to consider conceptual knowledge as in some ways similar to a set of tools.
>
> (Ibid.: 5)

A corollary of this argument is that the acquisition of inert concepts (e.g. algorithms, routines, decontextualised definitions – i.e. the stuff of many university courses) is of no use if the student cannot apply them. The analogy the authors use for students having inert concepts is those people who have a Swiss Army knife with a device for getting stones out of horses' hooves: they can talk knowledgeably about it, but would not know what to do if they saw a limping horse. We have to be careful with analogies. Many engineering students have no idea how to do a Laplace transform within a week or so of passing finals, but knowing of its existence and its function they can reassemble the heuristic knowledge they need when necessary. They know about the device, and given a limping horse it is easy to look up the heuristics of 'removing stones' they once knew. However, academic knowledge is not just the heuristics of 'removing stones', or 'doing Laplace transforms'; it has a broader and deeper functionality than that. The far greater problem is that students can exhibit competence in doing

Laplace transforms without having any idea of when to use them or why. They are good at removing stones, but they cannot recognise a limping horse in the first place. The distinction is important. As Brown *et al.* argue, we have to use our knowledge in *authentic activity*, i.e. genuine application of the knowledge; this allows us to build an increasingly rich understanding of the tool itself and how it operates. The reason for unpacking the analogy is that many lecturers would argue that they do indeed give students the opportunity to do 'authentic activity': to understand Laplace transforms you have to do lots of examples of them and use them in different problems. This is common practice in every engineering course and has its parallel in every other kind of course. The problem arises from the scope of 'authentic', the degree of embeddedness in the social and physical world. We have to help students not just to perform the procedure, but also to stand back from that and see why it is necessary, where it fits and does not fit, distinguish situations where it is needed from those where it is not, i.e. carry out the authentic activities of the subject expert. But these remain implicit objectives in most course descriptions, and that implicitness persists all the way through to the activities we prescribe for students. So one conclusion we can draw is that learning must be situated in the domain of its objective. If you want students to be able to recognise a limping horse, you must situate their learning activity within that domain activity, not simply in the domain of removing stones. This is a point we shall return to again.

As a further example of the value of situating learning, rather than decontextualising it, Brown *et al.* (1989a) demonstrate the unity between problem, context and solution when the problem is experienced, rather than given. A weight-watcher was trying to serve the correct amount of cottage cheese, worked out as three-quarters of the two-thirds of a cup he was allowed. After muttering about his college calculus course, he suddenly brightened and, certain that he had found the solution, proceeded to dump two-thirds of a cup of cheese onto a board, flatten it into a circle, cut it in four and serve three of the quarters.

> This sort of problem solving is carried out in conjunction with the environment and is quite distinct from processing solely inside heads that many teaching practices implicitly endorse.
>
> (Ibid.: 35)

This example gives rise to consternation among academics because it looks as though the weight-watcher's achievement is valued as more important than the more abstract knowledge of calculus. But the example is only used to demonstrate the 'sense-making' nature of naturally embedded activities; the weight-watcher is not being applauded. The point is that if formal education provided more naturally embedded activities, students could do their own sense-making. They are arguing against the decontextualising of knowledge by teaching abstractions:

> Our argument is that to the degree that abstractions are not grounded in multiple contexts, they will not transfer well. After all, it is not learning the abstraction, but learning the appropriate circumstances in which to ground the abstraction that is difficult.
>
> (Brown, Collins and Duguid 1989b: 12)

There is a distinction made, therefore, between teaching abstractions and enabling students to learn abstractions from multiple contexts. The latter stands between the extreme of the weight-watcher's purely situated knowledge, which is clearly not academic, and the purely abstract, which academic knowledge is often thought to be. The implication is that academic learning should occupy the middle position of an activity that develops abstractions from multiple contexts.

A CRITIQUE OF ACADEMIC LEARNING AS SITUATED COGNITION

Teaching practices that encourage abstraction from experience do not have to subscribe to an epistemology that places knowledge 'solely inside heads'. It is legitimate and necessary for teaching to go beyond the specific experience, to abstract the symbolic representation that allows the learner to use their knowledge in an unfamiliar situation. Situated cognition is attractive in well-chosen situations, but one of the reasons that education has evolved the way it has over the centuries is that situated cognition is not enough. Suppose the weight-watcher were trying to work out his share of a discounted car hire with a couple of friends and had to figure out the logically equivalent problem of one-third of 5 per cent off the total cost? The unity between problem, context and solution is not quite so apparent here. The point of an academic education is that knowledge *has* to be abstracted, and represented formally, in order to become generalisable and therefore more generally useful. It then empowers people like the weight-watcher to deal with quantities of things other than cottage cheese.

But how can students be taught to acquire an abstraction without it being taught directly as an abstraction? Some of the illustrations of situated cognition come from real teachers, and demonstrate what most practising teachers know, that concepts need to be grounded in experience and practice before they can be abstracted. It is common pedagogical practice at all levels of education to start with concrete examples, or to provide illustrative examples of general principles, but the way this is done determines whether it works or not. Again, the only way we can see how the idea of situated cognition applies is to go through an example in detail, and analyse the extent to which it provides an adequate account of academic learning.

The teaching of multiplication may seem a rather elementary example to use as an illustration for university teaching, but it works well for two reasons: because it reveals some interesting aspects of what it means to acquire an abstraction from multiple contexts, and it is an abstraction that everyone is familiar with.

Multiplication does not have to be taught as an abstraction. Brown *et al.* describe the approach of a teacher whose method is to make mathematical exploration continuous with everyday knowledge, and to help the learners towards the abstract algorithm in the context of real world problems and the stories the group creates about them:

> Lampert helps her students explore their implicit knowledge. Then in the second phase, the students create stories for multiplication problems. They perform a series of decompositions and discover that there is no one magically 'right' decomposition decreed by authority, just more and less useful decompositions [e.g. $24 = 8 \times 3$ or 6×4], whose *use* is judged in the context of the problem to be solved.
> (Brown, Collins and Duguid 1989a: 38)

It is clear from this example that situated cognition in the context of education is not concerned simply with learning about the world, but with learning about a way of looking at the world. Look at the dialogue they are describing:

Teacher: Can anyone give me a story that could go with this multiplication . . . 12 × 4?

Student 1:   There were 12 jars and each had 4 butterflies in it.

Clearly the learner has already acquired a way of interpreting 12 × 4, and also the usage of language such as 'story' and 'go with this multiplication'. This is not everyday language, it is already academic language, describing the notion of interpreting a symbolism. The teacher then draws a picture to represent jars, and another to represent butterflies.

Teacher: Now it will be easier for us to count how many butterflies there are altogether if we think of the jars in groups. And as usual the mathematician's favourite number for thinking about groups is?

Student 2:   10.

Grouping in order to count is a fundamental aspect of the nature of multiplication, but the learners are not grounding this aspect of their knowledge in the activity: it is being handed on as a precept, as the best way to do this kind of task. The choice of decomposition is not theirs but the teacher's. The focus here is on different ways of decomposing:

Teacher: Is there any other way I could group them to make it easier to count all the butterflies?

Student 6:   You could do 6 and 6.

Teacher: Now how many do I have in this group [of six jars]?

Student 7:   24.

Teacher: How did you figure that out?

Student 7:   8 and 8 and 8. [*He puts the 6 jars into 3 pairs, intuitively finding a grouping that made the figuring easier for him.*]

Now a student has offered a different decomposition, and the teacher can use this to show that the total is still the same.

Teacher: That's 3 × 8. It's also 6 × 4. Now how many are in this group [the other group of six jars]?

Student 6:   24. It's the same. They both have 6 jars.

Teacher: And how many are there altogether?

Student 8:   24 and 24 is 48.

Teacher: Do we get the same number of butterflies as before? Why?

Student 8:   Yeah, because we have the same number of jars and they still have 4 butterflies in each.

This is not strictly speaking an example of students discovering 'that there is no one magically right decomposition'. They are being led through a reasoning process planned by the teacher. They are shown that whichever way you group the jars, the total is the same. In fact, the more accurate interpretation is that 'authority decrees that there is no one magically right decomposition' and that this is the idea the teacher is trying to get across. Brown and his colleagues are justified in using this to exemplify good teaching, because the teacher is clearly aiming to make the idea of decomposition meaningful, but there is no question that she is also requiring the students to think about this activity in a particular way. The situation is very carefully constructed to act as a benign environment for learning about an abstract description of the world. But this extract does not demonstrate that the students do think about the activity the way she requires, nor that they have yet abstracted this knowledge from the multiple contexts set up for them. It demonstrates that students can do their own sense-making in this naturally embedded activity, but does not demonstrate the process of abstraction that is essential for academic learning.

Using situated learning as a metaphor for academic learning is interesting and powerful as an idea, because it analyses successful learning to understand how that operates, and then transfers that analysis to the academic context to see how it should be applied there. The problem with the analogy is that the learner stands in a different relation to the content of what is learned in the two cases. Learning in naturalistic contexts is synergistic with the context; the learning outcome is an aspect of the situation, an aspect of the relation between learner, activity and environment, so it is learning about that world and how it works. Those naturalistic contexts afford learning through situated cognition.

On the other hand, learning in educational contexts requires learning about descriptions of the world, about a particular way of looking at the world. The learner cannot relate to a description or to someone else's perspective as they can to an object. The weight-watcher could deal with hundreds of piles of cottage cheese successfully and never abstract the principle of proportional reasoning needed to deal with the car-hire problem.

Academic learning requires him to take a different perspective on those activities, to generalise from them to obtain an abstraction, a description of the world that does not consist in doing the activity alone.

Brown and his colleagues argue that we have to recognise the situated character of learning, and use it to devise ways of constructing a situation that is benign with respect to what we want students to learn. That is what Ms Lampert does, and what their extract demonstrates very well. But the analysis does not go far enough for the purposes of academic knowledge because it also has to address how that process of abstraction is to be done by the student. Multiple contexts may be necessary but they are not sufficient. Those children could be taken through hundreds of benign examples by the teacher, but while the teacher does all the planning, hands out precepts, and asks the questions, the students can easily fail to engage actively with her way of thinking. We have to address how learners are to engage with knowledge derived from someone else's experience.

ACADEMIC LEARNING AS A WAY OF EXPERIENCING THE WORLD

Some years ago, I contributed to a debate about the relationship between psychology and education, and made a specific request to the psychologists:

> Our problem is that at present cognitive psychology produces generalized, not content-specific principles and theories of learning . . . A general principle that describes, for example the importance of active manipulation, or of relating new knowledge to existing knowledge, is no help because it does not clarify the logic of the relationship between the cognitive activity and the content to be learned. We need cognitive psychology to tell us, in a content-specific way, how a natural environment affords learning. Then, perhaps, we can construct the means of access that will turn an unnatural environment into one that affords learning.
>
> (Laurillard 1987a: 206)

The psychology of situated cognition does provide a content-specific account of how a natural environment affords learning. It is valuable because it sees learning as essentially situated, and as requiring a non-dualistic epistemology. Analyses of how natural environments afford learning are used to construct descriptions of how an academic environment can do so too. The work on situated cognition does not, however, illuminate the essential difference between academic knowledge and everyday knowledge, and I want to pursue that point a little further.

In that earlier debate I drew a distinction between natural environments which afford the learning of 'percepts' in everyday life, and unnatural environments which are constructed for learning 'precepts' in education. Situated cognition makes the same distinction in arguing that the one type of environment should emulate the other, but does not elaborate on the nature of the difference. I argued that learning precepts is different from learning percepts because our means of access to them are so limited:

> We cannot experience structuralism in the same way as we experience good table manners. We cannot experience molecules in the same way as we experience dogs. Because we have to rely on the artificial structuring of our experience of precepts, via academic texts, for example, it is unlikely that the mechanisms we use in the natural environment will transfer directly to this unnatural environment. Thus our means of access to precepts becomes critical to our success in learning them.
>
> (Ibid.: 202)

The distinction between learning percepts and learning precepts is important for my subsequent argument about the nature of academic teaching but it is a difficult one to make, as Eysenck and Warren Piper pointed out in the debate:

> Choosing molecule as an example of a precept which cannot be experienced seems to overlook the degree to which people, when they imagine such entities, call upon what they have experienced so as to give such abstractions substance. Ping-pong balls and gravity are dragooned into service to explain the molecule . . . And while to Laurillard structuralism cannot be experienced like table manners, others might argue that that is precisely the way in which it is experienced, both being a protocol for going about a ritual task . . . One is led to conclude that there is no clear division between the natural and unnatural environments.
>
> (Eysenck and Warren Piper 1987: 209–10)

It is true that molecules can be experienced, but the very fact that we have to dragoon other such disparate experiences into service in order to experience them demonstrates how different that is from the way a dog is experienced. The point about structuralism is interesting because it probably could be experienced as a protocol, but I think academics want students to understand structuralism in a deeper sense than in being able to perform a ritual procedure. If students are simply acculturated into performing structuralism, then it will not also be available to them as an articulated idea, accessible to comparison with other approaches, and open to criticism. Academics want more to be learned than that which is already available from experiencing the world.

The whole point about articulated knowledge is that being articulated it is known through exposition, argument, interpretation; it is known through reflection on experience and represents therefore a second-order experience of the world. Knowledge derived from experiencing the world at one remove must logically be accessed differently from that known through a first-order experience. We need a specific example to clarify what this actually means for a teacher, and the classic one that emerges sooner or later in every discussion of student learning is the problem of understanding Newton's concept of force. Like any illustrative example it suffers from the fact that to appreciate what it tells us you really have to understand the concept, but it gains from the fact that it has been extensively researched, so we know a lot about the ways it is misunderstood.

We all experience force as an aspect of daily life, and we have multitudinous contexts from which to abstract a general idea about its nature. We learn the use of the word 'force' also in a number of different contexts, and learn to distinguish its use, as in 'police force', 'force it open', 'force of gravity', 'force them to do it', etc. Our knowledge of 'force' is situated and we have no great problem with it. The physics lecturer then offers some new ways of thinking about force, and using the word 'force'. We meet the idea of 'force acting at a distance', which is curious, but not unlike forcing someone to do something, and a falling apple interpreted as 'the force of the earth acting on the apple' which makes a kind of sense if you accepted action at a distance, but also 'the force of the apple acting on the earth', which makes no sense at all and had better be ignored. A reaction like this latter one dooms us never to understand Newton's idea of force. (More of this later.)

The problem is that we certainly use our everyday experience to help interpret the meaning of the physics lecture, and to an extent that helps. But it is important to go beyond that to attain the true scientific meaning. The physics lecture cannot offer any new experience of the world, however, to match this new idea. It offers only a different way of thinking about apples falling, of seeing them as being essentially similar to planets orbiting the sun, or atoms orbiting an electron. Every academic subject faces this same kind of challenge, to help students go beyond their experience, to use it and reflect on it, and thereby change their perspective on it, and therefore change the way they experience the world. That is why education must act at the second-order level of 'reflecting on' experience. Everyday knowledge is located in our experience of the world. Academic knowledge is located in our experience of our experience of the world. Both are situated, but in logically distinct contexts. Teaching may use the analogy of situated learning of the world, but must adapt it to the learning of descriptions of the world. I have termed this 'mediated' learning, after Vygotsky:

> A scientific concept involves from the first a 'mediated' attitude towards its object.
>
> (Vygotsky 1962: 102)

Teaching as mediating learning involves constructing the environments which afford the learning of descriptions of the world. The means of access to the two types of knowledge is different. The one is direct, the other mediated.

The contrast between experiential and academic learning is similar to the distinction made by Vygotsky between 'spontaneous' concepts, learned in everyday life and founded on concrete experiences, and 'scientific' concepts, learned in the classroom and developed through analytical procedures in a particular social context. As a psychologist, Vygotsky saw a synergistic relation between the two, where everyday concepts mediate between the world of experience and the world of analytical scientific concepts. He is able, therefore, to suggest how the development of scientific concepts ought to work, rather than describing, as an educationist would, how they appear to work, *and* how they fail to work. From his studies with children, he developed the educational theory for which he is now valued, of the importance of the social context in the development of scientific concepts, and their dependence upon the child's existing set of everyday concepts (Panofsky, John-Steiner and Blackwell 1990). The bulk of the current work based on his ideas concerns school-based learning, but the same kind of analysis is applicable at university level, as this chapter is intended to show.

Because academic knowledge has this second-order character, it relies heavily on symbolic representation as the medium through which it is known. This is usually language, but may also be mathematics symbols, diagrams, musical notation, phonetics, or any symbol system that can represent a description of the world, and requires interpretation. Students have to learn to handle the representation system as well as the ideas they represent. The difficulty of this has attracted a fair amount of attention at the level of school mathematics, but surprisingly little has been done on how students intepret teachers' language, how they read academic texts, and how they interpret graphical and symbolic information. Roger Säljö makes the same point in his analysis of 'the written code' as a medium for learning, fittingly subtitled as 'observations on the problems of profiting from somebody else's insights' (Säljö 1984). The problems stem from the fact that the two worlds, of everyday knowledge and academic knowledge, are not as synergistic and inseparable as Vygotsky suggested (see Panofsky *et al.* 1990), but are contrasting and separate:

> In scientific texts, new 'versions of the world', or fragments of such, are offered, and the act of learning through reading may thus be seen as containing an implicit commitment to transcend assumptions *vis-à-vis* reality for which we have a firm basis in terms of our own previous daily experiences. Our knowledge gained by personal experience and therefore 'true' in our everyday realm of life, may in our culture have to yield to an alternative mode of conceptualisation that links with a scientific 'version of the world'.
>
> (Säljö 1984: 31)

This contrasts with Vygotsky who sees a synergistic relation between the two, where everyday concepts mediate between the world of experience and the world of analytical scientific concepts.

In later chapters we shall look at studies of the problems students have with transcending their assumptions in order to acquire an understanding of somebody else's insights. In order to mediate knowledge we must understand how students deal with the means of access to it, i.e. symbolic representations, the written code.

Symbolic representation is also the means by which academic knowledge is assessed. It makes little sense to assess one's knowledge of the world through words and symbols (I can still remember the mesmerising difficulty of having to draw a diagram of the making of a stitch in needlework lessons). It makes perfect sense to assess one's knowledge of descriptions of the world that way. This further testifies to its second-order character, differentiating it from knowledge acquired directly through experience.

Before summarising the arguments made in this chapter, it will be useful to consider again the teachers' concerns we began with: 'critically assessing the arguments', 'compiling patterns to integrate knowledge', 'becoming aware of the limitations of theoretical knowledge in the transfer of theory to practice', 'coming to accept relativism as a positive position'. In the analysis of academic knowledge as being located in our second-order experience of the world, requiring mediation by the teacher, I feel we have not strayed too far from the focus of those concerns and the assumptions that underlie them. A computational model would not so easily embrace the sense of action they describe. Situated cognition certainly gives a sense of action, but not that sense of 'standing back' from the content that is implicit in what teachers want of their students. Academic knowledge is not like other kinds of everyday knowledge. Teaching is essentially a rhetorical activity, seeking to persuade students to change the way they experience the world. It has to create the environment that will enable students to learn the descriptions of the world devised by others.

SUMMARY

The chapter began by accepting that the aim of university teaching is to make student learning possible. Because academics are concerned with how their subject is known, as well as what is known, teaching must not simply impart decontextualised knowledge, but must emulate the success of everyday learning by contextualising, situating knowledge in real-world activity. However, academic learning has a second-order character, as it concerns descriptions of the world. So whereas natural environments afford learning of percepts through situated cognition, teaching must create artificial environments which afford the learning of 'precepts', i.e. descriptions of the world. The implications for the design of teaching are that:

- academic learning must be situated in the domain of the objective, the activities must match that domain
- academic teaching must address both the direct experience of the world, and the reflection on that experience that will produce the intended way of representing it

Thus teaching is a rhetorical activity: it is mediated learning, allowing students to acquire knowledge of someone else's way of experiencing the world. With that analysis of the nature of the task, we can now attempt to see how this might be done.

NOTE

1 All drawn from participants in workshops on student learning.

Chapter 2

What students bring to learning

INTRODUCTION

There is a many–one relationship between where students are at the start of a course, and where teachers want them to be by the end, not because they want to turn out identical replicas of themselves, but because there is a consensual aspect to the didactic process without which academic life fails in its responsibility to progress knowledge. We expect students to use their knowledge in a variety of ways, and to contribute personal and even original ways of thinking about their subject, but we expect them also to exhibit some point of contact with the consensus view of a subject: if they cannot agree on the substantive content, then they must be able to provide an acceptable argument for the opposing point of view. It follows from this combined personal and consensual character of academic knowledge that there are many ways of knowing a topic, and also that there are many ways of failing to know it.

The knowledge that students bring to a course will necessarily affect how they deal with the new knowledge being taught, and because this relationship has always been understood, the progress through an academic career has typically been governed by a student's acquisition of prerequisite knowledge; each new course builds on an assumption about what the student has already mastered. This is a dangerous assumption, as we shall see in this chapter. Mastery of the art of taking examinations designed to test knowledge is more prevalent than mastery of the knowledge itself. The teacher will often be building on sand. As teaching and assessment techniques improve, we could look forward to a gradual lessening of this problem, perhaps, were it not for the fact that other changes exacerbate the problem. Increased intake to university courses increases the likelihood that students will not have fully mastered all the prerequisite ideas in a subject area; and greater modularity in courses decreases the likelihood that they will have acquired those concepts that used to be considered prerequisite. It will continue to be necessary, therefore, for academics to understand not only where students should get to, but also where they are as they begin a course.

How can we know this? The educational system offers academics only one source of information, the examination result. It is hardly sufficient. Even the topmost grade obscures a multitude of sins of omission and commission in the student's knowledge and understanding of the detail of the subject. What are the different 'ways of knowing' that a whole class of students might bring to a topic? There are a number of studies of university students that tell us something about where they might be at the start of a course. In this chapter I shall introduce these studies as alternative sources of information for the academic to make use of. Like the examination system, they each use a particular methodological approach and therefore offer a particular kind of description of the student, and are therefore useful at different stages of the educative process. The examination system may be good for the selection process, but is no use at all to the academic who needs to know what kind of teaching the students now need to be able to cope with this new idea.

There are two fundamentally different ways of investigating what students bring to their learning of a topic. One approach considers student-specific characteristics, of which I have selected motivation, approach to study, epistemological belief and intellectual development as being the most interesting for our analysis. The other illuminates the task-specific aspects important for understanding: conceptions, reasoning processes and representational skills.

QUESTIONNAIRE STUDIES OF INDIVIDUAL STUDENT CHARACTERISTICS

Do students have individual learning styles or approaches to study which we should take into account? This is a question that intrigues many academics who think about how to design their teaching, and there are a number of studies that set out to answer it.

Individual student characteristics are explored in these studies as though they are independent of the context of particular learning tasks. The methodology is to survey or interview a sample of students, asking them questions about how they approach learning, how they define learning, how they organise their study, etc. Factor analysis of survey data, or content analysis of interview data into categories of similar responses enables the researcher to sort the student sample into different individual types and to correlate some characteristics with others, e.g. learning style and motivation. The methodology invites the emergence of individual characteristics which are necessarily independent of context, because that is the way they were collected, and which are therefore presumed to be present in the context of any learning task. The methodology cannot determine how important these characteristics are in the learning process.

The main difficulty in interpreting findings of this type is to decide how far we consider the characteristics discovered to be fixed and immutable for an individual. In Chapter 1 I argued that we should consider the learning process holistically, and knowledge as being situated and contextualised. This sits unhappily with the notion that students might have personality characteristics that determine the way they think, irrespective of the context. On the other hand, there is undoubtedly an expectation and an intuition on the part of academics that there are identifiably different ways of thinking, often linked to the type of subject being studied: course aims may be defined as being to help students 'think like a social scientist', or 'think like a technologist'. This expresses an intention to acculturate the student, rather than a belief in a personality type, but what about phrases like 'first class mind', or 'scatterbrain'? These express the idea that some aspects of thinking perseverate across a variety of contexts, and constitute an individual style of thinking. Clearly if there are such characteristic styles they would affect the way a learner responds to a particular task, and they would therefore be of interest to us.

Entwistle describes a study which asked students to indicate the extent of their agreement with a series of statements about their normal academic work, e.g.

I try to relate ideas in one subject to those in others, whenever possible.

I like to be told precisely what to do in essays or other set work.
It's important to me to do really well in courses here.
When I'm reading I try to memorize important facts which may
come in useful later.

(Entwistle 1981: 57)

Factor analysis of the results (e.g. for one study, 767 first year
students from three British universities) linked several items
together, which means that, for example, students who agree with
the second statement above (indicating extrinsic motivation) are
likely also to agree with the last one (indicating a superficial
approach to study). Another factor links, for example, a deep
approach to intrinsic motivation, and a third links, for example,
organised study methods to achievement motivation. In this way,
Entwistle is able to identify three types of motivation with these
three factors, which he characterises as 'personal meaning',
'reproducing', and 'achieving'.

The idea of pigeonholing students may seem like a convenient
simplification of the vast diversity of those idiosyncratic
individuals we are faced with, and I see no objection in theory to
attempting to describe people this way. It is always salutary,
however, to try to pigeonhole oneself in one of these categories –
do you think you are achievement-oriented rather than meaning-
oriented, or vice versa? The idea has a certain face validity when
applied to other people, preferably people you don't know too
well, but applying it to oneself illuminates the crudity of the
classification. There is a strong temptation to respond that 'it all
depends . . .' and that is probably closer to the reality; as Entwistle
and Ramsden pointed out, students are capable of variation as
well:

> It is possible to accept that there can be both consistency and
> variability in students' approaches to learning. The tendency to
> adopt a certain approach, or to prefer a certain style of
> learning, may be a useful way of describing differences between
> students. But a more complete explanation would also involve
> a recognition of the way an individual student's strategy may
> vary from task to task.

(Entwistle 1981: 105)

Although it is abundantly clear that the same student uses
different approaches on different occasions, it is also true that

general tendencies to adopt particular approaches, related to the different demands of courses and previous educational experiences, do exist. Variability in approaches thus coexists with consistency.

(Ramsden 1992: 51)

We do not have strong enough evidence of the existence of stable individual learning characteristics, whether motivation, learning style, or study pattern to need to abandon the idea that a student's approach is most meaningfully seen as being interactive with particular learning situations, and therefore context-dependent. That does not mean that there is no antecedent influence on what a student does during learning. The entire pre-history of their academic experience up to the time of a learning session can be implicated in what they do. How they do things already will play a part, but there are many ways in which they do things, and each individual student is probably more accurately described as having a repertoire of approaches of which one will be salient for a particular learning task. Moreover, part of Entwistle and Ramsden's research programme showed that students' approaches could also be influenced by their perceptions of teaching and assessment (Entwistle and Ramsden 1983). I would rather treat these approaches as being characteristic of the population as a whole, therefore, with all of them potentially available to all students as aspects of their interaction with the teaching, rather than make the much stronger assumption that they can be identified as personal characteristics of individuals.

EXPLORATORY STUDIES OF THE STUDENT POPULATION

Can we go more directly to eliciting what goes on for students at the start of a course? Exploration studies attempt to describe the characteristic ways of conceptualising and learning a topic that can be found in the student population. Many of these studies are also known as 'phenomenographic', because they produce students' 'descriptions of the phenomena' as results, in contrast to those that set out to 'explain' student behaviour.

I have begun this section with a conscious parallel of the description of methodology given in the previous section, to aid comparison.

Population characteristics are explored as though they are

dependent on the context of particular learning tasks. The methodology is to survey or interview a sample of students working on a particular task, either given by the researcher or occurring within their normal study. The students are asked questions about how they approach this learning task, how they think about it, why they do what they do, etc. Content analysis of interview or open-ended questionnaire data produces categories of similar responses which enable the researcher to sort the protocols into different types and to find common patterns of internal relations between characteristics of each protocol. The methodology invites the emergence of characteristics of the learning process which are necessarily contextualised, because that is the way they were collected, and which are therefore presumed to be applicable to the context of any learning task. The methodology elicits characteristics that are important in the learning process, but it cannot determine how consistent these are for individual students.

The 'phenomenographic' approach is grounded in the epistemology established in Chapter 1, which assumes that knowledge is relational, and therefore sets out to describe not what is known about x, as a natural scientist would, but how the idea of x can be experienced, where the relation is between knower and object. This makes it a particularly valuable methodology for educational purposes. In his original characterisation of phenomenography (Marton 1981), Ference Marton identifies what the scientist would ask, e.g.

> Why do some children succeed better than others in school?
> (Marton 1981: 177)

the answers to which might well be the content of an educational psychology course – and distinguishes this from what the phenomenographer would ask, e.g.

> What do people think about why some children succeed better than others in school?
> (Marton 1981: 178)

which is what the lecturer needs to know if they are to get the scientific answers across to the people they are teaching. It is not just the scientific knowledge the lecturer has to have, it is also the phenomenographic description of the ways the same phenomenon can be experienced by the students.

For educational purposes, we need to look at the varying conceptions of a phenomenon, which might be

> a common-sense conception of a phenomenon on the one hand and the conception used within a scientific framework for understanding the very same phenomenon on the other hand . . .
>
> (Säljö 1988: 38)

in order to map the range of ways an idea can be known. But there is no attempt at a reductionist explanation of these conceptions in terms of underlying psychological processes. A conception is not a property of an individual in the way a nose is; it is an aspect of their behaviour in the world and their experience of it. With that kind of epistemology it is impossible to expect that we can discover anything worthwhile about conceptions by looking at traces of how people carry out tasks, such as their written performance on subtraction problems. This gives us access only to their behaviour, not their experience. Without careful interviewing and observation it is impossible to interpret students' actions correctly. The power of the phenomenographic methodology is that it sets out to discover precisely what teachers need to know – the conceptions of reality that students have already acquired.

The phenomenographic method uses critical tasks within the topic concerned, probing interviews with students about their experience of carrying out those tasks, and comparative analysis of the protocols to reveal the main forms of conception. There is no expectation of being able to identify an individual with a particular type of conception, and it can happen that in the course of an interview a student will exhibit more than one conception. The analysis is not by individual, therefore, but is carried out in terms of the meaning of the conceptions invoked in the course of a student's explanation. Interviewing many students within a population will result in several forms of conception of one idea or topic. The relationship between these different conceptions is not clear, however. Some researchers see them as inclusive – a more sophisticated conception will logically include the lower ones. Others, myself among them, see them as being related not to each other, but to the history of the students' experiences with the idea. And others see them as defining a developmental progression, where each successive conception is better, in a similar way to the progression defined for scientific theories: they explain more, they are more productive. It is an intriguing fact of research on students' conceptions that they may sometimes bear a strong resemblance to earlier scientific theories – students have Aristotelian conceptions of motion, Lamarckian conceptions of evolution, phlogiston theories of combustion, Eysenckian theories of intelligence, for example, suggesting the delightful idea that the intellectual development of the individual recapitulates the development of the history of ideas (see Säljö 1988, Brumby 1984, Champagne, Klopfer and Gunstone 1982). There are studies that support all these views. I do not propose to decide among these just now. The important point, for my purpose, is that such an approach can illuminate for the teacher what their students might already know.

The remarkable conclusion from all these studies is that what students know can be described in a relatively concise way, as long as you penetrate to the level of what the concept means to the student. Brown and Van Lehn, in their study of subtraction procedures, found eighty-nine different ways of doing it wrongly (Brown and Van Lehn 1980). But by going to a different level of description, at the level of understanding, Resnick and Omanson (1987) found just two ways of misconceptualising subtraction. Looking at procedures attacks the problem at the wrong level. If a student borrows across zero incorrectly, we want to teach him not 'how to borrow across zero', but what 'borrowing' means. It is not just the formal manipulation of a procedural skill that we teach in teaching subtraction. The skill is inseparable from the knowledge it invokes. The most commonly identified problem with the teaching of arithmetic is that it divorces the process of subtraction from its meaning in action, as Brown himself argued in his later work (Brown, Collins and Duguid 1989a), already discussed in Chapter 1. It makes no sense to remediate a faulty procedural skill with reference to the procedure alone; we have to appeal to the conceptual apparatus that supports it as well. We have already established that knowledge is situated in action, and by the same token, action manifests knowledge; and this 'buggy' behaviour manifests an underlying conceptualisation that itself needs remediation. This means we must know how the student conceptualises all the aspects involved in the procedure: the action of borrowing, the representation of the task, the representation of the procedure, the concept of number, the concept of 'difference' and the concept of 'subtraction'. Students need practice in the interpretation and manipulation of the formal representations found in any academic subject.

Resnick has made use of the systematic definition of Brown and Van Lehn's (1980) 'buggy algorithms' (i.e. flawed procedures), but takes the view that the best thing to do with buggy algorithms is not to remediate them but to take them as revealing a fundamental infelicity in the way children think about number in the context of these tasks. It is this fundamental infelicity that should be remediated, thus pre-empting the formation of meaningless algorithms in the first place:

> if we look beyond the symbol manipulations of written arithmetic to what the symbols represent, the buggy algorithms look much less sensible . . . It seems reasonable to suggest . . . that a major reason that children invent buggy algorithms so freely is that they either do not know or fail to apply to calculation problems the basic principles relevant to the domain. If so, instruction focused on principles and on their application to calculation ought to eliminate or at least substantially decrease buggy performances.
>
> (Resnick and Omanson 1987: 49)

If you remediate one of the eighty-nine wrong procedures, you have another eighty-eight to contend with; but if you remediate one of the misconceptions, you avoid all the inherited bugs and faulty procedures as well. A methodology that searches for the fundamental misconceptions will yield far more valuable data.

We can follow the same argument at a more advanced level of the educational system. A nice topic for detailed analysis here is Newton's Third Law. Everyone misunderstands Newton's Third Law (including many of the people who teach it), and it is a good example of the difference between experiential and academic knowledge. This discussion is based on an extensive study of students' conceptions in mechanics, described more fully elsewhere (Ramsden *et al.*, in press, Bowden *et al.* 1992, Laurillard 1992a).

Using a phenomenographic approach, physics students entering and in their first year of university were interviewed about their solutions to five or six carefully selected problems. For one of them, they are asked to state Newton's Third Law (if they cannot remember it they are given a prepared statement of its canonical form: 'every force has an equal and opposite reaction'). They are then shown a diagram of a box resting on a table, and a box in mid-air and asked to use the law to describe the forces acting in the two situations (see Figure 2.1).

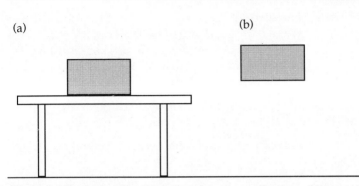

Figure 2.1 Students are asked to explain the application of Newton's Third Law for (a) the box on the table, and (b) the box falling to the ground.

The interviewer probes why they give the answer they do, how they define their terms, trying to obtain as complete a picture as possible of the way the student thinks about the problem. Of course, this kind of interview is a learning experience in itself, and not surprisingly, students often change the way they reason about the situation in response to mild but probing questions. To give a flavour of this kind of interview, I have reprinted a longish extract. The student begins with a definition of the law applied to the box on the table, which he later finds difficult to apply to the box in mid-air:

Interviewer: And in the case when it's falling, how does Newton's Law apply there?

Student: Well, umm, it's not at a constant velocity and it's not at rest . . .

Interviewer: Mm . . .

Student: . . . so there is a a net force, um, which is which is present and that's what is causing the acceleration.

Interviewer: And what is the net force?

Student: Um, it's the force of the gravity which is the mg force . . .

Interviewer: Mm . . .

Student: . . . minus the the component which is the resistance.

This is correct, but does not relate to the Third Law as it is not relating paired forces. Another student displayed the correct conception:

Student: The force of the earth, uh, box falling towards the ground, yeah, the earth on the box, is equal to the force of the box on the earth, but because the box's mass is so much less that the earth, it is . . . the box moves towards the earth.

Without the idea of the pairing of forces – box on earth, earth on box – the other student remains in difficulty:

Student: This case isn't applicable because the body is moving . . .
Interviewer: Mm . . .
Student: . . . and and it's not constant velocity.
Interviewer: So does Newton's Law sometimes work and sometimes not?
Student: Well the (laugh) you can't sort of say the law only exists for certain bodies. Um – it's gee (laugh) – yeah. I think I'll just, I can just say that, that the case which is just stated on this side is – um. See it's not the central situation so that specialised case doesn't hold on that side [*the block in mid-air*].
Interviewer: Mm . . .
Student: It doesn't mean that the forces don't exist.
Interviewer: Mm . . .
Student: It's just that, it's just that the the cancellation doesn't occur.
Interviewer: And because the cancellation doesn't occur?
Student: The, the, yeah, the effect that the cancellation has is to have made the body at rest or moving at a constant speed or velocity and because that hasn't occurred . . .
Interviewer: Mm . . .
Student: . . . then the, then the body is not in that situation.
Interviewer: And so?
Student: Yeah um well that, that case doesn't apply there.
Interviewer: Okay?
Student: Mm. Does that make sense?

Even without specialist background knowledge, it should be possible to see that this student is having difficulty in reconciling different bits of knowledge about physics: his definition of the law and its application to an instance, with his belief that the law should hold for all situations. His final question is an admission that indeed his reasoning does not make sense. Many of these interview sessions end up being a powerful learning experience for students. It should also be clear that analysis is not straightforward. Defining this student's conception of the law would be very complex, especially as it appears here as rather fluid in form, certainly not stable and bounded. We can discern within this dialogue, however, an aspect of thinking about the problem that is present in other interviews as well, namely the idea of the forces cancelling out:

> [The forces in the second case] are just the weight of the box acting down and there's air resistance acting up . . . The force acting down is bigger so that's why it falls down to the ground.

> It [the law] applies to when they're in equilibrium and at rest, but when the actual system is trying to reach equilibrium it doesn't apply.

The idea of forces cancelling out to give equilibrium is not relevant to the application of Newton's Third Law. The phraseology of its most common form, 'equal and opposite', sounds like the balancing of forces on a body, but this version neglects the additional idea contained in Newton's original formulation, that the forces are acting on different bodies ('the mutual action of two bodies upon each other'). The law expresses the idea that a force that does not have its counterpart cannot exist; it is not so much a property of the world as a definition of what he means by force. (It is rather like defining a mirror thus, 'for every mirror image there is an equal and opposite mirror image', in the sense that it is a tautology if you already know what a mirror image is.) To apply the law to the falling box, you have to recognise that gravity, the force of the earth on the box, presupposes the equal and opposite force of the box on the earth. What makes the box accelerate is its tiny mass in comparison with that of the earth. The earth is also accelerating towards the box, but its great mass makes its acceleration tiny in comparison with that of the box. The two forces are the same, however, and that is where 'equal and opposite' is applicable, not in any notion of balance which implies lack of motion.

This aspect of the students' conception cannot be construed as having any kind of logical relation to an expert conception. Once described we can begin to see its etiology in our everyday experience of force, in the language used to describe the law, in the problems set to students. Few textbooks quote Newton's Law in its original form, and in simplifying it, they often omit the very phrases that would help students see that their everyday conception of force is quite different. This is a 'pedagogic error', comparable to 'iatrogenic disease', and is avoidable if we become sufficiently aware of the contaminating effects of everyday language. However, at this stage I want to focus on identifying its presence, rather than preventing its existence.

In addition to the conceptualisation of the law in terms of equilibrium, we also found some students who conceptualised it correctly, using all three key components of the law, that all forces are paired, that paired forces are equal and opposite, and that they act on different objects, and they were able to apply this successfully to both situations. We also found a third form of conception, which did not insist on finding a pair of forces, and therefore explained the box in mid-air in terms of an unbalanced force of gravity:

> The second one, no table, so, ah, the box has still got gravity acting on it . . . and seeing there's no [other] forces coming from anywhere . . . it's just going to fall towards the ground with constant acceleration.

When challenged about how the equal and opposite forces mentioned in the Third Law could be applied to this situation, the student had little option but to reject Newton altogether:

> I'd only apply Newton's Third Law where there's no resulting acceleration for a thing, whereas this box is accelerating as it comes downwards, so I don't know, I wouldn't use Newton at all here.

This was not an isolated example, and given the lack of any sense of intellectual struggle in these cases, the interviewers were constrained to prolong these interviews a lot further to avoid this unfortunate conclusion becoming the learning outcome of the session.

This completes the analysis for this question, and leaves us with an outcome space of just three main conceptions of the law, as (1) including all three components, (2) neglecting the condition that the forces described act on different objects, (3) also neglecting the requirement that forces are paired. This is a complete description of the outcome space for this population of students, in the sense that it can account for all the explanations and reasoning processes students used. The three conceptions cannot be related to each other except via the definition of the law. They are well-ordered, in the sense that being wrong in type (2) is better than being wrong in type (3), but it is not obviously a developmental progression, where every individual has to go through each one. I prefer to keep the outcome space as empirically defined, therefore, and leave open the possibility that a different population of students could add to the number of ways of thinking about the Third Law.

This basic method can be applied to any subject area to clarify the alternative possible ways of thinking about complex concepts. Particular examples are: the law of diminishing returns in economics (Dahlgren and Marton 1978), the mole in chemistry (Lybeck, Marton, Strömdahl and Tullberg 1988), clinical diagnosis in medicine (Whelan 1988) and a much deeper analysis of the concept of subtraction (Neuman 1987). It should be clear from these studies and from the detailed analysis of one example above, that it is important for teachers to know how their students think. Without this we build on sand. Teachers must address and challenge those fundamental misconceptions, but first they need to know what they are. The methodology of phenomenography will tell us, but it is a labour-intensive task to undertake that kind of research for one topic at a time. In Chapter 4 we will look at the extent to which studies of this type can be generalised.

LONGITUDINAL STUDIES OF DEVELOPMENTAL CHANGE IN UNIVERSITY STUDENTS

The final aspect of what the student brings to learning derives from long-term studies of students that reveal the changes they go through over time. William Perry's study of Harvard undergraduates, carried out from the vantage point of the academic counsellor, documents the long intellectual journey from a basic dualism, regarding knowledge as facts that are right or wrong, dispensed by authority, to a generalised relativism and a commitment to personal values (Perry 1970). This study was carried out via long open-ended interviews with students, one for each year of their degree. The analysis looked at comparisons *between* students to generate the existence of different categories of epistemological belief, and at the changes *within* students to describe a developmental pattern. Both epistemological and ethical aspects were documented, the former developing from the dualistic position of knowledge as right or wrong, to a multiplicity of possible correct explanations, to the relativism of contextualised knowledge. There is a parallel in the ethical development, from seeing authority as responsible for what is known, to the solipsism of everyone being equally correct to a personal responsibility for the set of values one is committed to. Epistemological and ethical development do not necessarily stay in step with each other. When I analysed interviews with British Open University students studying the first year social science course, it appeared that some, being mature students, had already established a sense of a personal system of values and did not want to be told what to think. At the same time their epistemology told them that there were independent facts:

Student: They're going to tell me eventually what capitalism is
                . . . Well, I suppose they can leave it open for me to
                disagree, but I'd always assumed we were in a mixed
                economy, and the fact they're now saying *are* we a
                mixed economy surprised me, because I thought it
                was a mixed economy within capitalism . . . but it
                seems to me they're telling us all the time.
Interviewer: So what do you want?
Student: I don't know. I suppose what I want is to be presented
                with the facts and make up my own mind, which
                ultimately is what will happen, isn't it?

For this student the course focuses her attention on relativistic conceptions – *whether* our society is mixed economy or capitalist, not *which* it is – and yet she has no basis for deciding the issue herself. She is beginning to recognise the idea of relativism, but is unsure how to handle it:

> It seems to me that – I always get confused over things like this
> – that they're producing a model to explain how something
> works, but that the definition depends on how they explain it.
> So how am I to know? I suppose I look at capitalism and see if
> that explains the definition. Is that how it's supposed to work?

Students have to work out where they can locate themselves in this academic debate, and on what basis they can decide their view. They do not want to be told, but they want to know how they can know. It is a problem common to students in every subject area.

This kind of description of the student population differs from 'personality' studies in that all students are expected to go through all stages at some point in their academic career, though the pace of change may differ. Longitudinal studies differ from 'conceptions' studies because at any one time a particular student can be assigned to a particular stage, so in this sense, Perry's scheme identifies individual differences between students. What should the teacher do with developmental stages? Do we have to wait until a student is ready for a new way of thinking, or can we push them forward? Perry is clear:

> We cannot push anyone to develop, or 'get them to see' or 'impact' them. The causal metaphors hidden in English verbs give us a distracting vocabulary for pedagogy. The tone is Lockean and provocative of resistance. We can provide, we can design opportunities. We can create settings in which students who are ready will be more likely to make new kinds of sense.
>
> (Perry 1988: 159–60)

The student who began the social science course with the belief that individuals are responsible for their actions was resistant to structural explanations of vandalism:

> I thought some of the explanations that were given, I didn't accept them all – because they were bored – I don't necessarily think that's a good reason to kick in a telephone box. I think it's possibly just because they're vandals.
>
> (Laurillard 1982: 16)

The course tried to steer students away from individualistic explanations of this sort, but at the same time recognised them and addressed them. In discussing the question raised by the course, 'Is social science really just providing excuses?' the same student was able to acknowledge his earlier view and also recognise how it had changed:

> Yes this is an attitude that certainly I had very strongly when I just started up on the course. I think I'm gradually beginning to see the social sciences' point of view.
>
> (Ibid.: 16)

In this case the course created the setting in which this student was able to start making a new kind of sense. We shall return to how students' epistemological beliefs might affect teaching strategy in Chapter 4, and Chapter 3 shows how students at different developmental stages deal with intellectually challenging subject matter.

Finally we should consider Säljö's identification of five conceptions of learning, which also mark a developmental progression, but have been used to demonstrate that many students do not progress all the way through (Beaty, Dall'Alba and Marton, in press). His study was again interview-based, but instead of being longitudinal, it took interviewees from all age groups and stages of learning. Säljö's five stages (Säljö 1979) are compatible with Perry's nine, but they bring out what is implicit in Perry's analysis with respect to how students conceptualise the process of learning itself, as:

- the increase of knowledge
- memorizing
- the acquisition of facts, procedures for use in practice
- the abstraction of meaning
- an interpretive process for understanding reality

Their conception of learning is an important manifestation of a student's epistemology, being, quite literally, the way they believe they can come to know. It is important for teachers to know which one their students incline to, and to take responsibility for helping students develop this most fundamental aspect of what they bring to their learning.

SUMMARY

In this chapter I have made a division between studies of individuals' characteristics, characteristics of a student population, and longitudinal studies. The methodologies produced different kinds of data that will operate at different levels of description of the teaching process. Some can inform the curriculum planning level, e.g. how to address students' epistemologies, whereas others can suggest the language to be used in teaching, e.g. how to talk about 'force'. All the studies describe aspects of what students bring with them to learning a new topic. In summary these are:

- conceptions of the topic – teachers need descriptions of the ways students conceptualise a topic to be able to challenge their fundamental misconceptions
- representational skills – students need explicit practice in the representation of knowledge of their subject, in language, symbols, graphs, diagrams, and in the manipulation and interpretation of those representations
- an epistemology – teachers must enable students to develop their epistemological and ethical beliefs, and in particular, their conceptions of learning

These issues at least must be addressed later in devising teaching strategies, and will contribute to the generation of a teaching strategy in Chapter 4. Meanwhile, having considered what students bring to their study, Chapter 3 goes on to consider what they do when they study.

Chapter 3

The complexity of coming to know

INTRODUCTION

This is the point of the book at which we come as close as possible to what goes on while a student is learning. It is not easy to penetrate the private world of someone coming to an understanding of an idea, and much of this chapter will discuss the ways this can be done, as well as what is found out. I once caught myself wishing I could attach electrodes to students' heads to see what goes on when they learn. Never mind humanitarian principles of research investigation, or anti-reductionist beliefs about the nature of learning; it would be so wonderful to be able to see how their sense-making cognitive apparatus arrives at some of those weird outcomes. Retrospective interviews are a very unsatisfactory substitute. The fantasy deserves to be nothing more than that, but it does convey that sense of wanting to see the learning process from the students' perspective, in detail, in all its complexity, in such a way that we can make sense of it.

An insight into the student's view of the learning process would give us some basis for deciding on a teaching strategy. Chapter 2 elaborated the relevant features a student might bring to a learning session. We now consider what goes on within it. The teacher has to encourage 'mathemagenic' activities in the students. This is a term originally coined by Rothkopf to refer to those activities that 'give birth to learning', such as 'systematic eye fixations' while reading. The term defines 'truly, a student-centred approach' to instruction (Rothkopf 1970: 334), but it is a shame to confine it to the realm of such minute behaviours as eye fixations. The context of predominantly behavioural psychology within which Rothkopf was working constrained the application of his idea. He acknowledged the importance of cognitive processing but did not then have the means to take it further than one brief paragraph.

In the last twenty years, psychologists have done a great deal of research on processing, and with a different epistemological orientation we can extend Rothkopf's idea to its proper domain. The concept of mathemagenic activities expresses exactly the idea that there are activities the learner can carry out that will result in their learning. Encouraging these activities is the proper focus of a teaching strategy. So our task in this chapter is to consider what kinds of activities could be mathemagenic.

FINDING OUT WHAT HAPPENS IN LEARNING

The approach must be to look at what happens during the learning process and relate this to learning outcome. We need a methodology that provides a deep level of description of what is happening for the student when they learn, linking the way they think about the content to what they achieve as an outcome. Because of the focus on content, these studies have to investigate students working on particular learning tasks, and because of the requirement to illuminate their perspective on the topic, the methods have to include observation, interview and a trace of students' performance (written protocols, input to a program, dialogue, etc.). The interviews are not 'introspective', and the protocols are not 'think-aloud'. Both techniques derive from a different epistemological tradition in psychology: they require meta-level monitoring by the subject, which presupposes that this gives them access to an accurate account of the object-level activities involved in the task, and that meta-level monitoring is not itself used in the task. I had a graphic demonstration of the fallacy of the latter assumption when I first tried using think-aloud protocols for problem solving tasks. The typical pattern produced plenty of talk while the subject was figuring out how to go about the task, but the point at which they said something like 'Aha . . .' was followed by total silence until either they completed their plan of action or they got stuck again. It was as if the point at which the really productive thinking was happening did not allow them spare capacity for a meta-level account.

A better method is to allow the student to complete the task undisturbed, and to give a retrospective account of how they experienced it, much as one might describe an event witnessed. The student's account is not taken as an objective description of a psychological process, but as being itself a phenomenon which is to be analysed. The student performance protocols, e.g. worked problems or written explanations of a concept, are used by the interviewer to focus students' explanations of why they did what they did, and to provide a stimulus to recall their activity. The combination of protocol and retrospective interview is then analysed by the researcher in relation to other students' data and to the content of the topic discussed, to produce an account of what they learned and how. This procedure provides the kind of detailed insight we need into what constitutes the learning process.

There are several aspects of learning that have been investigated in enough detail to admit a general account that can inform teaching. Given everything I have said so far about the integrative nature of the learning process, the inseparability of knowledge and action, and of process and outcome, there is no logical ordering of parts of the process, as each part is constituted in its relation to the other parts. The particular aspects I want to focus on are characterised in a very general way to make them as widely applicable as possible: apprehending structure, integrating parts, acting on the world, using feedback, reflecting on goals. Each presupposes and is presupposed by the other; each combines content and action. Together they are meant to encompass the essence of the learning process. I do not mean 'there are five key aspects of learning . . .', but I do mean to suggest that the activities students engage in must be at least complex enough to address all five aspects if learning is to take place. The division is simply a convenience to make discussion more manageable. An integrative whole can be divided up in many ways, none of them more correct than the other; the difference is only in their utility.

APPREHENDING STRUCTURE

The most common method of learning in higher education is via acquisition, especially through lectures and reading. In Chapter 1 I argued that it is a peculiarity of academic learning that its focus is not the world itself, but others' views of that world. The idea that people can learn through listening to lectures, or from reading, most clearly expresses the fact that teaching is a rhetorical activity, seeking to persuade students of an alternative or at least elaborated way of looking at the world they already know through experience. This way of learning presupposes that students must be able to interpret correctly a complex discourse of words, symbols, diagrams, and pictures, all bearing a specific meaning that must be interpreted correctly if the student is to learn what is intended. How do students deal with this?

Meaning is given through structure. The Gestalt psychologists gave a clear demonstration of this with the famous picture that organised one way meant young girl, and organised a different way meant old woman. The same information, structured differently, has a different meaning. This is why I have begun by focusing on apprehending structure. In Chapter 1 academic teaching was linked to a didactic process that has as its goal a consensual viewpoint on the world, a particular meaning. For students to intepret a complex academic discourse as having a specific intended meaning, they must be able to apprehend the implicit structure of that discourse. A number of studies show that they fail to do this. Since deciding on the structure and how it is to be displayed is part of the teacher's instructional strategy, this needs elaborating.

Phenomenography is particularly successful at illuminating how students deal with structure and meaning because these studies focus on content. They have led to the identification of two contrasting approaches to studying a text: one is known as the 'deep approach', where the student looks for meaning, and processes the text in a 'holistic' way, preserving the original structure of the discourse and therefore preserving its intended meaning; the other is known as the 'surface approach', where the student focuses on key words or phrases and processes the text in an 'atomistic' way, distorting the original structure and therefore changing its meaning. There have been many studies demonstrating this contrast. Marton and Säljö, in their 1976 papers (1976a and 1976b), and Svensson (1977) at the same time, documented the earliest studies. More recent books by Entwistle (1981), Marton, Hounsell and Entwistle (1984), and Ramsden (1988 and 1992) document the many later ones, spanning a range of educational contexts and topic areas, though they are usually science-oriented.

Extracts from a (1977) study I carried out on students reading a social science text illustrate their different approaches to structure and meaning. Students were given an article by Bertrand Russell ('Can a scientific society be stable?'), in which he argues that a scientific society is not stable, and adduces a number of reasons for this. The connections made between science, population increase and instability are moderately complex, and Russell discusses several reasons for instability, so that there is a degree of information overload. Since the argument is complex enough to extend over the whole article, a deep approach is necessary to apprehend its structure and combine its parts to give the intended meaning. A surface approach would result in, at most, a list of unconnected points in the argument. Some students took a 'deep' approach to discerning the intended meaning:

> I was trying to remember the main points he was arguing. I tried to find out first what it's about from the introduction, and then went on to his reasons, which was what I was looking for, relating it to his title.

> I tried to understand his argument, see where it's leading, see if it makes sense.

and in their summaries of the text were able to preserve the original meaning by linking scientific progress to social factors:

> Because science is progressing and we can support large populations, the population growth will overtake scientific growth.

> He's basically advocating that in its present form the scientific society is unstable unless there is drastic population control and control of resources.

Other students described a 'surface' approach:

> I didn't read it deeply . . . I tend when I'm reading to forget what went before. I take it in at the time, but if nothing really strikes me I forget it.

> I just read straight through . . . I found I would think about it and carry on reading and find I'd have read the last few sentences again because I hadn't been concentrating on it . . . some bits go in easily, others don't.

Their summaries reflected this surface approach, being more

disjointed, and failing to preserve the original links between science and social factors:

It was about whether a scientific society could be stable.

It's basically about the ethics of science and how he doesn't reckon we will survive much longer unless man's wisdom increases.

Without attempting to discern the structure inherent in the text, these students were unable to unravel its complex argument, and were left with isolated statements lacking any clear relationship to each other. As we shall see repeatedly in these examples, the internal structure of academic ideas, arguments and conceptions tends to be complex, and usually more complex than the everyday conception of the same phenomenon. For example, Dahlgren and Marton demonstrate that the main difficulty with understanding the law of diminishing returns in economics lies in its second-order character, that it involves 'decrement of increment, i.e. change of change' (Dahlgren and Marton 1978: 28); Brumby shows that students of biology assign adaptive characteristics to changes in the individual, rather than to the more complex mechanism of changes to the species via natural selection among individuals (Brumby 1984). The typically greater complexity of the academic conception makes it extremely important that students attend to the problem of apprehending structure.

The same problem of appropriately apprehending structure will occur in the interpretation of discourse in any medium. To clarify some aspects of the argument an author will often appeal to experience and use a specific instance to illustrate an idea, but the description of that example will have its own complex internal structure embedded within the structure of the text as a whole. Discerning the structure is difficult, not just because of its complexity but also because it is rarely explicit. It is conveyed via syntax, conjunctions, and expressions such as 'in order to', 'not only . . . but also', 'instead', etc. For many of the ideas students have to grapple with, their only access to them is via text. Academic knowledge does not present itself through experience with the world. The link is more tenuous than that. Academic knowledge is related to the experience of the world it describes, but it also requires a great deal of contemplative reflection on that experience. Furthermore, the perspective described in an academic text is not a clear glass window onto the world. A closer analogy would be looking through the wrong end of some grubby binoculars adjusted to someone else's eyes. The student has to do a lot of work to discern the point being made. The principle–example structure, which is a common feature of teaching texts, is missed by many students whose attention is captured by the intriguing example (Marton and Wenestam 1979). The relational argument structure, also important for expressing a complex idea, will be unpacked to its constituent components but may never be reassembled.

I have elsewhere reported a study that applied a similar analysis to the rather different form of discourse of an educational television programme. Like lectures, a television programme is time-based, is not under student control, and has a particular intended meaning (or succession of meanings) conveyed through its structure. It is importantly different from lectures, and books, because images and language work together to express an idea and convey a message. Even so, a similar problem appears there too. Students were asked to summarise a twenty-five minute programme after watching it, and were then played key extracts of a minute or two and asked to say what point each one was making. Several students were able to interpret the extracts correctly, but their summaries showed they were not aware of the status of the extract in relation to the whole programme. Their integration of the component parts into a coherent whole did not preserve the original structure, and so distorted the intended meaning of the programme (Laurillard 1991).

I have focused so far on those teaching techniques that assume learning through acquisition, but the issue is just as important for other kinds of learning method, such as problem solving. The point of problem solving as a method is to enable the student to manipulate the internal relations within their conceptual knowledge, such as definitional relations, causal relations, forms of representation, mathematical relations, sign-signifier relations, etc., much as they would manipulate the world in order to learn about it. As a method of learning, the focus is not the solution but the relations between the problem statement, the solution, and all the intervening steps. The problem solving exercise has a structure and embodies a meaning, a description of the world. In this sense, the apprehension of structure is just as important in problem solving as it is in interpreting discourse. In a study of how students carry out problem solving (Laurillard 1979), different approaches again distinguished those who addressed the structure as a whole:

> First I had to decide on the criteria of how to approach it, then drew a flow diagram, and checked through each stage. You have to think about it and understand it first.

> You have to make a basic assumption to work through, then you work backwards to check your input, then forwards again.
> (Laurillard 1979: 399–400)

and those who made no attempt to deal with the overall structure:

> You don't need to look at the system, you don't have to interpret it. I looked up the formulae and made the calculations from those.
> (Laurillard 1979: 399)

For some students, the main focus of a problem solving exercise is getting the answer out. That will help them develop a facility for mathematical manipulation, but will not do very much to enrich their understanding. The process of selecting the equation that fits the variables given in the problem does not involve the student in thinking about the meaning of the equation, nor about the relation it expresses. In more general terms, without looking at the structure as a whole in relation to their task, the student will be unable to appreciate the meaning of the answer they have produced – whether they are reading philosophy, watching a social science programme, or doing a maths problem.

The mathemagenic activities relevant to this aspect of learning are already well-defined in the literature in terms of the 'deep' or 'holistic' approach, which characterises them as follows:

> Focus on 'what it signified' (e.g. author's argument, or the concepts applicable to solving the problem).
> Relate and distinguish evidence and argument.
> Organise and structure content into a coherent whole.
> (Ramsden 1992: 42)

Students may understand what it means to take a deep approach, and still find it difficult to organise the content into a coherent whole. Undoubtedly some examples of academic discourse, whether lecture, book or television programme, seriously obfuscate their meaning by pursuing a muddled or over-complex structure. Through understanding students' different approaches to structure and meaning we can design teaching to encourage the mathemagenic activities they need, such as a deep approach to apprehending structure.

INTEGRATING PARTS

The importance of the integrative aspect of learning has already been prefigured in the discussion of structure. The view of academic knowledge presented so far in this book constantly stresses its relational nature. Learning academic knowledge, therefore, requires activities that address and deal with relations. One of the most important is the sign-signified relation, which concerns the interpretation of symbol systems, whether linguistic, symbolic or pictorial. It plays a key role in the study of any academic subject. That is the focus of this section.

Academic study cannot do without special forms of representation – language, mathematics, diagrams, symbols – but how do students make sense of them? No subject area escapes the problem, because they all use at least language to represent ideas. However, there are few studies of the problem at university level. One example from science may serve to illustrate how students deal with it.

When I carried out a study on students learning about crystallographic projection, which represents the different shapes of crystalline matter as mathematical diagrams, there was plenty of opportunity to see how students cope with a new formalism in the form of a special diagram. One strategy is to treat it strictly as a procedure that does not need to be interpreted:

> It's about, um, representation of a unit cell of a close-packed hexagonal structure. It's a way of representing, well I'm not actually sure, but all I know is, it's a way of representing the atoms in the unit cell by means of 60° graph paper. And they just refer to the positions of the atoms. That's all I know, really, but that's all you need to know to do it. You don't need to know anything else.

Another student knew what he needed in order to grasp the meaning of these complex representations, but felt it was not available to him:

This doesn't fall into my particular method of learning, this handout business, because I don't learn things photographically. I can't look at something and remember it. I can't read something and remember it. The only way I can learn something is to do it. It's all done for us here and it's not fully educational for me. Instead of all these being drawn in, if these were exercises and we had to do work, then I'd get it straight away.

This student and the next one were both working hard at the subject, often devoting hours of study to trying to figure out how to interpret and draw these diagrams. It is a little like trying to understand a foreign language when you have only a cursory knowledge; once you miss the odd phrase, maintaining the sense of what the discourse is about becomes ever harder. What to the lecturer seems a logical progression through successively abstract diagrams that allow ever more complex crystals to be represented, seems to the student like utter confusion:

There are so many ways of describing one crystal, it seems illogical. We draw it naturally, the way you see it, then we're told to draw it in three-dimensional projection to see it that way. Now we're told to draw it in a circle. Totally illogical. Then we have to see not only how the crystal fits in the circle – and that looks nothing like a crystal to me – we have to see how it works in that diagram by drawing another diagram and another circle. It's very confusing, all the different terminologies for one crystal. It would be nice if we had one thing now that brought all these planes, this stereographic projection and this [diagram] and tried to relate them all and show exactly how they fitted, in a sort of sequence of events, whereas we've been given them totally separately.

This student demonstrates an awareness of what a deep approach would be, but he does not have the intellectual means to carry it out. He wants to have a sense of a coherent whole, he is trying to make sense of the diagrams in terms of the crystal it is supposed to represent, but the sign-signified relation is unintelligible so far, and he seems to have no idea that the point of the whole process is precisely to build a formalism that makes it easy to represent complex crystals and their orientations in the world. The lecturer, by the way, was unusually committed and reckoned by the students to be an excellent teacher. This is a non-trivial and persistent problem throughout higher education: students need help in practising the mapping between world and formalism, the ways of representing academic ideas and their interrelations.

ACTING ON THE WORLD (OF DESCRIPTIONS)

One of the most often quoted maxims about learning is the one which concludes 'I do and I understand'. All teachers recognise the importance of learning as an activity done by the learners. Teaching methods in use in universities therefore include many examples of learning through practice or imitation of practice (laboratory practicals, demonstrations, fieldwork, seminars, essays, problems, exercises, etc.). Action as an aspect of learning is not in dispute. But what are learners acting on when they are learning academic knowledge? Is it the same world they are acting on when they are learning experiential knowledge? I have already begun the argument in Chapter 1 that academic knowledge is importantly different from experiential knowledge, and this distinction becomes unavoidable when we consider this aspect of the process of learning. I contrasted second-order academic knowledge with first-order experiential knowledge, i.e. as being knowledge of descriptions of the world rather than knowledge of the world. The distinction is particularly important when we consider how learners are to access the knowledge. When the 'what' that is being learned is objects, behaviours, sensations, then experience serves as the access; when the 'what' is theories, descriptions, viewpoints, then the access can only be through some form of representation: language, symbols, diagrams, pictures. The actions learners must carry out can only be usage of language and symbols, therefore. Learning about dogs can be done through actions on the object: observation, touch, smell, interaction (offering a biscuit, throwing a ball), comparing these experiences with the same actions on other animals, etc., all done without recourse to any form of representation or use of language. Learning about molecules cannot be begun without recourse to representation of some kind.

In their paper debating this issue, Eysenck and Warren Piper suggest that students can imagine molecules as ping-pong balls, and in this sense they are experienced (Eysenck and Warren Piper 1987). Yes, but not in the way ping-pong balls are experienced.

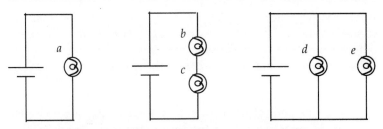

Figure 3.1 The bulbs in the circuits must be ranked according to brightness. (Based on Figure 3 in McDermott 1991: 308.)

The access to molecules is via an analogy, and this is a difficult trick, because setting up the correct analogy for a particular exploratory action on a molecule presupposes an understanding of molecules. Physics is notorious for alluring concrete analogies that lead you falsely. Electrical current is a nice example. Most people feel they have a rough understanding of current flow, using water flow as an analogy, but try using it to predict the answer to the problem shown in Figure 3.1, put by McDermott to an undergraduate physics class (McDermott 1991).

One form of the analogy assumes that the battery acts like a kind of waterfall (the greater the height the greater the voltage), and the bulb acts like a filter slowing the flow down (the faster the water flows the brighter the bulb). This means that the water flows at the same rate through a and b, but by the time it gets to c it has already slowed down a bit, so $a = b > c$. In the third situation, the same amount of water is divided, so the rate of flow through d and e is half what it is for a, so $a > d = e$. That is wrong: the right answer is $d = e = a > b = c$. The difficulty occurs in setting up the analogy. The rate of flow depends upon the relation between the voltage and the resistance, so an ever-replenishing waterfall whose rate of flow is not governed just by what you put in its way, but by the quantity of water available, is an inappropriate analogy. So an alternative analogy is composed to correct this: of traffic flow through bottle necks. A lane closed off in two places still yields the same flow through both places, so b now equals c. But they should also be the same as a, on this analogy. And since the traffic can divide through d and e, they should also receive the same flow as a – which makes them all equal. This analogy also fails. We need an analogy that embodies the fact that the current depends on the total resistance in the circuit, not just localised to a particular point. I hope you are suitably confused. Only one-eighth of the physics undergraduates got the correct answer, and were found to use a variety of unsuitable analogies (McDermott 1991: 308). The study makes the point that imagining concrete analogies is not a reliable way of gaining access to the experience of academic knowledge. Setting up the correct analogy is highly dependent on a good understanding of the concept being learned.

There is no equivalent of 'water play' for learning about electric current. An experience of water flowing faster as the bucket tips more steeply, of the conservation of amount, of watching the river flow, all enable us to develop an elaborated understanding of the concept of water flow, and to make reliable predictions about effects of actions on it. Our access to what electric current does when a circuit divides is available to us only via equations, definitions, language. Laboratory experiments are intended to provide 'current play' – and it is a fair bet that every person who reads this book will probably have carried out a school science experiment that put an ammeter across circuits wired up as in Figure 3.1 to demonstrate the effect above. But how does that trembling needle link into our mental model of electric current? It is a very tenuous link, hardly to be compared with the physical model of a water wheel spinning faster as you pour more water on it.

This kind of analysis is reminiscent of discussions in the philosophy of science about how scientists decide between theories. It is generally accepted that a decision about which theory is to be preferred can only reasonably be made when there is some basis for agreement about observables. Schoolchildren and physics teachers looking at an ammeter in a laboratory are rather like the Pope and Galileo looking through a telescope at the moons of Jupiter. In what sense is this a shared experience? What basis is there for a shared description?

If we move to a different subject area, such as the humanities, the same kind of analysis can be done. As Eysenck and Warren Piper (1987) pointed out (see Chapter 1), learning the concept of 'table manners' and 'structuralism' is similar because both are 'a protocol for going about a ritual task'. This is a fair point, except that understanding 'structuralism' embodies more than exhibiting certain behaviours. It is not sufficient that the student avoids referring to the author's intentions and employs a purely textual analysis, in the way that it is sufficient that a child avoids reading at the table and uses a knife and fork. Academic knowledge goes beyond behaviour because it has to be articulated in order to be available for argument, testing, improvement. The distinction parallels the difference between scientific knowledge and everyday knowledge, and the traditional divisions between education and training.

Acting on the world to learn about concepts is not a straightforward issue. Because academic knowledge is essentially knowledge through description, it follows that action on that knowledge has to be in the form of further descriptions using language or symbols, or manipulations of language and symbols. The actions are entirely contained in the usage of language or other forms of representation. Why else would academics consider written examinations an adequate way of assessing academic knowledge?

There are many learning activities students carry out during an academic course that do consist in learning about the world, in the sense that they increase their range of direct experiences which are then available for later analysis and reflection within the world of descriptions. Students of literature read novels, see plays; students of science look down microscopes to see substances in more detail; students of technology visit power stations to get a sense of scale and complexity; and all these direct experiences of the world then play a part in what a student brings to their learning of new academic material, as discussed in Chapter 2. Acting on the world is a component of academic learning, therefore, but does not adequately account for all that must be done. That is why the proper subject of this section is 'acting on the world of descriptions'.

USING FEEDBACK

Action without feedback is completely unproductive for a learner. As we learn about the world through acting on it, there is continual feedback of some kind, and if we can make the right connection between action and feedback, then we can adjust the action accordingly and this constitutes an aspect of learning. And it is not just getting feedback that is important, but also being able to use it. To the child who reads 'structural' we do not say 'accentuate the antepenultimate'; we say 'you mean "structural" ', because they can make a connection between that feedback and their action more readily. Feedback has to be meaningful.

There are two easily distinguished types of feedback, intrinsic and extrinsic, and both play an important role in learning. 'Intrinsic' feedback is that which is given as a natural consequence of the action. Clear examples of this are abundant in water play, as the physical world responds to the child's actions of filling, pouring, emptying, etc. Correcting pronunciation is another example: although not an inevitable response to the action, pronunciation is a social norm and feedback of this type is natural and probable in a social situation.

These examples contrast with 'extrinsic' feedback, which does not occur within the situation but as an external comment on it: right or wrong, approval or disapproval. It is not a necessary consequence of the action, and therefore is not expressed in the world of the action itself. Extrinsic feedback is the feedback that operates at the level of descriptions of actions, commonly used in educational contexts. It may or may not be helpful or meaningful. A simple 'right' or 'wrong' gives the learner no information at all about how to correct their performance, only that correction needs to be done. It may also not be obvious which aspect of the performance is wrong: are they saying 'wrong' because I mis-read it or because I mis-pronounced it? A more helpful form of extrinsic feedback would give the learner information about how to adapt their performance. An elaborated comment like 'accentuate the antepenultimate' offers a generalised rule from which the action '*struc*tural' can be derived. It is a description of an action, unlike intrinsic feedback which is response from the system in which the student acts, whether physical or social.

The key feature of extrinsic feedback is that it is external to the context of action. It refers to feedback that is not 'situated'. As an example, I shall draw on a tutor–student dialogue, published by Stevens, Collins and Goldin (1979), who use it to characterise tutor behaviour in response to students' 'bugs'. The dialogue concerns the causes of rainfall, and the student has demonstrated an understanding that rainfall comes from moist air cooling and condensing. The student then exhibits a misconception which the tutor corrects:

Student: ... the moist air cools, so the clouds can't hold the water, so it rains.
Teacher: OK, what causes the moist air to cool?
Student: It cools when the wind blows it and it lowers from the sky.

Teacher: What happens to the temperature of moist air when it rises?

Student: It gets warm.

Teacher: No. Warm air rises, but as it rises, it cools off.

(Stevens, Collins and Goldin 1979: 150)

The student has demonstrated a common misconception that the higher the air, the warmer it is. It is common knowledge that warm air rises, but this is interpreted as an attributional property of air that is high up. The tutor offers an alternative description of what happens, more complex in the sense that it describes a relation: as height increases, temperature decreases. This is a description of what could have been an experience for the student, obtained as extrinsic feedback on the student's description. If geography students were able to practise 'air play' as children can practise 'water play', then they could well develop a situated understanding of the relation, an equivalent to the generalised rule that 'as the angle of pouring increases, the water flows faster', along the lines of 'as air rises it cools'. The difference is that obtaining the feedback as a description and not as an experience means that from the student's point of view this result is not connected to any goal or action on their part. It is situated in the dialogue only, as feedback on their description. The dialogue offers further opportunity for action in the form of description, when the tutor asks how mountains could cool moist air:

Student: As it rises, or even if it doesn't rise, the cold mountains could cool it off.

Teacher: No, contact with a cold object does not provide enough cooling to an air mass to cause rain.

(Ibid.: 150)

The student appears to be aware of the possibility that the mountains could make the air rise, but is sufficiently uncomfortable with that conception at the moment to prefer the security of another common misconception, that the cooling is done by contact with something cold. The next opportunity to rehearse the newly-learned action of invoking the 'as it rises it cools' rule comes later in the dialogue when the tutor is trying to achieve transfer to the new situation of a non-mountainous region:

Teacher: What happens when the warmer moist air is blown off the water and hits the stationary cold air mass?
Student: It makes it rise.
Teacher: Right, why?
Student: Because warm air rises, and when this warm air rises with the cool air on top of it, then the air will cool and it will rain.
Teacher: Almost. The warm air rises over the cool air.

(Ibid.: 150–1)

Perhaps the student has now adopted the tutor's view that warm air rising is sufficient to cool it, but not to the extent of dissociating it completely from the cool air mass, which from the student's point of view still seems to have the function of helping the warm air to cool rather than helping it rise. The tutor makes the appropriate adjustment to the student's description.

The to and fro of this kind of dialogue makes a good match with the to and fro of interaction with the world, where action elicits feedback in the form of some event or behaviour, and adjustments to the action in the light of feedback elicit further feedback, enabling a refinement of the action to match what the world requires. In the dialogue, what is being refined is not actions in the world, but descriptions of the world, also a kind of action, perhaps, and undoubtedly experienced, but the experience is not of rainfall: it is of descriptions of rainfall.

The nature of feedback on academic learning will reappear again in the following chapters. At this stage I hope to have established the unity in the eyes of the student between, on the one hand, action with intrinsic feedback in the world as experienced directly and, on the other hand, action as description of the world with extrinsic feedback in the form of redescription. The tutor's role is essentially a rhetorical one.

REFLECTING ON GOALS–ACTION–FEEDBACK

It has been unavoidable in the previous sections of this chapter to include mention of the goal of the learning process. The presence of a goal is prefigured in the unity between action, feedback and integration; these aspects of the process only make sense with the direction provided by a goal. The link between them is only made if the learner can reflect on the relationships between them all: on what the feedback means for the action in relation to the goal to be achieved; on what the goal means for the action to be set up in the light of the feedback on the last action, etc. Reflection is not confined to the goal, but as an aspect of the learning process it must always attend to the goal.

There is not a great deal of work in higher education, or indeed at other levels of learning, that focuses specifically on the way learners handle the goals of a learning situation. It does receive considerable attention in work on information processing, particularly in relation to 'problem solving', where 'think-aloud' protocols are able to elicit descriptions of the meta-level activities associated with goal-setting, planning, revising, etc. The interviews conducted within the 'phenomenographic' method focus on the way subject content is perceived, but also ask for retrospective descriptions of how the task was accomplished, how the student perceived the goal, and how they used this in their execution of the task. Some of the early work on reading, which established the deep-surface dichotomy, used both textual analysis and retrospective accounts by students of what they were doing. The latter provided direct evidence of intentions such as 'looking for the meaning', 'trying to discover what the author wanted to put across', and conversely the absence of these intentions in a surface approach. This link made between intention, process and outcome is an empirical one, and demonstrates the importance for the learning process of the way the student interprets the goal of the task.

But whose goal is it? We keep returning to the essential unity of the learning process that requires mutual interaction between its various aspects, and in learning about the world through experience it is relatively straightforward to interpret the individual's actions as being goal-directed, where the goal is itself a product of the individual's interaction with the world, inextricable from the individual learning in that situation. This does not transfer very well to the academic learner, however. The goal of an academic learning situation is generally set by the teacher. The students may be aware of it, and may even share it, but they stand in a different relation to it in comparison with their goal-directed actions in the world.

A goal may be apparently agreed and shared, but the execution of actions directed to that goal may betray subtle differences in interpretation of the goal. Wertsch, Minick and Arns (1984) studied two different groups of adult–child pairs given the task of reproducing a model. They found that although all pairs achieved the match, the way they did it was dependent on the group they were in: in mother–child pairs in a domestic context the adult was more likely to direct the child's actions than in teacher–child pairs in a classroom context (Wertsch, Minick and Arns 1984). They interpret this result with the help of Leontiev's (1928) theory of activity, to suggest that although goal and execution are logically independent of each other, in the sense that a goal can be executed many ways and, conversely, an action can serve many goals, the regularity observed in the way a common goal is executed in two different ways in two different groups must be explained in terms of the way the activity is seen by the two groups. In the case cited, the mothers see the task as being to reproduce the model correctly, whereas the teachers see the task as being to instruct the children, hence the difference in the way the task was carried out.

What happens when students are solving problems set by a lecturer? In what sense are they able to maintain a unity between the nature of the task, the goal and their actions? I have reported elsewhere a study of how twelve students on a microelectronics course set about a problem solving exercise. The students reported retrospectively on their approach to a problem in microelectronics which asked them to write a device control program. The analysis of those protocols showed that the students were united in their perception of the task as being about providing the teacher with what he required of them, rather than as being about designing a program (Laurillard 1984). This was evident at the initial planning stage:

> I have to sort through the wording very slowly to understand what he wants us to do.

> I read through the notes to see what was familiar from the lecture, i.e. phrases or specific words that were repeated.
>
> (Laurillard 1984: 130)

and again at the operational stage, where they might be expected to focus purely on the content of the task:

> I thought of a diagram drawn in a lecture and immediately referred back to it. Then I decided which components were wanted and which were not and started to draw it out, more or less copying without really thinking.

> I decided since X was setting the questions block diagrams were needed.
>
> (Ibid.: 131)

and again at the final stage of checking back over the solution:

> I don't think the finished product was right but I decided it would do.
>
> I drew what I thought seemed logical although [I] was not satisfied as I couldn't really see how it fitted in . . . I didn't really do this exercise with a view to getting anything out of it. I felt it was something to copy down and nothing to understand really.
>
> (Ibid.: 132)

These were model students, who worked hard and conscientiously on a tough course, taught by an enthusiastic teacher. They cannot be dismissed as out of the ordinary in any way. But their perception of the task in hand is intriguingly contrary to what the teacher supposed was going on. The point of these exercises was to familiarise the students with the intricacies of this kind of program, to give them a feel for the way the control of the electronics device could be analysed. The teacher saw the exercise as a challenging logical problem in linking the features of the device to the capabilities of the microprocessor via the medium of a set of coherent and unambiguous instructions. The students saw it as a problem in matching the demands of the teacher, defined in the exercise as set, to the information available, encoded in the linguistic and pictorial forms of representation he used in the lecture, via the medium of symbols and diagrams. At every point the task, the goal and the operations are seen differently by teacher and students. I described the focus of the students' attention as being the 'problem-in-context', rather than the problem itself. This is similar to Wertsch's analysis of the theory of activity: the same task can be perceived as a different kind of activity by teacher and students, and therefore operationalised in a way the teacher may not expect.

This does not destroy the essential unity between goal and action. It is preserved in the mutual shift of focus of both goal and operations on the part of the students from the substantive problem to the problem-in-context. The teacher's goal is not their goal, so reflection on their actions in relation to their goal produces a different analysis than it would if they were concerned about getting a functional program written.

As a mathemagenic activity, reflecting on action in a learning task in relation to its goal is known to be important from the work on deep and surface approaches. We have seen from the above discussion that the teacher has some additional work to do, not just in setting the goal, but in helping to form students' perceptions of what is required and what is important in the task set, as well as encouraging students to do the reflecting.

SUMMARY

In this chapter we have looked at students' learning activities in terms of five interdependent aspects of the learning process. Students must address all these mathemagenic activities if learning is to succeed:

- apprehend the structure of the discourse – e.g. focus on the signified, relate and distinguish evidence and argument, organise and structure the content into a coherent whole
- integrate the sign with the signified – e.g. practise mapping between the two, practise the forms of representation of an idea, represent the discourse as a whole as well as its constituent parts
- act on the world and on descriptions of the world – e.g. relating knowledge to experience, relating theory to practice, extending experience of the world, manipulating the various forms of representation of that experience
- use feedback – e.g. both intrinsic and extrinsic feedback to adjust actions to fit the task goal, and descriptions to fit the topic goal
- reflect on the goal–action–feedback cycle – e.g. relating this to the message of the discourse, the structure of the whole

The division of the learning process into five aspects does not make them in any sense independent. Whichever way the process is divided up, it will always be necessary to see one aspect in relation to the others. Throughout this chapter I have repeatedly invoked one in the discussion of another, and this is inevitable. The five aspects chosen enabled me to make use of the research literature in an orderly way, and provide a framework for further discussion, but they are not meant to be seen as logically distinct.

It would be like trying to divide a society into mutually exclusive families. 'Family' is a useful category, but not an analytical one; each aspect of the learning process identified is constituted by its relation to the others.

Mathemagenic activities have been defined as those that give birth to learning, and encouraging these is an appropriately student-centred way of thinking about the teacher's task. We have looked at what count as mathemagenic activities for each of the five aspects of learning discussed, and considered also the activities that students engage in that are not mathemagenic. An awareness of both types will give us a grounding for devising teaching strategies in the next chapter.

Chapter 4

Generating a teaching strategy

INTRODUCTION

This chapter has the task of forming the bridge between what we know about student learning and what we should therefore do as teachers. That 'therefore' contains the assumption that there is some kind of logical link between the two. At the end of every study of student learning, and indeed of instructional psychology, educational psychology, and even sometimes cognitive psychology, there is an 'implications for teaching' section, which sets out the supposed link. In this chapter we shall look at some of these links and their resultant implications, but I feel I should issue a warning at the start that although this can be a respectable analytical process – going from what we know about student learning to what this means for teaching – it is not a logical one. It is clearly important to base a teaching strategy on an understanding of learning, but the relationship is fuzzy. The character of student learning is elusive, dependent on former experiences of the world and of education, and on the nature of the current teaching situation. What we learn from this will have an uncertain relation to what will happen in a new teaching situation. The dialectical character of the teaching–learning situation means that the connection will not transfer exactly to the different context of a new teaching strategy. We cannot tweak the teaching without altering the way the learning relates to it.

The nature of student learning described in all the previous studies embodies within it the nature of the teaching situation the students were involved in while being studied. That is why it was important not to decouple the description of learning from its content. However, it was usually decoupled from its context. In the one example I quoted in Chapter 3, where the context was taken into account (students on the microelectronics course), it became clear that there was a dissociation between the content and the context of the learning process (Laurillard 1984b): the students' problem-in-context had little relation to the substantive problem set by the teacher. This remains an unresolved issue for educational design, and I believe it is an important one.

The epistemological position laid out in Chapter 1, and everything that has followed, requires a relational view of knowledge and of learning, and emphasises the situated character of all types of learning. The bulk of the research we have to call upon, if it adopts this epistemology at all, does so in relation to content, rather than context. I do not wish to suggest that with enough funds and time we could establish complete and reliable connections between learning, content and context that would enable us to define reliable prescriptions for teaching strategies, any more than any other human science can do such a thing. Rather, the absence of research on the context of learning gives us an over-simplified view of student learning. So we are basing the design of a teaching strategy on an as yet minimal analysis of student learning. It can still be principled, however, and in this chapter I hope to clarify what makes it principled.

Chapter 2 showed that a teaching strategy has to address students'

- conceptions of the topic
- development of representational skills
- epistemological development

and Chapter 3 showed that a teaching strategy has to encourage students to carry out the following mathemagenic activities:

- apprehending the structure of academic discourse
- integrating parts of the process
- acting on descriptions of the world
- using feedback
- reflecting on the goal–action–feedback cycle

These, together with the subject matter content, are the only basis so far for generating a teaching strategy. These items were arrived at by considering the empirical evidence gathered from a selection of studies that investigated the outcomes and the process of learning in a particular way. None of the studies pretend to completeness of description of the learning process, nor are research studies carried out in a way that ensures they produce complementary coverage of what there is to be known about learning. The two lists therefore constitute a collection of things we ought to include, rather than an analysis of what we need to generate a teaching strategy. Given the lack of a logical relation between learning and teaching strategy, and this incomplete analysis of what a teaching strategy must include, it will be useful to look first at other attempts to derive strategies for effective teaching to see if they find a principled way of doing it.

I can identify in the current literature four distinct ways of handling this problem, deriving from different scientific traditions: (1) instructional design, deriving originally from behavioural psychology but increasingly incorporating findings from cognitive psychology; (2) intelligent tutoring systems design, deriving from cognitive science and applications of artificial intelligence; (3) instructional psychology, deriving from cognitive psychology and cognitive science; and (4) phenomenography, deriving from phenomenological psychology. Each one provides a link between an empirical base and a principle for design, so they can be compared from the point of view of the nature of that base, and the nature of the link made.

INSTRUCTIONAL DESIGN

The undisputed father of the field of instructional design is Robert Gagné, whose book *The Conditions of Learning*, first published in 1965 and now in its fourth edition, forms the precursor to all the current work. A recent analysis, *The Selection and Use of Media* (Romiszowski 1988), acknowledges the influence of his work, so it is worth looking at as an example of a principled approach to generating teaching strategies.

In the twenty-odd years since it was first published, Gagné's analysis has shifted from a grounding in behavioural psychology to using information-processing theory as its empirical base. The system itself underwent only relatively minor revisions and elaborations, however. This is because it has only a tenuous link to any empirical base. Gagné's approach is essentially a logical analysis of what must be the case, rather than an empirically-grounded theory. He begins with definitions of the general types of human capabilities that are learned: intellectual skills, cognitive strategies, verbal information, etc., a common-sense classification of what there is. He then describes the 'learning events' for each capability. These are derived from theoretical constructs generated by experimental studies in cognitive psychology, and based on information-processing theory. The constructs include, for example, 'short-term memory storage', based on studies of telephone number retrieval, and 'encoding', based on studies of memory of short passages of text. These 'learning events', together with the desired outcomes already defined as capabilities, are then used to generate the internal (mental) and hence external (situational) conditions for learning. For example, for 'defined concept learning', a sub-category of intellectual skills, the internal conditions are that the learner should (1) have access in working memory to the component concepts, and (2) have acquired the intellectual skill of being able to represent the syntax of the statement of the definition, i.e. distinguish subject from verb and object. The external conditions 'usually consist in the presentation of the definition of the concept in oral or printed form' (Gagné 1977: 134). That completes the analysis, and all the remaining combinations of capabilities and learning events are analysed in the same way to produce the same kinds of 'external conditions', i.e. the design of instructional events. The complete list of instructional events to be carried out by the teacher is:

- activating motivation
- informing learner of the objective
- directing attention
- stimulating recall
- providing learner guidance
- enhancing retention
- promoting transfer of learning
- eliciting performance
- providing feedback

They seem unobjectionable and have an intuitive logical appeal, which is probably why the approach has been so influential. However, its empirical base is constituted in the theoretical constructs of another discipline. Cognitive psychology has an empirical foundation, but one that is built for its own purposes. These studies of, for example, short-term memory are carried out in experimental situations, and in isolation from all the other components Gagné includes in the learning process. They are used to infer possible constructs to describe how the human brain works. These are then transferred to the context of an academic learning task, as though the transfer were unproblematic. The empirical base is insufficient, therefore, to provide a holistic understanding of student learning. There is no data in the theoretical development of this approach that derives from students learning in an instructional context. The theory may be used to generate teaching which is then evaluated, but this does not test the approach, only its instantiation in that piece of instruction.

A further problem with instructional design of this type is that the analysis into components of the teaching–learning process is not followed by any synthesis. Any relationship between cognitive strategies and motor skills, for example, is not considered. Gagné himself has recognised this recently in a paper with another of the key figures in instructional design, David Merrill. They begin by outlining what they see as the value of their approach:

> The procedure of working backwards from goals to the requirements of instructional events is one of the most effective and widely employed techniques. This approach requires the initial identification of a category of instructional objectives, such as *verbal information, intellectual skill, cognitive strategies* . . . From each of the single categories of learning outcome, the designer is able to analyze and prescribe the instructional conditions necessary for effective learning.
>
> (Gagné and Merrill 1990: 2, original italics)

This analysis deals with one objective at a time, so that the designer must plan for instruction 'at the level of an individual topic'. However, they acknowledge that this is sometimes an inadequate level of analysis:

> When instruction is considered in the more comprehensive sense of a module, section or course, it becomes apparent that *multiple objectives* commonly occur . . . When the comprehensiveness of topics reaches a level such as often occurs in practice, instructional design is forced to deal with multiple objectives and the relationship among these objectives.
>
> (Ibid.: 24, original italics)

Their solution is to add 'integrative goals' to the existing design theory, though without any perceivable shift in the underlying approach:

> We propose that integrative goals are represented in cognitive space by *enterprise schemas* whose focal integrating concept is the integrative goal. Associated with the integrative goal is an enterprise scenario and the various items of verbal knowledge, intellectual skills and cognitive strategies that must be learned in order to support the required performances ... a consideration of enterprises as integrated wholes may lead to a future focus on more holistic student interactions.
>
> (Ibid.: 29, original italics)

But it is not possible to effect a synthesis of those analytical components by simply drawing a circle round them, as the diagram in the paper does, and then naming it. 'Integrative wholes', and 'holistic student interactions' have to be derived from studies that look at interactions holistically. Their enterprise is word games; it is not science.

The influence of this kind of instructional design is enormous, however, which is why the approach must be considered. Perhaps it is the blandness of its conclusions that has permitted the largely uncritical acceptance of this way of tackling the task. Whatever the reasons, it is not a progressive force. It does not find out how the world is, it merely supposes. It is rather like reading a treatise on mediaeval physics, where theories, if they were built on anything other than supposition, were built on other theories, rather than on descriptions of the phenomena themselves. Gagné and Merrill begin their paper with these words:

> One of the signal accomplishments of contemporary doctrine on the design of instruction . . . is the idea that design begins with the identification of the goals of learning.
>
> (Ibid.: 23)

This may seem rather obvious for an idea dignified as a 'signal accomplishment', but its complete absence from much educational planning shows that it was worth saying. And getting widespread acceptance of such an idea is a worthwhile accomplishment. My argument is not so much against their conclusions as against their method. A progressive force in educational design theory would be one that cumulatively builds our knowledge of the phenomena concerned, and this does not. I think we can do better.

INTELLIGENT TUTORING SYSTEMS DESIGN

Intelligent tutoring system (ITS) design offers a different origin and approach to the generation of teaching strategies. Although relatively young as a field, having flourished only ten years or so, it has the distinction of having attracted substantial funding and some clever people to work on the task of designing computer programs that can embody teaching strategies. Its vigour as a field of research depends partly on funding for artificial intelligence in general, of which it is still a branch, and partly on the persistence of the belief that success in this enterprise will enable teaching programs to be generated more efficiently. It is important for its potential future influence, therefore. For my purposes it is also an example of a way of approaching the task in hand.

In a recent paper, Stellan Ohlsson has argued that the goal of artificial intelligence (AI) in education is not to build successful instructional systems, but to 'contribute to the development of a learning theory with clear and specific prescriptive consequences' (Ohlsson 1991: 6). The field is not sufficiently unified to take any one view as representative, but Ohlsson's argument is a useful one to study in detail because it has a clear methodological focus, that establishes the claim that AI in education can provide a principled way of developing a teaching strategy.

Ohlsson begins by pointing out that evaluating an ITS (and the argument applies to any teaching method) is useless, because the particular topic, the particular student population and the particular social environment investigated all change, so that the lessons learned from such an evaluation are almost useless:

> The multitude and volume of instructional topics and student populations imply that we ought to give up the idea that we will one day have pedagogical knowledge about every topic and every student population . . . We need a theory that enables us to work out an optimal set of instructional experiences, messages, and interactions, given a topic, a student population, and certain resources . . . a generative theory from which we can derive successful instructional designs as needed.
>
> (Ohlsson 1991: 7)

A generative theory for instructional design constitutes the kind of principled generation of teaching strategy I am looking for. But if it is not to be based on pedagogical knowledge of topics and students, what is it based on?

Ohlsson describes the link between learning and instruction in terms of a hypothesis about learning, and a model for how learning would be triggered, given this hypothesis, which together logically imply a particular instructional strategy. It is a theory that begins and ends in the mind of the researcher. At no point does a student mind affect it. The construction of the model itself contains the prescriptions for instruction. Something similar happens with the use of 'subject matter representations' of the type used in expert systems (e.g. Anderson 1981) to develop learning theory:

> The expert model of the Geometry Tutor . . . was based on the *implicit assumption* that a geometry expert searches the same problem space as a beginning student, except faster and better . . . because they have heuristics of how to search the relevant problem space . . . Learning consists, *one naturally concludes*, in the acquisition of those search heuristics.
>
> (ibid. 1991: 12, my italics)

No intrusion of a real student so far. It is still supposition. The supposition is then tempered by empirical studies:

> But careful analysis of protocols revealed that geometry experts sometimes solve proof problems without going through all the necessary steps . . . The expert module of the Geometry Tutor was based on a false assumption about learning: learning to construct geometry proofs does not consist in acquiring heuristics for searching the basic proof space of geometry, but in changing the representation of geometric knowledge such that those heuristics become unnecessary.
>
> (Ibid.: 12)

But again, no data from students. The conclusion is not valid. From expert protocols it is only possible to conclude that '*having learned* to construct proofs does not consist in *using* heuristics'. Ohlsson draws the correct conclusion about student modelling:

> Student modeling algorithms . . . are, in fact, implementations of particular assumptions about learning.
>
> (Ibid.: 13)

This is a much better description of the components of an ITS.

The implementation of assumptions does not itself contribute anything to the development of learning theory, however, and although it offers 'clear and prescriptive consequences' for instruction, they derive from a logical analysis, not from empirical studies of students.

There is a considerable epistemological gulf between AI researchers and educationalists. As John Self points out, ITS philosophy, with its persistent 'transmission' model of education:

> runs counter to almost everything of significance in twentieth century educational philosophy ... The ITS philosophy derives from a commonsense theory of knowledge, which holds that items of knowledge exist in an objective sense in the external world and that we can acquire knowledge from the world, via our senses or teachers, or ITSs. But according to most contemporary epistemologists, all knowledge, even in the natural sciences, is conjectural. Knowledge grows only through criticism.
>
> (Self 1989: 4–5)

Building ITS design on an 'education as growth' model enables Self to suggest some interesting features for such systems, e.g. Socratic tutoring techniques, reflection as meta-level architecture, belief logics as the basis for belief revision, co-operative dialogues, and so on. These ideas sound much closer to the epistemological base I have been working to, although the empirical base remains elusive. In his discussion of evaluation of ITSs, Self draws an analogy between ITS design and aircraft design. The goal is a mathematical theory of ITS from which designs may be formally derived; aspects of the theory are tested not in the real world, but in environments specifically designed to test aspects of the theory ('ITS wind tunnels'). As in Ohlsson's analysis, evaluation is not used to develop the system, but the theory:

> the long-term goal should be to eliminate empirical evaluations, not to embrace them within the design process . . . [as] an interim strategy we derive [designs] by observing the (simulated) ITS in a simulated world. It is the same idea as deriving economic predictions from a programmed model of the economy, rather than by axiomatic deductions from a

theory of the economy, and certainly rather than by empirical experiments in the real world.

(Self 1989: 10)

The appeal to economic theory hardly strengthens the case, as we collectively struggle with the consequences of poor economic predictions, but the important point is the nature of this methodology. It is more like a kind of mathematics than science. It explicitly eschews empirical evaluation data. The fun of it, for both Ohlsson and Self, and I suspect for most AI researchers, is in the purely theoretical enterprise of thinking up the ideas, thinking up ways of implementing them in a system, and using its performance to develop better ideas. That is a valid enterprise, and it will enable the field to develop program structures that may well be useful to educational designers, just as mathematical structures are useful for engineers. But I do not accept this as a valid way of generating teaching strategies, because the methodology can tell us nothing about student learning, nor about the teaching of students. Its role is to contribute ways of implementing teaching strategies that are developed by other means. An ITS, used as a means of instantiating theories about learning and teaching, should be a useful research tool. Building a computer program that instantiates a particular teaching strategy both enforces precision on the formulation of the strategy, and offers, as Ohlsson suggests, a reliably consistent means of testing it on several different student populations. But it does not offer a principled derivation of a teaching strategy because ITS design, like instructional design, does not attempt to link it to empirical data about students' learning.

INSTRUCTIONAL PSYCHOLOGY

In his overview of American instructional psychology, Robert Glaser discusses both the instructional design and the ITS approaches, but identifies instructional psychology as the field that will derive the connections between learning theory (from cognitive psychology) and instructional theory, to produce prescriptive principles of instruction (Glaser 1987). For each type of experimental finding or theoretical construct delivered by cognitive psychology, he indicates the way that instruction might make use of it. The empirical base therefore consists of experiments in human cognition. This is augmented by previous and current learning theories to suggest teaching strategies. Implicit in the range of examples he gives are only two different kinds of links between the empirical base and the teaching strategy, however: (1) using the differences between good and bad student performance to define instructional targets, and (2) using results of experiments on different task conditions to specify helpful instructional conditions. We look at each in turn.

Glaser presents findings that indicate what counts as expert knowledge, defining how this differs from that of novices. These studies do not tell us how novices become experts, only how the two differ, so the only possible link to teaching strategy is to define what it must focus on. Examples are:

Knowledge organization and structure:
– elements of knowledge become increasingly interconnected so that proficient individuals access coherent chunks of information;
– so structuredness and accessibility to interrelated chunks of knowledge become targets for instruction.

Depth of problem representation:
– ability for fast recognition of underlying principles is an indication of developing competence;
– so instruction might concentrate on attaining the understanding and depth of representation appropriate to stages of learning achievement.

(Glaser 1987: ix–xiii)

These studies specify what the instruction should focus on, but without any information about the transitional process or the transitional stages they cannot prescribe how the instruction should be carried out. However, they do enable the focus of instruction to progress beyond the identification of topics to a more detailed description of how they should be known (e.g. that chunks of knowledge should be more interconnected).

For the second type of link between empirical base and teaching strategy, Glaser describes a number of studies that look at subjects' performance under different task conditions. There is a direct empirical link made here to what instruction should do, which is given by the nature of the conditions. An example illustrating this approach is to find the task conditions that improve performance efficiency, and then use these to prescribe the instructional strategy:

> Automaticity to reduce attentional demands:
> – when sub-tasks of a complex activity make simultaneous demands for attention, the efficiency of the overall task is affected;
> – so in the development of higher levels of proficiency, basic skills should receive enough practice to become automatized, so that conscious processing capacity can be devoted to higher level processes.

(Ibid.: xi)

It is a plausible prescription, similar to Gagné's, that the teaching strategy should rehearse component skills first. Glaser augments this with more detailed prescriptions using Schneider's training guidelines, based initially on experimental studies of controlled and automatic processing of 'letter set' search and detection tasks. These later led to research on instruction in higher-order skills such as electronic trouble-shooting. The guidelines are specific to skill training and include instructional prescriptions such as 'design the task to allow many trials in short periods of time', 'present information for a component skill in a context that illustrates the large task goal'. Of course, as Schneider points out, these prescriptions are derived from experiments in particular kinds of high performance skill, and the findings may not transfer to other contexts. The conclusion that must be drawn, therefore, is that the link between task conditions and improved performance must be empirically determined for each instructional case.

It is not a promising outlook for the 'prescriptive' future of instructional psychology. The empirical base provided by novice–expert studies only identifies what the teaching should focus on, not how it should be done. And the one area that does offer prescriptions, experimental studies of varying task conditions, does so with provisos that they may not apply in other contexts. They do suggest instructional strategies that might succeed elsewhere, which is reasonable and helpful, but hardly 'prescriptive'.

Glaser also describes specific teaching strategies such as Collins and Brown's cognitive apprenticeship, and Anderson's ACT theory, but does not analyse how these are generated from any empirical base. We are left with just two types of link between empirical base and teaching strategy, therefore:

1 From descriptions of the differences between novice and expert derive the types of knowledge structure, forms of problem representation, problem features and subject matter conceptions that should be focused on.
2 From studies of different kinds of performance under different task conditions, deduce the instructional conditions most conducive to learning.

The teaching strategy that can be generated depends upon the type of empirical study that was done, focus of content for the former, localised task conditions for the latter. Beyond that, the generation of teaching strategy is a creative process informed by what we know from research, but not determined by it. The 'prescriptive principles that can guide the design of instructional techniques and materials' that Glaser looks towards (Glaser 1987: vii) will be a long time coming. The studies he covers are suggestive rather than prescriptive, and do not promise ever to be more than that.

PHENOMENOGRAPHY

Given that the methodology of phenomenography, as discussed in previous chapters, contrasts with that of instructional psychology, it will necessarily contrast also in the way it uses data. Its empirical base derives from discovery rather than hypothesis-testing; it uses qualitative rather than quantitative data; and it produces descriptions rather than explanations. It can hardly aim to be prescriptive in defining the implications of its findings, therefore. The term used instead is 'co-operative' (Marton and Ramsden 1988). When research is co-operative rather than prescriptive it follows that the nature of the link between empirical base and teaching method must turn away from defining what the teacher must therefore do to the student, and towards defining how teacher and student should interact.

Marton and Ramsden list eight teaching strategies deriving from a collection of phenomenographic studies. This is the most extensive list of recommendations based on phenomenographic methods, so it is the best representation to date of what the method can achieve in terms of implications for teaching:

1 Present the learner with new ways of seeing.
2 Focus on a few critical issues and show how they relate.
3 Integrate substantive and syntactic structures.
4 Make the learners' conceptions explicit to them.
5 Highlight the inconsistencies within and the consequences of learners' conceptions.
6 Create situations where learners centre attention on relevant aspects.
7 Test understanding of phenomena; use the results for diagnostic assessment and curriculum design.
8 Use reflective teaching strategies.

(Marton and Ramsden 1988)

The first three and the sixth are prescriptive about what to tell students, focusing more on how to present than on how to interact. Numbers (4) and (5) work better because they assume the kind of interaction between teacher and student that gives the teacher access to what the student's conceptions are, and then prescribe how the interaction should continue thereafter. Numbers (7) and (8) prescribe different forms of interaction, allowing students' views to be represented and taken into account in the approach to teaching and assessment.

Marton and Ramsden's recommendations are in the spirit of a more co-operative approach to the way both educational research and teaching should be carried out. Their discussion of each one shows how the empirical base can be used to generate the strategy they define. Implicit in this discussion are two distinct ways of linking research results to implications for teaching:

1 from descriptions of the internal structures of different conceptions, deduce how teachers and students should make their conceptions explicit so that they can be compared and contrasted.
2 from descriptions of the differences between successful and unsuccessful teaching, deduce the characteristics of successful teacher–student interactions.

They look similar to those distilled from Glaser, but there are important differences. Firstly, because phenomenographic studies produce descriptions of the internal structures of students' and experts' conceptions, they clarify what aspects of the conceptions should be focused on in the interaction, how students relate to the ideas, and how the dialogue should be conducted. This is richer material than is produced by novice–expert studies. Secondly, the descriptions of differences in teaching are based on studies of real teachers teaching real students, so the abstraction of generalities can be carried out at the level of the relation between teacher–student–subject, and does not have to move so far away to the level of conditions–person–task. For both types of link, the research prescribes not the action the teacher must do to the student, but the form of the interaction between teacher, student and subject matter. This is why I believe phenomenography offers the best hope for a principled way of generating teaching strategy from research outcomes.

Academics will need a less generalised level of description of the recommendations than those listed above. In applying these types of link to the research outcomes listed at the beginning of this chapter, therefore, I shall attempt to preserve the content of the original findings, to ensure that the strategies derived are usable.

A PRINCIPLED APPROACH TO GENERATING TEACHING STRATEGY

Returning to the list of findings to be addressed by a teaching strategy, I want to reconsider these in the light of the principle, expressed above, of using them to deduce the form of interaction between teacher, student and content. This shift in focus from what the teacher should do, to how they must set up the interaction, reflects the fact that we cannot generalise these findings, only the methodology (Marton 1988). We cannot claim to have sorted out once and for all what students need to be told if they are to make sense of topic X. No matter how much detailed research is done on the way the topic is conceptualised, the solution will not necessarily be found in new ways of putting it across. The new way of telling may sort out one difficulty, but it may well create others. All we can definitely claim is that there are different ways of conceptualising the topics we want to teach. So all we can definitely conclude is that teachers and students need to be aware of those differences and must have the means to resolve them. The only *prescriptive* implications are that:

- there must be a continuing dialogue between teacher and student
- the dialogue must reveal both participants' conceptions
- the teacher must analyse the relationship between the student's and the target conception to determine the focus for the continuation of the dialogue
- the dialogue must be conducted so that it addresses all aspects of the learning process

There is no escape from the need for dialogue, according to this analysis. There is no room for mere telling, nor for practice without description, nor for experimentation without reflection, nor for student action without feedback, etc. This very 'prescriptive' implication from phenomenographic studies is compatible with my analysis of the nature of academic knowledge in Chapter 1. If you accept that academic knowledge is knowledge of descriptions of the world and will become known through operations on descriptions, then teaching must be seen as a rhetorical process. So the implications of research must be about how to conduct the dialogue with students.

The findings on what students bring to learning (see Chapter 2) can be used to decide on the selection of content and the way it should be focused on. For example, the rainfall example reveals a mismatch between the tutor's 'as air rises it cools' conception, and the student's 'warm air rises' and 'cooling happens by contact' conceptions, which suggests a focus for a teaching strategy. But the identification of a mismatch does not suggest what should be done about it. Similarly, McDermott's study of electric current reveals an inappropriate use of the water flow analogy, which implies the teaching should focus on what governs the flow of current, but again it cannot be specific about how this should be done (McDermott 1991).

Moving from conceptions to forms of representation, we know, for example, from Resnick's studies that students have trouble interpreting the signs of the subtraction procedure (Resnick and Omanson 1987). That finding provided the focus for a 'mapping' teaching strategy, designed to help students practise mapping between a real-world event and its mathematical representation. We know from the results of the experiment that the strategy was not successful, but the data collected is not informative about why. Because of the experimental–prescriptive paradigm she uses,

Resnick supplies only quantitative data on students' performance, rather than the kind of qualitative data that was used to state the original research problem and develop the teaching strategy. With a descriptive–co-operative paradigm, the interaction resulting from the new teaching strategy itself would have been the new data, yielding new qualitative descriptions of the students' learning, not just the quantitative measures of the students' performance. Qualitative data of this type builds our knowledge of how students think.

The findings on the aspects of the learning process students need to address (see Chapter 3) will be the best source of ideas about how to conduct the interaction around the selected focus. Table 4.1 elaborates each aspect of the process to show what roles student and teacher should play in the interaction.

Table 4.1 Student and teacher roles in the learning process

Aspects of the learning process	Student's role	Teacher's role
Apprehending structure	Look for structure Discern topic goal	Explain phenomena Clarify structure Negotiate topic goal
Integrating parts	Translate and interpret forms of representation Relate goal to structure of discourse	Offer mappings Ask about internal relations
Acting on descriptions	Derive implications, solve problems, test hypotheses, etc. to produce descriptions	Elicit descriptions Compare descriptions Highlight inconsistencies
Using feedback	Link teacher's redescription to relation between action and goal to produce new description	Provide redescription Elicit new description Support linking process
Reflecting on goal–action–feedback	Engage with goal Relate to actions and feedback	Prompt reflection Support reflection on goal–action–feedback

To see how usable this analysis is, I shall apply it to two particular learning problems for which the literature tells us something also about the success of the teaching strategy used. In each case we look at how the teacher-student interaction is conducted, in terms of the five aspects of the process listed above.

How rainfall occurs

Taking the dialogue between tutor and student already outlined in Chapter 3 as an example of an interaction designed to help the student change their conception, how would the above analysis be applied?

1 There *is* a continuing dialogue between teacher and student.
2 The dialogue *does* reveal both participants' conceptions.
3 The teacher *does* analyse the relationship between the student's and the target conception to determine the focus for the continuation of the dialogue.
4 The dialogue *does not* address all aspects of the learning process.

It is not just conducting a dialogue that is important, but how it is conducted. This particular dialogue fails to address several of the essential aspects of the learning process, as listed at the end of Chapter 3. First, in that exchange there was no opportunity for the student to 'apprehend the structure' of the tutor's discourse. It would be a difficult exercise from the transcript, and next to impossible in the cut and thrust of a conversation, to discern the totality of the tutor's point of view, the key planks in his argument, the nature of the connections between them. The representation of the tutor's knowledge structure in the original paper involves nine propositional nodes and seven connecting relations of three different types. This remains only implicit in the kind of dialogue I quoted in Chapter 3.

Other aspects of the process are better. The tutor certainly provides an interactive environment that allows the student to act on descriptions; he elicits descriptions from the student relating in different ways to the descriptions he offered. The student is asked to explain phenomena ('. . . it rains – yes, why?' 'Because the moist air cools and the clouds cannot hold the water'), to make predictions about new situations ('Can you guess what the average rainfall is like on the other side of the mountains?' – 'It's probably heavy'), to compare analogous situations ('What is the relation between mountains and cold air mass?' – 'The cold air mass stays low'). This is exactly what that peculiar phrase 'acting on descriptions' is about: making connections between propositions, offering re-articulations, deducing new propositions. There is also feedback, in the form of extrinsic feedback on the student's hypothesis, a new description ('The cold mountains could cool it off' – 'No, contact with a cold object does not provide enough cooling') (Stevens, Collins and Goldin 1979: 150). The student then has to link this feedback to the goal and action to produce a new description. It is clear what his action was – his hypothesis about cooling by contact – but not so clear what the topic goal is, because this has not been explicitly negotiated. The current tutor-set goal is to explain the role of the mountains in cooling the air, and if he shares this goal he now has a reason to look for an alternative hypothesis, since 'cooling by contact' has been rejected as inadequate. The tutor follows this with feedback relevant to his current goal: 'Rainfall is almost always the result of cooling due to rising air', and then sets up an opportunity for the student to apply this: 'How do you think the mountains might affect the rising of the moist air?' So the tutor is making good connections between the student's description (action), feedback and goal, but the student is not in control, and may not be following those same crucial links, which may be why the 'cooling by contact' bug appears to surface again later in the dialogue. The tutor does not support the student's reflective process of using the feedback to modify their description in relation to the goal.

The aspect of the process that integrates the different parts together does not work very well for the student because the tutor is directing it according to his goals, which remain un-negotiated with the student, and are never reflected upon. This is a common feature of the 'Socratic dialogue', of which this is meant to be an example. It is worth taking time to elaborate this a little further, because it is a respected teaching strategy taking the form of dialogue and so it should fit my purpose well. Yet, interestingly, it fails the application of the above principles.

Brown and Atkins, in their discussion of effective teaching, use Socratic dialogue as an example of the goals of 'enhancing intellectual and oral skills, of developing attitudes and of improving understanding of oneself and others' (Brown and Atkins 1991: 51), and Socrates as 'the great proponent' of small group teaching. The illustrative example they use is from Plato's

Symposium (Hamilton 1951), in the dialogue with Agathon. They quote, with approval, an interaction in which Socrates engages in a kind of rhetorical bullying:

Socrates: You said, I think, that the troubles among the gods were composed by love of beauty, for there could not be such a thing as love of ugliness. Wasn't that it?

Agathon: Yes.

Socrates: Quite right, my dear friend, and if that is so, Love will be love of beauty, will he not, and not love of ugliness?

Agathon agreed.

Socrates: Now we have agreed that Love is in love with what he lacks and does not possess.

Agathon: Yes.

Socrates: So after all, Love lacks and does not possess beauty?

Agathon: Certainly not.

Socrates: Do you still think then that Love is beautiful if this is so?

They omit Agathon's immediate admission of humiliation:

Agathon: It looks, Socrates, as if I didn't know what I was talking about when I said that.

as well as the remainder of the dialogue which shows Socrates being apparently magnanimous in victory, but condescending, nonetheless:

Socrates: Still, it was a beautiful speech, Agathon. But there is just one more small point. Do you think that what is good is the same as what is beautiful?

Agathon: I do.

Socrates: Then if Love lacks beauty, and what is good coincides with what is beautiful, he also lacks goodness.

Agathon: I can't find any way of withstanding you Socrates. Let it be as you say.

[Is this really what we want from our students?]

Socrates: Not at all, my dear Agathon. It is truth that you may find it impossible to withstand; there is never the

>slightest difficulty in withstanding Socrates. But now
>I will leave you in peace.
>
> (Hamilton 1951: 78–9)

Is that a fitting conclusion for a tutorial? Is this an interactive style
to be emulated by tutors? Hamilton, in his introduction, has a
more realistic assessment of the Socratic method, pointing out that
he employs upon Agathon:

>the instrument of philosophical inquiry that is peculiarly his
>own, the method of question and answer, of which the first
>stage consists in reducing the interlocutor to 'helplessness', the
>admission that his own existing views upon the subject under
>discussion are completely mistaken.
>
> (Ibid.: 18)

The goal for Socrates is Truth, to be achieved through
philosophical inquiry. That is not the same as a goal of enhancing
the intellectual skills and understanding of others. Perhaps his interlocutors could achieve his level of understanding by imitating his
method. But in essence it is a strategy that softens them up to the
point that they are ready to capitulate to anything he says: 'Let it
be as you say.' It is extremely authoritarian. The Socratic method
is not, as it is often described, a tutorial method that allows the
student to come to an understanding of what they know. It is a
rhetorical method that puts all the responsibility on, and therefore
assigns all the benefit to, the teacher. To appreciate the true value
of a dialogic interaction to the student, we have to look at the
totality of what the student says. In both Socrates' original, and in
the rainfall dialogue, removal of the teacher's role reveals just how
minimal the student's role is. They engage actively at a localised
level only, the overall structure remaining inaccessible to them,
and therefore the overall meaning is in danger of being lost to them.

We can conclude from this that a tutorial dialogue must be
carefully managed to be successful from the student's point of
view, addressing all the 'mathemagenic activities' as well as
selecting the right focus.

Problem solving in genetics

Given that I am aiming to arrive at a principled way of generating
a teaching strategy that will be useful for a range of teaching

contexts, the principle derived has to be tested against several kinds of applications. Repeating this kind of detailed account for many examples will test the patience of the reader too far, so for this chapter I will present only one more, and further illustration will come in later chapters. The principle should be applicable to any subject area and to any kind of academic learning. How to apply it may not always be transparently obvious, however.

A study of students learning about genetics through problem solving forms a nice contrast to the earlier example, and has the advantage of having been thoroughly researched. Slack and Stewart describe the research history of the identification of conceptual difficulties, consequent prescriptions for improving teaching, and attempts to use computers to promote learning. Some conceptual difficulties were identified as originating from the kinds of problems typically set by textbooks. Their own work provided students with a computer simulation environment which offered problems that were closer in style to the activities of professional geneticists – e.g. reasoning from effects to causes, rather than predicting offspring from initial population conditions. The simulation provided students with a population of organisms and they had to explain the genetics of the population by carrying out selective breeding to produce offspring on which they could perform statistical tests. They could make their own decisions about whether they had enough data and how to interpret the test results. This is a fair simulation of what a geneticist would be doing, and brings the student much closer to active experimentation and biological reasoning than the standard textbook problems did.

All the elements required for the learning process seem to be present here, so the simulation should represent a principled teaching strategy: the students have access to the complete problem structure of explaining the genetics, they decide on task goals (albeit within the global teacher-defined topic goal), they act on the population, obtain feedback on those actions, and are able to reflect on their achievement of the task goal in relation to those actions and the feedback. It seems fine, but in fact this is a careless interpretation of the principle. Manipulating the parameters of a simulation – controlling inputs and seeing the resulting outputs from a model – does not itself constitute a goal–action–feedback unity in terms of the topic goal of describing the genetics. If the goal is to learn how to explain the genetics of the population, then the feedback must be about how well their explanation does that. As it is, the students' work is too close to the scientist's: their goal is to offer a description of the genetics, but they receive no feedback from the simulation program on how good their description is. Their job as students should be to learn about how the scientist sees the world, not do the science.

What did the students learn in this case? Slack and Stewart recorded what students did, and what they said in thinking aloud while solving the problems. Their analysis revealed a number of continuing misconceptions and failures in reasoning which they summarise as follows:

> It is evident from our research that while computer simulations make it possible to offer students experiences in reasoning from effect to cause, and provide opportunities to make hypotheses and to generate and interpret data, they do not of themselves improve problem-solving performance and under-standing in genetics. In order for this to happen teaching must be designed so that these educational goals are explicitly addressed.
>
> (Slack and Stewart 1989: 312)

They deduce from this a new set of prescriptions for instruction, among them the following:

- promote genotypic thinking – it is important for students to have a 'big picture' of the structure of genetics, to realise that genes map to traits, to think about a trait as a variable concept and a variation as a value concept
- promote qualitative thinking – students should realise that a great deal of data analysis can and should occur before considering the more quantitative aspects, and they should be taught to look for cues in the data
- promote general problem-solving heuristics – teach students content-independent problem-solving heuristics, such as generating hypotheses from redescription of data, checking results, asking themselves what they learned

From the direction of the argument in this chapter it should be clear that these are useful findings in that they identify with considerable precision (far more so in the original paper than it would make sense to include here) the nature of conceptual and reasoning difficulties students experience with the subject. It should be equally clear that prescriptions of this type will not be a once and for all solution. We would not be so naïve as to expect such a thing, of course, and the continuous iteration offering gradually better teaching that this article describes is an excellent way to teach. The flaw is only in the nature of the prescriptions; they describe what is to be taught. When teachers use them to teach new things to their students, all the difficulties inherent in the way teaching is received and understood by students will persist for these new topics too. Students will not suddenly switch to being the model of holistic, deep, and epistemologically sophisticated learners. Every finding on student learning I have marshalled in the previous chapters will be attendant upon these new topics as well. The point is not just to change what is taught, but also how it is learned. Teaching must create a learning environment in which the complete collection of mathemagenic activities is available, and their unity preserved at every level of description of the learning situation; i.e. conceptual structure, actions, feedback and goal must relate to each other so that integration can work. Prescriptions for teaching must identify the structure of the range of conceptions, as these authors do, but must also describe how the dialogue is to be conducted, which they do not.

The conclusion from this case is that the four prescriptions listed above for a principled teaching strategy must be refined to make sure they are applied the right way to a particular learning situation. There is a continuing dialogue, in a sense, with a computer simulation, but the design is not such that the students' conceptions are revealed to the program. The case demonstrates a continuing dialogue, in a sense, with the teacher, in which students' conceptions are revealed and analysed, and used to determine the focus of further teaching, but the duration of the dialogue is several research projects. The computer environment does address all aspects of the learning process, but not at the same level of description. For example, the feedback was good enough for science but not for learning.

The case makes clear the need to separate out the nested levels of academic discourse and the experiential learning it refers to. The goal–action–feedback cycle may be supported at the latter level without the former.

SUMMARY

This chapter has sought a way to generate a principled teaching strategy, given what we know about the characteristics of student learning. Three very different approaches were considered. 'Instructional design' theory and 'intelligent tutoring systems' theory are both logically-principled, not empirically-based. The prescriptive nature of instructional psychology allows only restricted conclusions to be drawn about either the topics that need to be addressed, or the contexts within which particular instructional conditions will work. These are informative, but not prescriptive, and neither do they tell us anything about how students learn.

I found phenomenography a more fitting approach. The co-operative style is more democratic, giving full representation to students' as well as teachers' conceptions, and if it prescribes anything, it does so at the level of how the resulting dialogue should be conducted. The best expression of an empirically-based teaching strategy so far, therefore, is as follows, where the requirements generated throughout the chapter are organised into four general categories of description. The learning process must be constituted as a dialogue between teacher and student, operating at the level of descriptions of actions in the world, recognising the second-order character of academic knowledge, and having the following characteristics:

Discursive
- teacher's and student's conceptions should each be accessible to the other
- teacher and students must agree learning goals for the topic, and task goals
- the teacher must provide an environment within which students can act on, generate and receive feedback on descriptions appropriate to the topic goal

Adaptive
- the teacher has the responsibility to use the relationship between their own and the student's conception to determine the focus of the continuing dialogue

Interactive
- the students must act to achieve the task goal
- the teacher must provide meaningful intrinsic feedback on the actions that relates to the nature of the task goal

Reflective
- the teacher must support the process in which students link the feedback on their actions to the topic goal for every level of description within the topic structure

It may seem a little legalistic, but democracy is a serious business. It is prescriptive, but aspires to prescribe a form of interaction between teacher and student, rather than action on the student, and in this way provides a structure capable of its own improvement. The claim for this higher level of prescription is the strong one, that it should not fail. It will be difficult to apply, and might be misapplied, but it should result in improved quality of learning. In the remaining chapters this way of generating a teaching strategy will be used to direct the selection, design and implementation of teaching methods.

Part II

Analysing teaching media

INTRODUCTION

This section has the task of examining what the various teaching methods and media have to offer education. Having arrived at a perspective on teaching and learning that sees the process as inescapably and essentially a dialogue, this may appear to rule out any contribution from teaching methods other than the one-to-one tutorial. Whatever you may think of the approach developed over the last four chapters, it has something to recommend it if it derives the one-to-one tutorial as the ideal teaching situation. Sadly, the one-to-one tutorial is rarely feasible as a method in a system of rapid expansion beyond a carefully selected élite, so we look to other methods to provide the same effect more efficiently.

The familiar methods of teaching in higher education are there to support learning as it is commonly understood to occur: through acquisition, so we offer lectures and reading; through practice, so we set exercises and problems; through discussion, so we conduct seminars and tutorials; through discovery, so we arrange field trips and practicals. These methods, if practised in combination, are capable of satisfying most of the constraints imposed by the teaching strategy derived at the end of Chapter 4. Feedback on students' actions is the weakest link. This is handled within the assessment procedures adopted for set work, and within supervised practicals and tutorials, but is not guaranteed, is usually not closely associated with the actions, and tends to be more extrinsic than intrinsic. I do not accept, however, that these methods are *essentially* unable to yield the ideal form of the teaching–learning process. Paul Ramsden, in his recent book on teaching in higher education (Ramsden 1992), seems more pessimistic. Having developed an extensive analysis of what must be required of the best teaching methods – that they must involve students in actively finding knowledge, interpreting results and testing hypotheses – he notes the sharp contrast between these and the methods that traditionally place authoritative information before students and leave the rest to them:

> The reader will now I hope be able to see one step ahead in the argument and confront the inevitable truth that many popular methods, such as the traditional lecture–tutorial–discussion– laboratory–class method of teaching science and social science courses, do not emerge from this analytical process unscathed. In fact, not to put too fine a point on it, many teaching methods in higher education would seem, in terms of our theory, to be actually detrimental to the quality of student learning.
>
> (Ramsden 1992: 152)

On the other hand, he certainly does not see any salvation in the technological media:

> Computers and video in higher education have so far rarely lived up to the promises made for them ... No medium, however useful, can solve fundamental educational problems.
>
> (Ibid.: 159–61)

In the remainder of his book, he retrieves the position for many of the more traditional methods, or at least for a combination of them, by describing better ways of doing them, with examples of how the traditional methods can, with careful planning, meet the requirements of good teaching:

> In short, a teacher faced with a series of classes with a large group of students should plan to do things that encourage deep approaches to learning; these things imply dialogue, struc- tured goals, and activity ... Teaching is a sort of conversation.
>
> (Ibid.: 167–8)

It is possible, then, to examine the ways traditional methods can meet the requirements derived from the research on student learning, and I believe it can be done in the way Ramsden suggests. I also agree with his point that no one medium can solve the problems, as will become clear. But given what we agree is the essentially conversational character of the teaching–learning process, what kind of role can the various media possibly play, since most of them cannot support conversations at all? Moreover, media may even be *defined* as transmitters, the very opposite of what we need:

> We define 'media' as the *carriers of messages, from some transmitting source* (which may be a human being or an inanimate object) *to the receiver of the message* (which in our case is the learner).
>
> (Romiszowski 1988: 8, original italics)

So how can the use of media possibly fit with an epistemology, such as the one explored in this book, that argues against a transmission model for education, and against the idea that knowledge is an entity separable from knower and known? It will mean a redefinition of 'media' at the very least.

CATEGORIES OF MEDIA FORMS

There are many attempts in the literature to categorise and classify the forms of media, none of which is very illuminating or useful for our purpose here. Classification of forms is a notoriously difficult task, even when we can expect there to be some kind of guiding principle inherent in their existence and formation. The development of educational media has an odd mix of engines driving it – technological pull, commercial empire-building, financial drag, logistical imperatives, pedagogical pleas – and between them they generate a strange assortment of equipment and systems from which the educational technologist must fashion something academically respectable. None of the media discussed in this section was developed as a response to a pedagogical imperative, and it shows. They do not easily lend themselves to pedagogical classifications.

The point of a good classification system is that it should be powerful enough to embrace the ideal as well as the actuals, and thereby make the shortcomings of the actuals apparent. A classification system that starts by classifying what there is will fail in this, and that is why the current attempts are unsatisfying. Chapter 4 ended with principles for generating a teaching strategy, and that is where a classification of educational media should begin.

The categories defined at the end of Chapter 4 reflect the interdependent relationships between all the aspects of the learning process previously defined. To recap, the educational media can be classified as 'discursive', 'adaptive', 'interactive' and 'reflective' when the following conditions are met:

Discursive: both teacher's and students' conceptions are accessible to the other and both topic and task goals can be negotiable; students must be able to act on, generate and receive feedback on descriptions appropriate to the topic goal; the teacher must be able to reflect on student's actions and descriptions and adjust their own descriptions to be more meaningful to the student.

Adaptive (by teacher): the teacher can use the relationship between their own and the student's conception to determine the task goals for the continuing dialogue, in the light of the topic goals and previous interactions.

Interactive (at the level of actions): the students can act to achieve the task goal; they should receive meaningful intrinsic feedback on their actions that relate to the nature of the task goal; something in the 'world' must change observably as a result of their actions.

Reflective: teachers must support the process by which students link the feedback on their actions to the topic goal, i.e. link experience to descriptions of experience; the pace of the learning process must be controllable by the students, so that they can take the time needed for reflection when it is appropriate.

To illustrate these different processes as they occur in real teaching, I have applied them to a one-to-one tutorial in what I hope is an accessible topic. This is not, I'm afraid, another excursion to the primary classroom. It is an edited extract of a remedial maths session for UK undergraduate technology students.

Topic goal: to represent correctly cancellation of algebraic quotients.
Task goal: simplify $(ca + b)/c$.

Student:	$\dfrac{ca + b}{c} = a + b$	*Action on task.*
Teacher:	Can we just look at this bit again?	*Indirect extrinsic feedback on action.*

	Let's turn this into a real problem. Suppose you've got six apples and six bananas and you divide them between six people, what does each person get?	*Adapts task goal to real world task.*
Student:	One apple and one banana.	*Implicit intrinsic feedback from imagining action in world.*
Teacher:	OK, and we can write 'six a's plus six b's shared among six' down as (6a + 6b)/6, and that comes to a + b. OK?	*Extrinsic feedback. Redescription of action as mathematical representation. Checks description is shared.*
Student:	Yes.	*Agrees description.*
Teacher:	Now, can you write down something similar for dividing four apples and one banana between four people?	*Adapts topic goal to check that S does share principle for describing real world action. Selects example to match form of original task.*
Student:	[writes] (4a + 1b)/4. Is that it?	*Reflects on T's earlier redescription. Presents own redescription of imagined action as mathematical representation.*
Teacher:	Yes, terrific. So four apples, and a banana, what would they get each?	*Extrinsic feedback. Adapts task goal to carry out imagined action in the world.*
Student:	One apple and a quarter of a banana . . . Ahh.	*Reflects on interaction, and on description of events as mathematical representation.*
Teacher:	Right. Can you write that down? Write down the whole thing.	*Adapts topic goal to check that redescription of event as mathematical representation is shared.*

Student:	[writes] $= a + \dfrac{b}{4}$	*S redescribes own representation of action.*
Teacher:	Good,	*Extrinsic feedback on redescription.*
	so you can't just cancel one of them. The four divides both the terms on the top line.	*Redescription of T's conception.*

The teacher's focus throughout the dialogue is not on the real world task -- equally, the student's ability to share out objects is not in doubt. The point is to help the student learn to represent the real world mathematically – to acquire the academic knowledge of how to represent experience. The 'thought experiment' with apples and bananas is sufficient interaction, and the student's reflection on that imagined interaction, together with their discursive interaction at the level of description, enables the student to arrive at the teacher's way of looking at the world of apples and bananas. The student is learning how to represent the world, not how to act on the world.

The list of required media characteristics is meant to encompass a complete specification of what is required of a learning situation and what can be offered by combinations of media. Figure II.1 represents adaptation (activities 5 and 10) and reflection (11 and 12) as internal to both teacher and student, and characterises the two levels of their dialogue as discursive, i.e. interactive at the level of descriptions (activities 1 to 4), and interactive at the level of actions (activities 6 to 9).

This 'conversational framework' for describing the learning process is intended to be applicable to any academic learning situation: to the full range of subject areas and types of topic. It is not normally applicable to learning through experience, nor to 'everyday' learning, nor to those training programmes that focus on skills alone, all of which tend to occur at the experiential interactive level only. Cognitive psychologists will argue that experiential learning has adaptive and reflective components as well, which is probably a good model, but the 'conversational framework' identifies those as conscious processes accessible to the learner to consider and modify. This is important, because it makes it possible for both teacher and student to change the way they use them. The reflection we do as children on the internal

TEACHER   MEDIUM   STUDENT

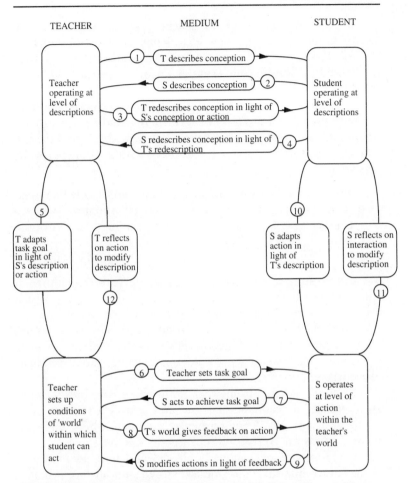

Figure II.1 The 'conversational framework' identifying the activities necessary to complete the learning process.

structure of the language we are experiencing, for example, is not necessarily under our conscious control. There we may do it, but as academics we must do it: as students of a subject, we must consciously stand back from our experience and then, having reflected upon it, argue about it. A critical perspective, necessary for academic understanding, is not a normal adjunct of learning at the level of experience. The two levels are also observably different – the one being action on the world, the other being talk about those interactions with the world. In the context of education, the distinction is an important one.

The characterisation of the teaching–learning process as a 'conversation' is hardly a new idea. I have already quoted Paul Ramsden's statement that it is a sort of conversation. Gordon Pask formalised the idea in Conversation Theory some time ago (Pask 1976), including the separation of 'descriptions' and 'model-building behaviours', and the definition of understanding as 'determined by a two level of agreement' (Ibid.: 22). Vygotsky drew the same kind of distinction between the 'spontaneous' concepts of everyday learning, and the 'scientific' concepts of the classroom:

> The inception of a spontaneous concept can usually be traced to a face-to-face meeting with a concrete situation, while a scientific concept involves from the first a 'mediated' attitude towards its object.
>
> (Vygotsky 1962: 108)

Most interesting ideas have their counterparts in the culture of Ancient Greece, as does this one in the 'Socratic dialogues', which are still referred to as epitomising the tutorial process, as we discussed in Chapter 4. The 'conversational framework' as set out above has at least face validity, therefore, and serves both to clarify the second-order character of academic learning, and to define its essential components.

The conversational framework outlined here defines the core structure of an academic dialogue and relates it to content in terms of a topic goal. Any particular dialogue, where the topic focus shifts as the conversation proceeds, would be mapped by a series of 'nested' conversational frameworks, where the topic goal breaks down into sub-topics, or switches to a parallel topic before returning to the main topic. The dialogue may never actually include action-in-the-world; it may only refer to former experience or 'thought experiments' as in the remedial maths dialogue above, but the core structure still remains two-level. Similarly, the dialogue may never take place explicitly between teacher and student. It could be a purely internal dialogue, with the student playing both roles. This kind of process is manifest in the research interviews described in Chapter 2, where students talk themselves into realising that they fail to understand the point, and in clarifying this fact may sometimes see their way past the cognitive block. For learning to take place, the core structure of the conversational framework must remain intact in some form: the dialogue must take place somewhere, the actions must happen somewhere, even if it is all done inside the student's head. That is where it has to be when learning is done by reflecting on lecture notes. The question before us now is the extent to which the educational media can support the conversational framework and thereby assist the learning process.

In the following chapters each of the principal educational media are analysed in terms of the conversational framework to see how far they serve the needs of a principled teaching strategy, using evidence from evaluation and design studies in the literature where possible. I have selected the main types of educational media, and divided them into their canonical forms, the orthodox, unadulterated way of using each one. This allows us to focus on their essential pedagogical characteristics, and by distinguishing them from each other to identify the unique contribution made by each one. It is hard to find any of these existing in their canonical form, of course, as designers recognise the limitations and each medium is used in combination with another, to the extent that hybrids, such as interactive video, acquire an identity of their own. Another way of dealing with the limitations of a particular medium is to introduce design features to overcome them, such as Rowntree's 'tutorial-in-print' idea to make books easier to learn from (Rowntree 1992). For each medium, therefore, some of the add-ons and the hybrids will be discussed as well.

Chapter 5

Audio-visual media

INTRODUCTION

The audio-visual media include print (both text and graphics) audio, usually audio-cassette, audio-vision (an audio-cassette talking accompanied by some separate visual material), broadcast television or film, and video cassette. These are distinguished from the computer-based media and the teleconferencing media discussed in the following chapters.

There should be some significant pedagogical consequence of the differences between the various types of media. That is what we try to discern in this chapter, for the audio-visual media, using the framework defined in Figure II.1. To what extent can the audio-visual media support the essential activities students must engage in during the learning process? The chapter ends with a table comparing the media covered.

LECTURE

The lecture is under consideration here only to provide a baseline for the classification. It is neither interactive nor adaptive; it does not encourage reflection by the student, and only the teacher is able to communicate their conception. It therefore puts a tremendous burden on the students to engage in the full range of mathemagenic activities: they must do the work to render the implicit structure explicit to themselves, must encourage themselves to reflect on the relationship between what the lecturer is saying and what they previously understood, decide if it is different and how the difference is to be resolved, and check that this is compatible with everything else the lecturer said, thus initiating their own reflective activities, retrospectively, using their notes of the lecture. Their personal redescriptions are then displayed in tutorial discussions or essays which later elicit feedback from the teacher to complete the 'discursive' loop. It can be done, but opportunities for breakdown or failure are numerous.

Some lecturers acknowledge these limitations, and use techniques designed to address the activities omitted in the canonical form of one person talking to many for fifty minutes. Questions to students set tasks for them, where their answers allow the lecturer to refine their descriptions and explanations. Questions from students provide the discursive mode that gives the lecturer an insight into how they are thinking about the topic. Buzz groups allow students to reflect on how their understanding relates to the lecturer's description. Techniques such as these restore the lecture to something a little closer to the ideal of the one-to-one tutorial, but its inevitable one–many format maintains its position as very far from the ideal.

Why aren't lectures scrapped as a teaching method? If we forget the eight hundred years of university tradition that legitimises them, and imagine starting afresh with the problem of how best to get a large percentage of the population to understand difficult and complex ideas, I doubt that lectures will immediately spring to mind as the obvious solution. Their success depends upon the lecturer knowing the capabilities of the students very well, and on the students having very similar capabilities and prior knowledge. Lectures were defensible perhaps in the old university systems of selection of students on the basis of standardised entrance examinations, but more open access and modular courses make it most unlikely that a class of students will be sufficiently similar in background and capabilities to make lectures workable as a principal teaching method. The economic pressures forcing open access also dictate larger classes, yet open access makes those teaching methods hopelessly inefficient.

Academics will always defend the value of the 'inspirational' lecture, as though this could clinch the argument. But how many inspirational lectures could you reasonably give in a week? How many could a student reasonably absorb? Inspirational lectures are likely to be occasional events. Academics as 'students' typically think little of the method. It is commonplace to observe that the only valuable parts of an academic conference are the informal sessions. For the individual learner, the lecture is a grossly inefficient way of engaging with academic knowledge. For the institution it is very convenient, and so it survives.

Alternatives to the predominance of the lecture method at university level have been practised successfully for years in distance learning universities such as the British Open University. These have relied on a combination of media-based learning, occasional tutorials, and correspondence with tutors. For the campus-based university the balance could well be similar, but with the advantage of more opportunity for contact with the tutors and with other students. In the remainder of this and the following chapters, we shall test the educational media against the conversational framework defined earlier to see how far they can support the required activities for students to learn, and what therefore would be an appropriate balance of media and methods for a university not enfeebled by tradition.

PRINT

Print is easily the most important educational medium, in terms of proportion of teaching delivered that way, in both distance teaching and campus universities. This is because of its logistical rather than pedagogical advantages: it satisfies only one of the requirements of the conversational framework, that the teacher can describe their conception. Logistically, it shines: it is the easiest medium to design (single author), to produce (established publishing mechanisms), to deliver (bookshops and libraries), to handle (light and portable), to use (random access, contents, indexes). Logistics change with technological and cultural changes, however, so we have to be clear about the true extent of the pedagogical characteristics of print to be able to judge these against its changing comparative logistics.

Print is similar to the lecture in that it can support only the description of the teacher's conception, but has the key advantage that, like most educational media, it is controllable by the student. They can control the topic focus: they can re-read, skip, browse, go to another topic via the index or contents page, and in doing so control the pace of delivery of the material. For students with contrasting academic backgrounds, self-paced study is important.

The second principal advantage over the lecture is that it will be more complete and better presented than the notes the student took. When I was teaching as a maths lecturer I once took a look at a student's notes, and saw reference to a '$\partial\partial\partial$ function'. Intrigued by this I asked him what it meant. He had no idea but claimed that I ought to know as I had written it on the board. It turned out to be my badly-written 'odd function'. The implications of this were horrifying: not only did the transmission of my knowledge fail, it was also clear that he did not even expect it to succeed, and moreover, knowing it had failed did nothing to remedy the fact, and moreover accepted his fate. It was probably around this time that I began to question the whole idea of the transmission model of education, although my immediate solution was the one that many lecturers adopt routinely, of distributing prepared notes. This combination of lecture and print has almost become the canonical form of the 'lecture'. The point of the lecturer's presence, in this case, can only be to provide what Hodgson calls 'the vicarious experience' (Hodgson 1984) where the lecturer, through their presentation skills, enables the student to see the subject from their point of view, to see why they are enthusiastic about it, to see what is elegant or pleasing, to see how it makes sense of the world. Good writing can put all that into print, however, so it remains difficult to see the point of having lectures at all. At least the printed notes are accurate, and are more easily controlled by the student than the lecture.

Print still has the disadvantages of failing to be interactive, adaptive or reflective, and this has been a particular concern of authors of teaching texts and academics in distance learning institutions such as the British Open University. To counter these essential deficiencies of the printed format, a number of design features have been adopted:

1 The statement of *learning objectives* as a way of clarifying the topic goal.

2 The use of *in-text questions* and *activities* to provide a form of interaction, where students are asked, for example, to write down their own point of view before reading on to see how the writer reacts to each of the points they might have expressed.

3 To improve adaptivity, the provision of *supplementary texts* for students who need to spend more time on some aspects of the work.

4 The provision of *self-assessment questions* (SAQs) to help students reflect on what they know.

The combination of activities and SAQs enables print to be more discursive, by inviting the student to describe and even redescribe their conception in the light of further reading. It is not fully discursive, of course, because it is not possible for the teacher, as author, to redescribe their conception in the light of the student's description. Some texts do this pre-emptively, by predicting possible misconceptions and addressing those, which is an excellent way to write a teaching text, and diminishes the constraints of the medium.

Even the modest print medium can be improved considerably over its canonical form, therefore, and although it still fails to satisfy all the requirements for an ideal teaching strategy, the students are given some support for what they have to contribute themselves.

The structure of the discourse for both lectures and print remains essentially implicit, and there have been attempts, following the investigations of the 'surface approach' to text, to help students take a 'deep approach' to apprehending the structure, in an attempt to negotiate a shared understanding of what the topic goal is. The 'in-text activities' referred to above sometimes take this form. Evaluation studies of these design features have not been particularly encouraging (see, for example, Lockwood 1992) and appear to suggest that the solution does not lie in a design fix alone, but depends also upon the student's appreciation of the idea of the 'deep approach' itself, their conception of learning, and their perception of the learning context. The addition of in-text activities and all the other add-on features discussed above do not in themselves change the format of the medium – it is still print, and only print, and therefore open to the same distortions as the original simple text. The students have to imbue an activity with a different status, have to acknowledge that it invites them to stand back from the text and reflect upon it, and then do that. But there is nothing in the format of the print medium that *requires* them to do it. And many of them choose not to. Only a small proportion of students actually write something down when asked to do so in an activity (Lockwood 1992), whereas all of them produce an essay, which is another way of getting them to reflect upon the text. The essay is more successful in terms of the proportion who do it because it represents a structural change to the format of the medium. The addition of a marked essay allows the print medium to establish more links in the chain of 'display teacher's conception (text)' – 'set task (essay question)' – 'action (write essay)' – 'feedback (marks and comment)'. The chain has to endure over a long time-span, however, and the dialogue between teacher and student that this represents is similarly attenuated, so the combination is far from ideal.

AUDIO-VISION

The audio-cassette as a medium is underrated by the textbooks on educational media. Its principal contrast with the lecture is that it is more controllable, though less so than print, being difficult to browse or index. Its principal contrast with print is that it uses the auditory channel rather than the visual, which means it has the tremendous potential for students who cannot easily read, that it makes the world of print available to them. The lecture loses little, pedagogically, by being transferred to audio-cassette, and gains in giving greater control to the student. Moreover, the audio-cassette can offer at least a vicarious experience of discussion, such as a recorded tutorial, or academic debate. Can, but rarely does, because it is so under-used. The disadvantage of audio, for sighted students, is that it provides nothing for the visual channel to focus on. That is why 'audio-vision' is a more acceptable medium, as well as offering more scope pedagogically.

The hybrid 'audio-vision' uses the auditory channel in combination with something for the visual channel to focus on, usually print. Thus it creates an additional representation in print of the descriptions being given in sound (Durbridge 1984a). Since print is not just text, but also pictures and diagrams, the print can provide an iconic or graphic version of the verbal description. The 'vision' part does not have to be print, it may also be material – one example from a geology course is a piece of rock, where the audio cassette talks the student through an examination of its look and feel; another example from a technology course is a computer program, where the audio talks the student through their actions on the computer and provides an interpretation of the screen at each stage. If the audio is being used to set tasks which enhance and interpret students' experience of the world, then the medium achieves a degree of interactivity. I defined 'interactive' as requiring something to change in the 'system' as a consequence of the student's action, and clearly, if they are operating a piece of equipment, or cutting a piece of rock, then they are changing the state of the world and seeing the consequences. Moreover, since the audio commentary is designed to interpret these (presumably) known consequences, the student is receiving tuition at both levels of experience and description of experience, making the medium a surprisingly powerful one. This combination of description and analogue representation will surface again in the discussion of video, a much more complex medium, but it is worth remembering that for static images, objects, and controllable actions, the audio-vision combination can be a very effective educational medium.

Print and audio, in their canonical forms, offer little. They cannot be discursive, in the sense of being able to comment on the student's representation of the topic, and even in combination they cannot easily incorporate adaptivity or reflection by the teacher. These have to come from the student. However, the audio-vision combination, where the visual part is some kind of action on the world, can achieve interactivity, so that both levels of discourse are addressed.

TELEVISION

Broadcast television has been a solution to certain special educational conditions, such as widely distributed campuses in Australia, Canada, the Philippines, or widely distributed students in distance learning universities. With more widespread introduction of cable television and satellite broadcasting, as the communications infrastructure develops, there is an increase in this form of delivery of the lecture, extending also to training and continuing education as companies with widely distributed organisational networks find it worthwhile to use the medium. Like the lecture, it is neither discursive, interactive, adaptive nor reflective, and is not self-paced. Its principal contrast with lectures is the form of representation it can use: dynamic analogue images as well as language.

The power of television to assist in the difficult trick of conveying a particular viewpoint on the world is frequently underestimated. Academic knowledge consists in descriptions of the world, and these descriptions represent a particular way of experiencing the world (see Chapter 1). Much of the work a lecturer has to do involves finding ways of conveying the peculiar characteristic viewpoint of their subject. Television (and film, which I take to be equivalent for this discussion) is peculiarly able to convey a way of experiencing the world, because it provides a vicarious experience through dynamic sound and vision, and moreover uses a number of technical devices to manipulate that experience. Salomon has called these devices 'supplantation', in the sense that they supplant a cognitive process (Salomon 1979). For example, a 'zoom' from long shot to close-up supplants the process of selective attention; a 'pan' supplants the process of shifting attention; a 'montage' supplants the process of association of ideas. These are powerful rhetorical devices. Add to these the production decisions about what to film and where to point the camera, and the potential for establishing a point of view is clear.

For the academic who wants to convey a complex theoretical idea, television can offer a way of supplanting the process the student has to undertake in coming to an understanding of the meaning. I would have great difficulty in trying to describe a Riemann surface to non-mathematicians, but if you were to see the sequence where trick photography is used to make a man seem to get smaller as he walks along a radius crossing concentric circles which gradually get closer together, then you would know what it is in a way you could not from words alone. The sociologist trying to get students to take an objective look at the world, and see vandalism not just as something perpetrated by youths, but as an aspect of the way we all live, uses a series of shots of industrial waste, ugly hoardings hiding a beautiful tree, a house covered in stone cladding, the destruction of a cottage to make way for a by-pass – these are all representations of what the academic sociologist means by describing vandalism as an aspect of the structure of society rather than the product of agents. It is possible to see these sequences as simply extending students' experiences of the world, and television certainly has that function. By bringing the world to the student's study it becomes possible for them to experience vicariously a variety of actions on the world: fieldwork (climbing a volcano and inspecting samples), experimentation (add another chemical and watch the reaction), interpretation (compare one part of a painting with another). But these define purely logistical, delivery roles for television, whereas given enough resources the students would engage in these experiences directly. The 'supplantation' devices are convergent with the way we see in that medium, being developed over many years as the cinematic medium shapes and is shaped by our cultural responses. 'Supplantation' allows our perception of the world through television to imitate our perception of the real world. As television offers a 'vicarious perception' of the world, it acts as a solution to the logistical problem of enabling large numbers of students to experience that aspect of the world directly.

The more interesting role for television as a unique pedagogical medium exploits its rhetorical power. Television as a public information medium necessarily has its rhetorical power constrained, in the interests of balance and objectivity, as if such a thing were possible. In educational broadcasting, given my position that academic knowledge is essentially rhetoric anyway, the medium can legitimately fulfil its potential.

There are not many studies of the rhetorical aspect of educational television. The literature in the field is overwhelmingly concerned with technical devices to aid recall of local propositions within a programme (e.g. Kelley, Gunter and Buckle 1987, Davies 1989, Golden 1990). From all that has gone before it follows that it should not be seen as primarily a means of transmitting information. It is a poor informational medium anyway, because it is not controllable, so the viewer is too easily swamped with information; alternatively the information is meted out in digestible quantities, which then makes it inefficient. It hardly matters if students fail to remember some constituent item within a sequence or programme; if the medium is being used as I have argued it should be, to persuade the viewer of a line of argument, or a way of seeing the world, then the important question is whether they understood the point being made.

In a study of students learning from social science programmes, for example, I found that often they did not. The internal structure of the programme was elaborate and yet obscured from the students, so they found it difficult to discern the overall meaning conveyed through that structure (Laurillard 1991). Their summaries of the programmes focused on local meanings of particular sequences, especially those represented most evocatively through vicarious experience, instead of talking heads. For some of the programmes, however, the students' summaries were very accurate, i.e. they were similar to the message the producer and academic were trying to put across. These were identified as programmes which had an 'image–argument synergy' for the overall message (Ibid.: 19). The term is meant to express the closeness of correspondence between the academic's description of the world, and what the viewer experiences through the on-screen images. Television can provide an analogue representation of an idea normally expressed through language, e.g. 'states can be violent' can also be expressed as images of war, riot police, capital punishment. When it does that, either within a sequence or at programme level, the 'supplantation' achieved is of a different kind from the 'vicarious perception' I described earlier. Here it supports the students' cognitive efforts to discern the meaning embedded in the implicit structure of the discourse itself. 'Image–argument synergy' ties the experience (the image) to the description (the argument), synthesising both levels of the academic discourse, and giving the students a 'vicarious conception', i.e. the way the teacher thinks about the topic.

When this more elaborate kind of 'supplantation' succeeds, the medium scarcely needs the other rhetorical props of interactivity and adaptivity to bring the teacher–student dialogue to a consensus. Of course, the same can be true of a lecture: an idea may not be so difficult that students need such props; alternatively, the inspired lecturer finds a way to convey the idea well enough through language alone. However, if the idea is too complex, or unfamiliar, then its alternative representation as some televisual analogue may help, where supplantation via image–argument synergy attempts to replace the entire rhetorical cycle necessary for learning to take place.

Television is engaging and powerful, and those advantages can be exploited effectively to assist student learning, but it is not a reflective medium, partly because it is not controllable by the student. Reflection has to come later, in a tutorial discussion, or prompted by printed notes with SAQs for the individual learner. In its canonical form, however, television covers at most three of the required activities within the conversational framework: the teacher's description, the teacher's set task, and intrinsic feedback on the teacher's actions.

VIDEO

The principal contrast between broadcast television and video is the relative controllability of the latter, making it adaptive by the student. Some researchers have referred to video-cassette plus exercises as 'interactive', but I believe this over-states the case. I have defined interactivity as involving intrinsic feedback on what the student does – the information in the system should change as a result of their action. Nothing in the video changes when a student rewinds it, just as nothing in a book changes when you turn a page. The epithet 'interactive' is applied to video because a cassette allows students to carry out activities in between watching sections, and to carry out analytical exercises on the video material itself. These are excellent ways of using video cassette, and of exploiting its controllability, but they are not interactive in the strong sense, and are essentially the same kind of activities as reading a book, re-reading it, analysing passages, doing activities between reading, etc. The medium cannot itself provide intrinsic feedback on what the student is doing. It is 'active video' perhaps, but not 'interactive video'.

Video has the same ability as television, however, to bring together experience and description of that experience, and being self-paced, can enhance this further with the opportunity for students to reflect on what they are doing. Nicola Durbridge, in an evaluation of video use at the British Open University, observed this in the way a set of videos of children doing mathematics were used in a course for teachers:

> Thus, the video can be described as having two aspects to its full meaning. One is the *sense* of the problems of doing mathematics, the other involves a *critical appreciation* of these problems. Students need to respond in two ways to understand the whole; they need to be receptive to the stimulus of the 'real-life' sound plus vision and to show a sympathetic but instinctive understanding of it; they also need to pursue a rational enquiry into its fuller meaning along the lines prompted by the notes and voice-over elements.
>
> (Durbridge 1984b: 234, original italics)

In fact, she found that the voice-over technique was less successful than the notes, because students were 'more engrossed with the action' on screen, and felt the simultaneous instructions to focus on particular content were distracting and off-putting. The synergy between image and argument may only work when the image is given time to be 'sensed', or the event experienced, and there is separate time for the argument to be 'critically appreciated', or the concept described.

Although this form of 'active' video gives students set task goals at the end of short sections of video, there is no feedback on their actions. Durbridge highlights students' sense of frustration with this aspect of work on video cassettes:

> There is also clear evidence that if questions and directives are highlighted ... they will need to be supported by some indication of the answers or observations students might make. Without such support many students felt both frustrated and anxious about the quality of their learning.
>
> (Durbridge 1984b: 240)

This is the disadvantage of a medium that is neither fully discursive (giving extrinsic feedback) nor fully interactive (giving intrinsic feedback). However, Durbridge does suggest ways in which 'pre-emptive' extrinsic feedback can be offered, e.g. where the academic's version of the answer, or their comment on an expected wrong answer, is written at the end of the notes, or summarised at the beginning of the next video section, in much the same way as print may comment on what a student is presumed to have done in an activity. Students need to know what they are meant to be learning, and need to have a sense of when they have achieved what is expected. The non-interactive media must attend to this aspect of the learning process, even though they cannot support it fully.

The only advantage of video over television is in the self-pacing provided by greater learner control, which at least allows students to reflect on the interaction they have witnessed, making this available to the activity of modifying their description, should they be invited to do this by additional instructions or notes.

SUMMARY

Table 5.1 summarises the characteristics of the media discussed in this chapter. I have included SAQs because they offer a way of enhancing any medium, providing no less than six of the required activities. The table enables us to see how combinations of media can cover the conversational framework more fully than the canonical forms.

The table can be read as a way of deciding how to cover the range of activities required by the conversational framework, but it does not decide between the media. It does not say 'choose

Table 5.1 Summary of audio-visual media characteristics

	Print	AV	TV	Video	SAQs
1 T can describe conception	✓	✓	✓	✓	O
2 S can describe conception	O	✓	O	O	✓
3 T can redescribe in light of S's conception or action	O	O	O	O	O
4 S can redescribe in light of T's redescription or S's action	O	✓	O	O	✓
5 T can adapt task goal in light of S's description or action	O	O	O	O	O
6 T can set task goal	O	✓	✓	✓	✓
7 S can act to achieve task goal	O	✓	O	O	✓
8 T can set up world to give intrinsic feedback on actions	O	✓	✓	✓	O
9 S can modify action in light of feedback on action	O	✓	O	O	O
10 S can adapt actions in light of T's description or S's redescription	O	✓	O	O	✓
11 S can reflect on interaction to modify redescription	O	✓	O	✓	✓
12 T can reflect on S's action to modify redescription	O	O	O	O	O

television rather than print because it gets more ticks'. The decision on media choice is more complex than that, involving both the obvious presentational properties of the medium (e.g. that television presents dynamic visuals better) and the logistics of development and distribution, to be discussed in Chapter 11. The table should rather be read as a way of indicating which activities are unsupported by a particular medium. Once this is clear, the teacher can decide on how best to deal with it – by adding another medium, by offering tutorial support, or by assuming that students can provide the additional activities for themselves. Analysing the audio-visual media in terms of the conversational framework allows the academic to design their teaching with a more realistic expectation of success.

Chapter 6

Hypermedia

HYPERTEXT

Hypertext brings us to the first of the computer-based media. Hypertext is a 'computer-based software system for organizing and storing information to be accessed nonsequentially and constructed collaboratively by authors and users' (Jonassen 1991: 83). The information items are 'documents', in the most general sense of the word, and may include text of varying length, pictures, diagrams, short animation sequences, sound bites, etc. The links between these items are associative links constructed by an author (see Figure 6.1): with a particular document on the screen (e.g. a map of a country), the author decides to link part of this (e.g. the name of the capital city) to another document (e.g. a picture of the capital city).

The author highlights the capital city name, uses a software option to identify this as an item (also known as a 'button') to be linked to another item, then uses the database functions of the software to find the other document (the photo) and identifies this to the software as the other end of the link. Thereafter, whenever the author or any subsequent user arrives at the first document (the map), they will see that part of it (the capital city name) can call up (by clicking on it) another item (the photo). Users can also create links, in the same way. They may prefer to link the capital city to a document containing a file of factual data, and may either retain or disconnect the link to the photo. Thus users can either navigate the database according to the author's links, or create their own.

This very simple linking structure is general enough that a hypertext system can emulate a rich variety of interactions with an

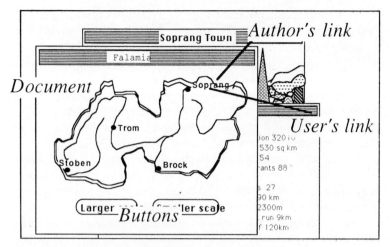

Figure 6.1 Organisation of a hypertext database, showing documents, buttons and links.

information database. With hard disc storage and the storage capacity of a compact disc, the database accessed by the hypertext software can be vast, unless it contains images, in which case it is merely large, e.g. 100 photos on one compact disc. The capacity of this type of system, and the ease of authoring the links between nodes has created great excitement in the world of educational media because it appears to solve the perpetual problem of how to create sufficient good quality courseware. Being so simple to use, teachers can create their own courseware very easily. This very simple linking structure between nodes of information is all it is, however. How does it stand up to the requirements for a teaching strategy?

Hypertext, accessing a text database, is not interactive, because there is no intrinsic feedback on the user's actions: the inform-ation in the system does not change as a consequence of the user's actions on it; it only changes if they change the system itself, by changing the information or the links directly. So it is no more interactive than writing in the margins of a book, or editing the book yourself, or annotating it with your own references to another point in the book. It would not be possible for the student to tell if they had made an inappropriate link – the system remains neutral with respect to anything they do. Because it gives no intrinsic feedback, nor has any specific goal, being simply a connected database, hypertext can be neither adaptive nor reflective.

Hypertext is controllable by the user, and this is the medium's real strength. The indexing, referencing, searching and editing tasks are very well supported by the options and iconic forms used in these systems. The use of mouse clicks and pull-down menus to move around a large database makes accessing and displaying an item of information very convenient, and the flexibility of the system for the user makes it easily customisable. The other principal virtue of hypertext is that it makes the structure of its topic completely explicit and highly accessible. What there is is easily available, usually in a variety of ways, and if the structure does not suit the user's way of thinking about the topic, then they may change it to suit their purposes better. As an information storage and retrieval system it is a very well-designed medium.

But as an educational medium, enabling the student to develop their academic understanding, it has little to offer. The claims made for its potential in education should be examined with care, because on the one hand it is nothing more than a small but beautifully connected library, and on the other hand, by its very nature, it undermines the structure of the 'texts' it uses and reduces knowledge to fragments of information. Jonassen lists some of the claims made for hypertext. Are they justified?

One such claim is that 'learners in college courses can browse through interconnected knowledge bases in lieu of textbooks' (Jonassen 1991: 84). Hypertexts are interconnected information bases, but a knowledge base is more than an information base. I have already defined academic knowledge as having a second-order character, being known through descriptions of experiences of the world. Within this account, clearly knowledge is not the same as information. It is useful to have a clear distinction between the two concepts, because 'information' is already clearly defined as a particular kind of abstract entity used to describe a wide range of behaviours in the world. An information-processing account of the world offers a particular perspective on how to describe events, not just cognitive processes, but anything, from the workings of a washing machine, to management of a company, to weather-forecasting. The success of this perspective has allowed computers and information technology to pervade many aspects of our life. 'Information' is the unit of currency in all these transactions. It allows us to reduce our interactions with machines, with colleagues, with nature, to a complex network of simple links between information fragments:

no matter how apparently complex it is, the system can be seen in terms of the transfer of information. Each level of description of the network can be reduced to a more elementary level of description. The whole process is perfectly reductive. The information that lies at the bottom of all this is unrecognisable from the top level of the action we experience. Each fragment of information only makes sense in the context of its local network. So 'information' is an important and powerful concept, which we cannot do without. It should not be adulterated by confusing it with something else we need as well.

Academic knowledge as I have defined it is not reductive; it is unitary, indivisible. In education, we want to preserve the relationship between what is known and the way it comes to be known, so the notion of a fragment of information has no place in that kind of analysis. Knowledge of rainfall is not adequately expressed as an associative network of fragments of information: even a simple statement such as 'as air rises it cools' cannot be expressed as an *association* between two component fragments. Knowledge of rainfall will be developed through using that relation in a variety of contexts, as the dialogue we looked at in Chapter 3 tried to do. If there is any relationship between knowledge and information, it is contrastive, the one unitary/holistic the other elementary/atomistic. Knowledge is information already transformed: selected, analysed, interpreted, integrated, articulated, tested in application, evaluated. The definition of academic knowledge I am working to has never separated out the components of knowledge into information and processes. An information-processing account does do that, and the implication is that hypertext would be an acceptable way of representing knowledge and is therefore an acceptable vehicle for acquiring knowledge within that paradigm. For the representation of academic knowledge, however, its reliance on *associative* links between information fragments makes it unacceptable. In constructing the articulation of a particular perspective on the world, which is what academics do when they write books or papers or prepare lectures, the links between separable bits are not merely associative. The argument in an article, or even a paragraph, cannot be expressed in that way, the links are logical or rhetorical. Whalley makes a similar point in reflecting on transferring a normal academic text to a hypertext form:

It is important to note that the paragraphs were written, or at least rewritten, to be able to stand alone. Whilst this makes graphical and hypertext versions of the text possible, it is quite noticeable . . . that this has the effect of making them rather boring to read as prose, as there is no use of the connectives to link the ideas between paragraphs . . . it lacks the subtlety of the many linguistic devices possible.

(Whalley, in press)

Most of the ideas we are concerned with in education are more complex than can be expressed by an associative network. When knowledge networks are constructed to represent some kind of academic knowledge the links defined between the nodes are many and various (e.g. in the Stevens, Collins and Goldin 1979 rainfall example) – even within the information processing paradigm it cannot be done by association alone. One example quoted by Jonassen uses the relation 'is a component process of' to link 'needs assessment' to 'instructional systems development' (Jonassen 1991). But the link is much more complex than that. The original text linking the two would undoubtedly take a strong line about the importance of 'needs assessment', and would discuss where in the 'development' process it should come and how it would relate to the other components, expressing the full complexity of all the important links between the two 'nodes'. In the hypertext system, these points may be made within the documents associated with each node, but then the true internal structure has not been made explicit. The hypertext zealot will answer this by saying 'ah but it could be'. Perhaps, but unpacking that complex structure into an explicit form generates an extremely complex network that would be difficult to navigate, and even more difficult to keep track of as you do so. The display of a network makes it explicit but does not make it known. The student still has to do a great deal of work to internalise its structure and interpret its meaning, just as they do with the implicit structure of text.

So what sense can we make of 'interconnected knowledge bases in lieu of textbooks'? Textbooks are already interconnected knowledge bases. The interconnections they use cannot be represented as simple links. Hypertext cannot replace textbooks. Moreover, shoehorning a textbook into hypertext format will distort the internal structure of its argument and the discourse will lose its meaning. Hypertext effectively destroys the knowledge represented in textbooks.

Hypertext may be oversold as a means of acquiring knowledge, but can it offer something as a means of constructing knowledge? This is also a frequent claim:

> The collaborative creation of hypertext knowledge bases by learners is an example of a constructivist learning activity; that is, learners are actively engaged in constructing knowledge.
>
> (Jonassen 1991: 89)

But what this means is that students can type in their own 'documents', and make their own links. This is precisely the same kind of activity they do when they annotate a textbook. It is a good thing for students to do, as it means they are taking responsibility for an aspect of the learning process, the description of their own conception. But hypertext does not provide anything more than wider margins (since documents entered by a student can be any size). In particular, it does not offer feedback on their description (except in the format where buttons are used for selection of multiple choice items, discussed in Chapter 8), so it is not a discursive medium. Neither does it offer the opportunity for action on the world or on a simulated world. The only action offered is the manipulation of descriptions: the text available in the system can be annotated, interlinked, and edited, which allows the student to 'redescribe their conception' in the light of further analysis of the teacher's conception as embodied in the database. But there is no extrinsic feedback on what they do – the 'teacher' (here the hypertext system) cannot offer any comment on what the student expresses. And there is no task set, no other kind of action by the student. The case for hypertext as an innovative pedagogical medium is confined to its limited discursive capabilities.

Its logistical advantages are clear for information retrieval, however. With the voluminous storage now available on hard discs it is possible to provide access to extensive, if localised bodies of information. Twenty books are probably enough for any one task, if they happen to be well chosen. However, the inclusion of any audio or video material, which is increasingly seen as desirable, drastically reduces the storage capacity, so while the available material is certainly extensive, it does have to be very well suited to the task in hand, and in that sense is 'localised'. For someone who needs instant easy access to a large body of related material, a hypertext system will be valuable.

However, this kind of activity is more likely to be done by the scholar than the novice. It is easy to see why academics love the idea of hypertext, but is it appropriate for their students? Browsing, or scanning, or hunting down a piece of information from an extensive resource all play a rather small part in learning academic knowledge. The learner is more likely to be working on a smaller scale, to need help with discerning the structure and through it the meaning of a particular text being studied. This is where hypertext fails to support the learner, for the reasons outlined above – it provides no feedback at either the level of action or the level of description. It is not a stand-alone learning medium. It needs additional support from the teacher, just as library work does.

Scholars delight in the capabilities of these systems, because prohibitively time-consuming research tasks are made feasible, and therefore accessible, and therefore accessible also to the undergraduate. Hypertext can change the curriculum. If students can now, with a few key presses, call up every instance of Homer's references to 'Helen', or every paragraph in which 'Helen' occurs as well as 'beauty', then comprehensive textual analysis becomes possible. But what must concern the academic teacher is not so much the information retrieved by the student, but the use of that information – the transformation wrought by the student to render it as knowledge. The number of references used in the analysis is far less important than the quality of the analysis, if what you are teaching is how to do textual analysis. Once it indicated diligence, perhaps; now it indicates access to a powerful system.

Only in so far as students are seen as needing to do extensive library work does hypertext offer a useful tool, assuming the appropriate database is available. These systems should not be invested with greater powers than they have. Their attractiveness and logistical convenience makes it likely that they will be used increasingly to replace other information retrieval systems, but it would be absurd to suppose they can replace anything else. Hypertext systems will be fascinating and motivating for students able at last to act like researchers in their field, but it will be very easy for them to produce extensively documented rubbish unless the focus is kept firmly on the quality of the knowledge they generate from these systems.

MULTIMEDIA RESOURCES

As an information retrieval system, hypertext, in its most generic form, can access 'documents' consisting of information stored in any form, including audio and video, stored in digitised form on hard disk, or on a compact disc. It is possible, for example, to link animations to static diagrams in a text, to link a clip of video to a descriptive paragraph, an audio recording of foreign language pronunciation to words or pictures, and so on. The combination of a hypertext system with audio-visual media to give 'multimedia' brings together the best of both. It is easier to create image–argument synergy in a system that can handle both text and visuals, and since that feature of video referred explicitly to an *associative* link between image and argument – the identification of one with the other – it follows that this is precisely where the associative links offered by hypertext can be valuable.

With an interface well-designed for searching and displaying the audio-visual material stored, multimedia systems offer some intriguing challenges. When a student is studying an idea that requires discrimination of visible properties, e.g. by comparing exemplars and non-exemplars of a concept, discerning family resemblances among objects etc., then access to easy comparisons is valuable. In his analysis of what multimedia ought to be, David Clark encapsulates the case for accessible visual databases as follows:

> At the heart of all acts that combine to permit the revelation of a new idea lies the act of comparison. Surely we never wish to see a picture in isolation – we always require the juxtaposition of images.
>
> (Clark 1991: 78)

The act of comparison may well be ubiquitous, though it will not always depend upon images. None the less, when the idea being studied does have this character, then it is true that we require juxtaposition, and this simple fact demands fast access to the relevant data, under user control, and a multimedia resource is very good for that. This is the only sense in which a multimedia database can support interactivity: the learner can compare juxtaposed 'documents'. The student engages in actions on a very particular world, the world of documented data. That is why these systems are important in education, where the world of documented data assumes great importance. With access to the original data on which an author's thesis is based, the student has it in their power to check and challenge that thesis, by calling up, for example, data additional to that studied by the author. The inclusion of sound, photographs and video in a multimedia system enables the student to observe aspects of the real world not possible in hypertext alone.

One of the largest multimedia databases is about Ancient Greece, developed by the Perseus Project at Harvard. It brings together texts, archaeological maps, photographs of sites, and of artefacts, all accessible through an interface allowing all the manipulation tools of hypertext. The editor in chief, Gregory Crane, describes the changing role of the 'reader' that this kind of medium offers:

> A richly documented publication, such as the hypermedia museum catalog . . . will, superficially at any rate, undermine the author's authority. Readers can see at least some of the evidence underlying the author's conclusions, and a greater number of readers will be able to challenge those opinions.
>
> (Crane 1991: 49–50)

Perhaps an author refers to Achilles' warlike image; the student may check this by deciding on a task goal to test whether he is always depicted as warlike, and to achieve the goal by calling up photos of Greek vases depicting Achilles, an action that is carried out in a few key presses. The system provides intrinsic feedback on that goal-directed action in the form of displays of images of Achilles, which the student must interpret as warlike or not. If a few appear not to be warlike, then this act of juxtaposition of documents – author's text with additional images – permits the revelation of the new idea, that Achilles may have another side to him, which can then be developed as a challenge, with supporting evidence, to the author's original thesis. There is nothing revolutionary about these activities for the academic, but easy access to original data creates the possibility that students may also do them. And that *is* revolutionary, for every academic subject, because every subject creates a world of documented data, and students must be able to act on that world. Now they can interact with it in the way a scholar could.

What this offers the student is still essentially a library, however, because a multimedia resource fails to be either adaptive or reflective. The teacher (i.e. the system) cannot offer redescription in the light of what the student describes in their annotations of the text, because these are not inspectable by the system; the teacher cannot adapt or set task goals, and cannot reflect on the student's actions on the system, which are also not inspectable by the program in a multimedia resource. Students' use of such systems will need further support from a tutorial dialogue with the teacher, therefore, if they are to be sure they have interpreted their findings correctly, and have set themselves appropriate tasks.

Multimedia databases should not be oversold. They offer more than hypertext because the addition of sound and vision allows observation of the real world, albeit a very restricted one, filtered through the selection process for the creation of the database. Like hypertext, multimedia databases cannot offer stand-alone teaching, and could easily provoke fruitless searches, non-selective data collection, misinterpretations of data collected. They *only* enable students to explore large quantities of data, making them the equivalent of a small library, or a lot of travel money. None the less, the multimedia database has several advantages over print:

- it can make available the data from which the supporting evidence of an existing thesis is selected
- it can make available the data from which the supporting evidence for a new thesis might be selected
- it offers wide margins for annotations, enabling the student to describe their own conception as it relates to items in the database

That is a significant advance on the normal textbook, or library. The pedagogical claims for multimedia resources should stop there.

SUMMARY

Having considered hypertext and multimedia in relation to the conversational framework defined in the introduction to Part II, we can broadly summarise those they can support, as in Table 6.1.

Hypertext and multimedia have similar pedagogical characteristics, although multimedia allows a limited form of action on the world, in the form of observation and comparison of

Table 6.1 Summary of hypermedia characteristics

		Hyp	M-m
1	T can describe conception	✓	✓
2	S can describe conception	✓	✓
3	T can redescribe in light of S's conception or action	O	O
4	S can redescribe in light of T's redescription or S's action	✓	✓
5	T can adapt task goal in light of S's description or action	O	O
6	T can set task goal	O	O
7	S can act to achieve task goal	O	✓
8	T can set up world to give intrinsic feedback on actions	O	✓
9	S can modify action in light of feedback on action	O	✓
10	S can adapt actions in light of T's description or S's redescription	O	O
11	S can reflect on interaction to modify redescription	O	✓
12	T can reflect on S's action to modify redescription	O	O

documented aural and visual data. Where the data is purely textual, the interaction is taking place at the level of descriptions of the world in any case, so I have confined hypertext to the non-interactive category. When the world is itself textual, as in poetry criticism, for example, then a hypertext system could be counted as interactive in the same sense as the multimedia database is for the world of Greek vases, though this is a rather special case. Neither form of hypermedia succeeds in supporting all the activities required to complete the learning process.

Chapter 7

Interactive media

SIMULATIONS

A computer-based simulation is a program that embodies some model of an aspect of the world, allows the user to make inputs to the model, runs the model, and displays the results. The model could take several forms: a system of equations, for example, for describing coexisting plant populations (Golluscio, Paruelo and Aguiar 1990); a set of procedures, for example, for guiding a rocket (Brna 1989); semi-quantitative models to support reasoning about the direction of change in a system (Ogborn 1990); a set of condition–action rules, for example, for operating a nuclear power plant (see Figure 7.1, from Moyse 1991).

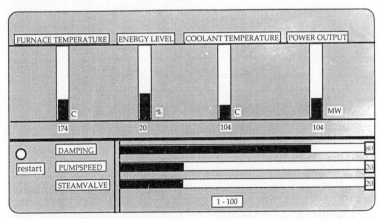

Figure 7.1 The screen for the simulated power system. Subjects mouseclick in the horizontal bars to set the related control. Readouts of the system state are given in the vertical bars. (From Moyse 1991: 26, Exhibit 1.)

The program interface allows the user to make inputs to the model, which may take the form of selecting parameters to change, choosing parameter values within a range, or choosing when to change parameters. The users' inputs to the model determine the subsequent behaviour of the model, which is then displayed, either as numerical values, a diagram, a picture, an animation, or as a description of its new state. From this very general description it should be clear that a simulation is possible for anything that can be implemented as a model relating two or more parameters, where changes to one parameter produce changes in another.

There is occasional terminological confusion when 'simulation' is used to refer to a program that runs a model without any input from the user – the program generates its own input to the model, and the user simply watches. This is certainly a simulation, but since the usual usage within education is *interactive* simulations, it is reasonable to reserve the term 'simulation' for those, and to relegate the non-interactive ones to the term 'animation' or 'demonstration', as they could equally well be shown on the non-interactive medium of video.

Simulations are useful for representing complex relations. There would be little point, for example, in simulating a model of an aspect of the economy, such as 'increasing inflation leads to increasing unemployment', as the relation is simple enough to understand from the description alone. A more complex relation, such as 'there is a phase difference of 12 months in the rate of change of inflation and that of unemployment', might be better understood by non-mathematical students if they could see what happened to unemployment figures, in either numerical or graphical form, as they change the inflation figures. A simulation represents actions and events in a simulated world.

The computer-based simulation is the first medium we have considered that is interactive, in the sense that it gives intrinsic feedback on students' actions. The actions are inputs to a model, not descriptions, so the simulation is allowing the student to have a particular kind of experience; it is not operating at the level of *descriptions* of experience. A simulation is controllable by the student, because by selecting parameters to change, they effectively determine the topic focus. For example, in a plant population simulation they can decide when to stop investigating the effects of rainfall and move on to looking at effects of pollution.

Or within their investigation of rainfall, they can look at conditions for stable equilibrium, or effects of competition below the equilibrium point (see Golluscio *et al.* 1990). The decision about topic focus is the student's, not the teacher's. This is not a dialogue with the teacher, even indirectly through the program. There is no sense in which the teacher can make decisions about the level of the students' understanding on the basis of their actions, and thereby suggest a new topic or task focus. It is therefore not adaptive by the teacher at the task level. The student may well have come to the wrong conclusion about the feedback from the system, and their decisions about future actions may reveal this, but the system does not judge their actions or make decisions about what they should do next, it only responds via the model, to their input. It is interactive in the sense that the system gives intrinsic feedback on their actions. But it does not comment on them, or discuss them, so it is not discursive.

The negotiation of the task goal is not so straightforward. One simulation could be used to serve many different learning goals: to give students a sense of the relations between certain parameters, a feel for the appropriate range of values for a parameter, an understanding of what constitutes a critical condition, and so on. The design of the interface to the simulation will affect how well the particular goal is communicated to the students, or the degree to which they can select the goal. Many simulations are designed to be quite neutral with respect to how they are used, so that the user can decide what to investigate, and decide when they have satisfied their intention. They can also be designed to offer several goals from which the student can select one. If this is done, then both student and system know the goal, and that makes it possible for the program to comment on the attainment of the goal. For example, if the goal is to find the conditions for stable equilibrium of two plant populations, then the program can provide two types of feedback, as shown in the fictional example in Figure 7.2.

Firstly, it can display the results of the input according to the model – e.g. the plants die (population A) or survive (population B). Secondly, it can inspect the current parameter values input by the student, the state of the system, and the goal, and with all these known to it, can comment on the validity of the student's input with respect to the state of the system and the task goal. The comment would be in the form of pre-programmed text, and

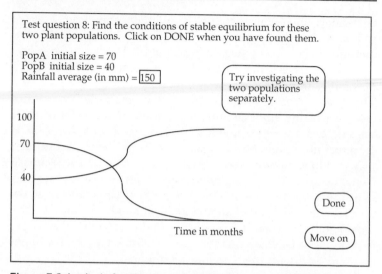

Figure 7.2 Intrinsic feedback as graphical display showing results of student's action in assigning rainfall average. Extrinsic feedback appears in the form of comment on the action in a pop-up window.

when each definable combination of input values, system state and goal occurs, it could trigger the appropriate text description (e.g. 'try investigating the effect of rainfall on the two populations separately'). That kind of design would enable the simulation to be adaptive by the teacher to expected student problems. It is not the canonical form of the simulation; with this, it resembles a tutorial (see Chapter 8). The explicitness of the goal is critical: with it, the simulation can encourage reflection on the goal and its relation to the action and the feedback, and can comment on the student's action; without it, where the student simply explores 'what if' questions, reflection is not encouraged because there is nothing specific to aim for, and comment is not possible.

Simulations support a kind of experiential learning, but the students' actions are confined to quantitative descriptions and comparisons – they have to decide on the values of parameters, and reason about the amount by which their goal is missed and therefore the amount by which to change their inputs. The inter-parameter relations they can posit to help in this reasoning will be quantitative, along the lines of 'more X gives less Y, so try a bit more X to get Y down a bit' (see, for example, Moyse 1991, Laurillard 1978). Many people, myself included, have referred to simulations as giving students the opportunity for qualitative reasoning. In fact, much of their reasoning will be quantitative, albeit vague, because the only form their actions take is to determine the quantities of parameters. However, it can also be qualitative, as Moyse has shown. He found an important dichotomy in the way the use of a simulation was set up for students. Those given a 'structural' model describing 'the flow of energy through the system' were far more likely to reason qualitatively, referring to real world knowledge, than those given a 'task–action mapping' model describing 'a list of control movements which would achieve operational goals' (Moyse 1991: 25). Qualitative reasoning, incorporating knowledge of real world objects or processes produced comments like this:

> I have increased the speed of the coolant going round the system and it's bringing down the temperature again.

> I'm going to try and stop the furnace from cooling too much, by clicking on the damping allowing it a bit more air by going down towards zero.

> (Moyse 1991: 27–30)

On the other hand, the task–action mapping group justify their decisions using instrumental reasoning referring only to quantities and processes explicitly represented on the screen, so that the actions remain uninterpreted:

> Power is going down, we need to increase the steam valve.

> We are getting nothing like the power we need. Open steam valve up, about, put it up to fifty.

> (Ibid.: 29)

In this latter group, had the quantities been given different labels, their conversation would have been identical, save the labels. The content was irrelevant to them; only the quantities were figural. The structural description given to the other group, with the focus on the behaviour of the system rather than quantitative control, elicited more real world, qualitative reasoning. Purely quantitative reasoning is not inevitable in simulations, therefore, but a more interpretive approach may have to be encouraged, as it is not elicited by the mere operation of the simulation. I reported a similar finding from an evaluation study in engineering, where students spent much of their time 'number-hunting', trying to find the exact value of a parameter that produced the critical effect (Laurillard 1987b). The dialogue was of the pure 'up-a-bit, down-a-bit' form that Moyse reported for his task–action mapping group. In fact the internal relations between the parameters in many simulations are too complex to be determined with any accuracy from these kinds of numerical experiments, so it cannot be about establishing the underlying equation. Instead, lecturers using simulations provide detailed notes which set out the derivation of the model, and students may refer to this symbolic description to help them make their decisions. By doing this, they can tell that one parameter is affected, for example, by an exponential, and needs to be increased a great deal before it has a noticeable effect on another. This is a valuable educational tool for encouraging something like Resnick's 'mapping strategy', because it enables students to relate the mathematical symbolism on paper to the behaviour of the system as represented on the screen, either graphically or iconically. If this works, then they begin to achieve better coverage of the learning process, as this is now focusing on descriptions of the simulated world, not just on actions within it.

Access to the teacher's conception within a simulation is a matter of design decision. Simulations are based on a model, and in most the model remains hidden in the depths of the program, inaccessible to inspection by the student. It is common for a teaching program to be issued with accompanying notes that state the model, and even, if the students are supposed to have some mathematical competence, its derivation. The model *is* the topic structure, so it exists in an explicit form in the program code and on paper somewhere. It may be a system of equations, as in the plant simulation; it could be a set of rules, consisting of statements such as '*if* patient has a temperature, *then* call Procedure A, *else* ask Question Y'. The complexity of the explicit form is usually the main reason for creating a simulation from it, so that students can become familiar with it by investigating the behaviour it models rather than by inspecting its explicit form. But having both forms of access – explicitly via the equations or rules, and implicitly via the behaviour of the model – gives the student a better chance of turning their experience of the world (actions on the model) into descriptions of the world (the formal statement of the model).

A simulation is not discursive: it provides no opportunity for teacher or student to describe their conception. The student is therefore not invited to reflect on the interaction to modify their description, and their conception remains implicit in their actions.

Simulations address many aspects of the learning process, but in their canonical form they fail to address interaction at the level of descriptions, adaptivity of task focus, and reflection, but because they contain the explicit model it is not too difficult to build a more sophisticated form of 'tutorial-simulation' that can support the teacher's (program's) reflection on the interaction as well. An example is Moyse's system in which

> A partial interpreter, or simulator ... is used to produce an execution history in terms which allow its interpretation through any of the required [available] viewpoints. This facilitates a range of tutorial interactions and allows the student to choose a viewpoint which is suited to their current [topic] goals.
>
> (Moyse 1992: 207)

As the program has a model of the system, and can record all the student's input to the system, it can be programmed to use that information (the execution history) to help the student reflect on the interaction that both program and student have been party to. In practice, simulations are often embedded in a teaching context that supplies these other aspects of the conversational framework in other ways:

- students use it in pairs, so use dialogue to interact at the level of descriptions
- the equivalent of the 'lab sheet' provides the teacher's pre-emptive task focus for what they do with the program
- students describe their conception in the form of a write-up on their work on the simulation, rather like a lab report on an experiment
- the teacher gives extrinsic feedback in the form of comments on the write-up

In this way teachers improve the canonical form of the simulation by adding to it the medium of print, and student discussion. The difference that collaborative work makes to the coverage of the learning process is very important, as we shall see again in Chapter 9, and can lift a very limited educational medium to one that covers many aspects of the learning process.

MICROWORLDS

A further terminological difficulty attends the usage of 'microworlds'. Some authors refer to simulations as microworlds, an understandable confusion, because it is a feature of simulations that they allow the user to act within a 'little world'. Microworlds made their biggest impact in education in the form of Logo, Seymour Papert's programming language for geometry. In his book 'Mindstorms', Papert describes the reasoning behind the development of a Newtonian microworld, and in doing so, expresses exactly the difference between a microworld and a simulation. What makes microworlds interesting is that they appear to address explicit description of the student's point of view:

> Direct experience with Newtonian motion is a valuable asset for the learning of Newtonian physics. But more is needed to understand it than an intuitive, seat-of-the-pants experience. The student needs the means to conceptualize and 'capture' this world . . . The Dynaturtle on the computer screen allows the beginner to play with Newtonian objects. The concept of Dynaturtle allows the student to think about them. And programs governing the behaviour of Dynaturtles provide a *formalism in which we capture our otherwise too fleeting thoughts.*
>
> (Papert 1980: 124, my italics)

The formalism provided as an essential feature of a microworld allows the student to express their description of some aspect of the world in a form understandable by, and therefore inspectable by, the program. The simulation offers no such means of representation, only actions encoded as option choices of parameter changes.

However, microworlds are very similar to simulations in the sense that they allow the user to act in a simulated world, and experience that world from the perspective of, in this case, Newton. The little world the user inhabits, for both media, is one that has been highly constrained by the designer. Using the plant population simulation is quite unlike acting in the real situation, where the student might be disposed to look at, say, the flowering periods of the two plants, or to regard them as peacefully coexisting. In the simulation, the user has no choice but to see the two species as competing: all the decisions they are invited to make concern conditions affecting competition, and the feedback plots the changes in size of the two populations over time. The students are therefore unable to experience aspects of this world that the designer is not interested in. They may still ignore or misinterpret the data, of course, but they cannot avoid looking through the biologist's spectacles. Similarly, in the design of the Dynaturtle and the programming language that governs its behaviour, Papert constrained what students could do with it, so that their view of this microworld incorporated the perspective he wished them to take.

The key difference between the simulation and the microworld is in the way the student interacts with it. The microworld provides a mediating mechanism for acting in its world, namely a programming language. This provides a level of description of what is happening in that world. To use Papert's physics microworld, a student has to describe their actions in the form of a set of commands, then run them as one would a program, and the result is either the intended behaviour or something unexpected. The feedback operates at the level of the description. Consider an example in Logo geometry: a student types in a set of commands to draw a square (e.g. forward 100, right 90, forward 100, right 90, forward 100, right 90), then runs it, and the computer draws three sides of a square (see Figure 7.3).

What does that feedback do? It provides a comment on their description of the action, i.e. that it is too short, and therefore indicates what kind of change they have to make to it. Having perfected the description of a square (by adding another 'forward 100'), they can adapt and develop that to produce more elaborate

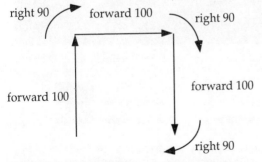

Figure 7.3 The feedback on an incomplete representation of a square as the sequence of commands: 'forward 100, right 90, forward 100, right 90, forward 100, right 90'.

outcomes in the microworld. If they create a model or program
with variables (e.g. 'repeat X(forward Y, right Z)'), they can then
investigate its behaviour under different initial inputs, using the
model as one does in a simulation. A more sophisticated design,
such as that in Figure 7.4 (from Sellman 1991), displays an iconic
representation of the sequence of events (the orbit), a numeric
representation of the input (parameter values at the bottom of the
screen), and a symbolic representation of the student's description
of the events (the program statements).

The students creating the program clearly have a different kind
of learning experience from anyone who only uses what they have
created. The difference lies in whether the action exists as a

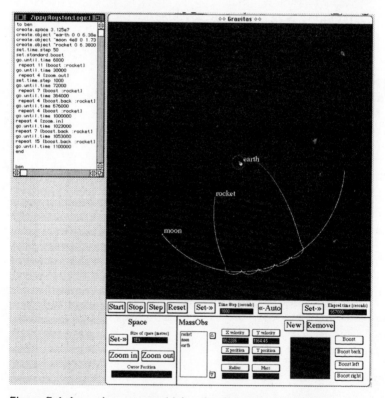

Figure 7.4 A user's program driving the discovery learning
environment 'Gravitas' to navigate a rocket from Earth to Moon and
back. (From Sellman 1991: 9.)

description, and can be 'captured' for inspection, reflection and revision resulting from feedback, as in a microworld, or whether it remains a fleeting thought captured only as part of the memory of the action, as in a simulation.

I hope the structural difference between simulations and microworlds is clear from this. The feedback at the level of description is important if we want an educational medium to address all aspects of the learning process, and the microworld is the only medium discussed so far that attempts to do this in any way. The way it does it is problematic, however. The form of description is peculiar. A program is a formalism, designed to overcome the barrier to understanding of a mathematical formalism:

> It bypasses the long route (arithmetic, algebra, trigonometry, calculus) into the formalism that has passed with only superficial modification from Newton's own writing to the modern textbook.
>
> (Papert 1980: 124)

Papert's primary concern is not in fact to provide the student with a means of describing actions in the world, but to provide the means for them to enter the Newtonian way of thinking without having to use mathematics as the medium:

> We shall design a microworld to serve as an incubator for Newtonian physics. The design of a microworld makes it a 'growing place' for a specific species of powerful ideas or intellectual structures.
>
> (Ibid.: 125)

Thus Papert wants to give students direct access to the physicist's way of experiencing the world, enabling them to develop an intuitive grasp of the correct Newtonian conceptions. This is more compatible with the idea of academic knowledge as 'situated cognition' than as second-order descriptions of the world. It seeks *experiential* knowledge of the world, just as a simulation does, rather than *articulated* knowledge. None the less, surely the programming language feature of the microworld fits the requirement I developed earlier for a teaching strategy that can interact at the level of descriptions? Papert's concern was that the formalism should be intelligible to the student; my concern is that it should also function as a description. But is a program the right kind of description? I previously referred to descriptions as though they were purely language-based. The characterisation of academic knowledge as being second-order, standing back from experience of the world, articulating what is known, all presuppose language as the vehicle of expression. And yet academic knowledge is not only represented through language. The more usual alternatives are mathematical symbolism and diagrams, which also, of course, can be carried through the medium of print. When the computer becomes as ubiquitous a medium as the book, why should academic knowledge not be expressed also through the medium of a program?

This is close to the mission that Papert expresses in his book, that learners of all ages should be taught computational modelling as a powerful intellectual tool: being able to program a system is as good a way of knowing it as being able to describe it mathematically or in language. Is it though? Papert quotes a teacher as saying 'I love your microworlds, but is it physics?' and he seriously considers the question it raises about how far one should attempt to reconceptualise classical domains of knowledge (Papert 1980: 140ff). His main argument is that turtle physics is closer to the spirit of real physics than the physics of the stereotyped classroom where formulae are meaningless rituals. It is a good defence, but is it close enough to real physics? Or to take the discussion beyond just physics: is computational modelling within a microworld an adequate representation of the existing academic knowledge? The reader can probably sense my implicit 'no' in answer to all these questions. The reason lies in what is embedded in the design of the microworld. That is where the real physics is. Reading the description of the development of any microworld, be it physics (Sellman 1991) or music (Holland 1987), it is apparent that tremendously hard thinking about the subject has to be built into the way the program objects are designed. The user will use these building blocks of programmable objects, or commands, or rules, to create a system that models some theory of the real world; they cannot be just anything. They are theoretical constructs, peculiar to the theory of the world that is being built. Once they are designed, students can build with them and explore how they work. Then they have access to that special world, defined by the theoretician, and can learn about it in the way we learn about the real world by experiencing and acting on it. The computational model they devise brings them closer to an intuitive understanding of what goes on in that world, but does not help them express it, because the programmable objects are a truncation of the real physics into manipulable chunks. So my answer to the teacher's question is no, I do not think this is physics, at least not academic physics, any more than playing with real bricks is academic physics. I do accept Papert's argument that the microworld provides students with the experience of this perspective on the world that will be useful for thinking about academic physics. And this is now reminiscent of the video analogue of an academic idea – it affords a particular way of experiencing the world. The microworld is better because it is more controllable by the student, it is interactive, it is adaptive by the student, it supports reflection, and it supports interaction at a certain level of description, but not the one I specified in defining a teaching strategy. I have to define more closely what I mean by description. It has to be a complete description of the system, not one that relies on a knowledgeable compiler to interpret it.

It is important to be clear about the nature of the learning experience each style of medium offers, because in the consideration of individual examples it is very easy to be distracted by the particular content, or the particular implementation. Many of these systems are extremely attractive, especially to teachers and experts who already understand the subject very well, and see immediately the potential for discovery and play that they offer. But we are considering them here from the point of view of benefit to learners who have all the usual conceptual difficulties. What is the real pedagogical significance of a microworld for them? It is designed, remember, to help them become familiar with a world which is normally only accessible through mathematics. A Logo-type microworld makes exploring Newtonian objects and motion as much as possible like exploring the behaviour of building bricks in the real world. That is the whole point, as defined by Papert. The metaphor is entirely apt. But to what extent is the child playing with bricks, even if noting down a record of the moves made with them, doing physics? This is coming to an intuitive understanding of the world, it is learning about the world through experience, and the analogy follows through to the physics students using the Dynaturtle – they are learning about the Newtonian world through experiencing it. So it is not academic knowledge they are acquiring, but experiential knowledge. I would not deny its importance, or its value to the student who then uses this in building their academic knowledge, but it is important to be clear that they are not the same. This is what accounts for Papert's teacher's anguish – it is not physics. But the reasoning that students are doing while operating in a microworld, is helping to build their personal theory of that world, just as the child builds theories of the physical world by playing with bricks.

So does the structural difference between simulations and microworlds have any pedagogical significance? I think it lies in the fact that a simulation does not support the student's description in any form, whereas a microworld permits the student to express their concept as a sequence of commands, and to check this against feedback from the interaction. It supports a special and limited form of description of their conception, therefore, which is important because it encourages them to reflect upon the interaction. The absence of this in a simulation means that students may easily 'see what happens if . . .', but *only* see, and not reflect on what they see. Without reflection, the simulation, for all its interactivity, then has no better status than the usual run of events, contributing little to new understanding.

MODELLING

A modelling program invites the learner to create their own model of a system, defined mathematically, which it then runs, allowing the output to be compared with stored data of a real world system, or the program's own model. It contrasts with a simulation because the student manipulates the model itself, not just parameters within a given model. For example, Figure 7.5 shows a program where students define the equation to be plotted in order to find the best fit to a given set of case study data.

A modelling program contrasts with a microworld because the student defines a mathematical model directly, it is not buried within the design of objects. In a modelling program the program merely interprets formulae (or rules), it knows nothing about any subject matter, unlike the microworld. A physics microworld can only be used for physics; a modelling program can be used for anything that can be modelled. There is a considerable interface design problem in getting the program to interpret the learner's description of the model, and this is the clever part of designing such a program. Perhaps the best known commercial program in

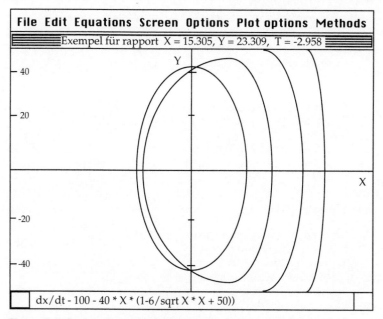

Figure 7.5 Screen from modelling program for moments of inertia. (Based on Figure 1 in Laurillard *et al.* 1991: 26.)

a Macintosh environment is 'Stella', although students find it difficult to operate. Defining a suitable description language or representational system for students to express their conception of an idea, or model a problem, is a complex design task (see, for example, Reusser 1992). A simpler solution is to offer a template for defining an equation, such as offering a polynomial for which the user can specify the coefficients. This would not do for exponential forms, of course, so most modelling programs would have specially-designed templates for particular uses. The job of the program is then simply to interpret the student's model and plot the resulting graphs in the specified range.

The program may also contain its own model, or data, for a particular topic, which it can compare with what the student has done. If so, it can prompt some reflection on the student's outcome in comparison with the goal. Since the program has access to the student's model, it could also be programmed to comment on particular characteristics of its relationship to the known model, assuming the topic goal is known, although in existing programs this is rarely explicit. This is a plausible

Table 7.1 Summary of characteristics of interactive media

		Sim	MW	Mod
1	T can describe conception	O	O	O
2	S can describe conception	O	✓	✓
3	T can redescribe in light of S's conception or action	O	O	O
4	S can redescribe in light of T's redescription or S's action	O	O	O
5	T can adapt task goal in light of S's description or action	O	O	O
6	T can set task goal	✓	✓	✓
7	S can act to achieve task goal	✓	✓	✓
8	T can set up world to give intrinsic feedback on actions	✓	✓	✓
9	S can modify action in light of feedback on action	✓	✓	✓
10	S can adapt actions in light of T's description or S's redescription	O	✓	✓
11	S can reflect on interaction to modify redescription	O	✓	✓
12	T can reflect on S's action to modify redescription	O	O	O

extension, but certainly not part of the canonical form, which remains neutral with respect to anything the student tries. It supports an explicit representation of the student's model, but in mathematical and graphical form only. It gives feedback on the student's action by running the model, and is fully controllable by the student.

The structural form of a modelling system is the same as a microworld. The only difference is in how the student's conception is expressed: in a microworld as a code describing actions in the world; in a modelling system as a mathematical representation of those actions. Here there would be no doubt in the teacher's mind that this is 'doing physics', and that is because the focus of the students' talk is on how to express the already known behaviour of a system mathematically. If the aim is not to merely experience the world but also to explain it, then the modelling program is the closest so far to supporting the learning of academic knowledge.

SUMMARY

Having considered simulations, microworlds and modelling programs in relation to the conversational framework defined at the beginning of Part II, we can broadly summarise those activities they can support as in Table 7.1.

The main differences between these interactive media concern the expression within the system of the student's conception. None of them succeed in supporting all the activities in the complete learning process, but they are the only media so far to offer interaction at the level of action in the world, albeit a simulated one. The link between this and the student's redescription, which is elicited by microworlds and modelling programs, makes them pedagogically very valuable, as long as the remaining learning activities can be covered by other means.

Chapter 8

Adaptive media

INTRODUCTION

'Tutorial programs' and 'tutoring systems' differ from all the previous media forms because they embody an explicit teaching strategy. Both are premised on the assumption that it is possible for a computer program to emulate a teacher. In Chapter 4, I drew the conclusion that the ideal teaching system was a one-to-one teacher–student dialogue. We now begin to consider whether it is possible to achieve that ideal without very high staff–student ratios, with a computer program acting as 'teacher'. Given the aspirations of this type of medium, we must expect it to come close to covering all aspects of the learning process earlier identified as being essential. The basic design of such a program is to:

- specify a learning objective
- offer a brief introduction to the topic
- set a task according to a strategy for achieving that objective
- interpret the student's performance on the task
- use this to select the appropriate feedback
- use the student's performance so far to select the next task

At the very minimum, therefore, the tutoring program offers extrinsic feedback on the student's actions, and an adaptive task focus related to previous actions and the overall goal.

There are some programs that masquerade as 'teaching programs' that are not adaptive, that simply set tasks on demand, give extrinsic feedback, and total a score of some kind. Cynics may claim this emulates normal teaching very well, and apologists defend it on the grounds that it gives students plenty of much-needed practice in certain kinds of task. Neither defence will do. We do not go to the enormous trouble and expense of developing computer-based teaching without aiming for some kind of ideal in the process; and practice for improvement is more efficient if the tasks are adapted to the learner's needs. So I only consider adaptive tutorial programs here.

TUTORIAL PROGRAMS

Tutorial programs in their canonical form do not set out to express either the teacher's or the student's conceptions explicitly. Because of the limitations of the computer as a presentational medium, it is not best used to offer initial teaching, unless it can be expressed in few words and simple diagrams. Tutorial programs have tended to assume some previous initial teaching of the topic, and to focus instead on the practice of related tasks. The teacher's conception is implicit in the form of the feedback given, but this does not make it available to the student to inspect in its totality.

The teaching strategy embodied in the tasks put to the student is usually designed to elicit known misconceptions, so in that sense there is an intention to make the student's conception available to the program, but because of the limitations of computer interface styles, these are extremely constraining on how students are allowed to express their ideas. The most risky style is also the most common – the multiple choice question (mcq) technique. This is perfectly acceptable in those cases where all possible answers to the question can be listed for the student to select from, e.g. yes/no questions, or questions of the form:

> How do increases in government spending and in private investment compare with respect to their effect on aggregate demand:
>
> (a)   Only government spending shifts aggregate demand.
> (b)   Only private investment shifts aggregate demand.
> (c)   Both shift aggregate demand.
> (d)   Neither shifts aggregate demand.

As there is no other possible answer to the question as phrased – logically it has to be one or the other – the mcq technique works well as a way of communicating the student's answer to the question. Compare this with another way of asking about the same topic:

In comparing an increase in government spending to an increase in private investment, we can correctly say that in the short run:

(a)   They will both shift aggregate supply.
(b)   They will both shift aggregate demand.
(c)   Government spending is inflationary; private spending is not.
(d)   Government spending must equal taxes; private investment must equal saving.

(Saunders 1991: 259)

This is much more hazardous as a way of gauging the student's answer, because there are many possible ways of answering this more open question – the particular ones chosen do not cover all logical possibilities. This means the student's own way may not be represented. Therefore they must consider each answer in turn for its plausibility. In doing so, they will be likely to postulate a reason why each answer might be correct – 'government spending must equal taxes' sounds sensible, so that must be the right answer. Even if they end up selecting the correct answer, that reasoning cannot be expunged; it could be what they remember best, even though they may never have thought of it without prompting. The mcq technique therefore runs the great pedagogical risk of inviting students to make sense of wrong answers. At least with the first example above it does not introduce ideas they could not have thought of.

On the other hand, the first example fails to identify those students who have the conception that spending increases aggregate supply. The only way to elicit this conception without also inviting it is to rephrase the question, and use keyword identification of an open-ended answer, a technique known as a 'concealed multiple choice question'. This would work as follows. Ask the question 'What else increases when government spending increases?' and compare the string of letters input by the student to the strings 'supply' and 'demand'. If any part of the input matches 'supply', then the program assumes that they believe that supply increases with government spending. The matching algorithm may be more sophisticated, e.g. allow mis-spellings of 'supply'; or allow certain synonyms. However, with this method it is always possible for the student to get a right answer which the program cannot recognise. The feedback should therefore be cautious about right/wrong judgements. A common solution is to say something non-judgemental, but making explicit the correct answer, such as 'In fact it increases demand'.

Whatever form of elicitation of student conception is used, it should be designed to allow the student to express what they think as closely as possible.

It is possible, of course, to link a tutorial to other media that do allow expression of the teacher's point of view. The advent of high resolution screens and 'multimedia' capability for personal computers radically changes the presentational qualities of the computer screen, and 'multimedia' tutorials can now include presentation of the teacher's conception using audio, video and print. However, the explication of a difficult or complex theory or concept, if it needs to be expressed in those forms at all, typically requires a sustained narrative. The style of study required for apprehension of the structure of a narrative, and through that of its meaning, is not compatible with the style of study required for computer programs. Because programs are minutely controllable and interactive, the student inevitably expects continual prompting, whereas a passage of text or a video sequence requires sustained attention, but no action. I do not want to term this contrast 'active/passive', as if when reading or watching a video students are passive. They are necessarily mentally active in using these media if they are to experience anything at all. However, with a computer program they are constantly required to react – perhaps 'active/reactive' is a better formulation of the contrast. In any case, moving from the tutorial medium of continual interchange, to a presentational medium of continual receptivity is a disquieting jump for students. For that reason, the video used in conjunction with tutorials is usually chunked in very small clips, of a few seconds or so. Text as well, aside from the difficulties of reading text on a screen, is kept to short passages in well-designed programs. If it is not, there is an observable tendency in students to ignore it, or to become impatient with it. The availability of audio and visual media within tutorial programs makes little difference, therefore, to the communication of the main idea or message of the topic goal. They are more likely to be there to serve the task goals, e.g. to enhance the experience of some aspect of the world, than to express the teacher's global understanding of the topic in the narrative form that would be appropriate in a video or a chapter of a book.

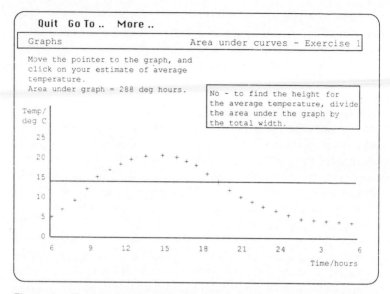

Figure 8.1 Tutorial feedback giving a hint on how to find the average 'y' value, given the area under a graph.

The adaptive characteristic of tutorial programs is the main feature that distinguishes them from the previous media. The others, in their canonical form, cannot be adaptive, whereas the tutorial necessarily is, otherwise it is not a tutorial. Adaptivity means that the program uses the student's performance on previous tasks to decide what task should be set next. For example, in a tutorial to teach basic numeracy, students are given problems in the interpretation of the 'average temperature' of a house. If they fail on two of these, this is assumed to indicate that they are not making just slips, but have an underlying difficulty. The program branches to a separate section that gives them help in understanding what 'average temperature' means, as in Figure 8.1.

This embodies a teaching strategy of the form: surface errors indicate underlying conceptual difficulty so set tasks to change their conceptions. The program also makes decisions about how many practice examples a student needs, on the basis of the frequency of their errors, and suggests they do more before moving on to a different topic, or taking a test. This embodies a strategy of the form: if they make some errors but get most right, they need more practice. Thus adaptivity acts at the level of deciding what task to set, and how much practice to offer on each one. In order to be adaptive, the program must collect and store relevant information on the student's performance. This need be no more than a database logging, e.g. tasks attempted, categories of response, cumulative scores, response times, etc., depending on what kind of performance is sought.

Tutorial programs should be fully controllable by the student because although the teacher's adaptive strategy may be generally effective, it may not be so on every occasion as far as the student is concerned. They may be aware of their mistake, or bored with an exercise, so there should be no compulsion to follow the teacher's advice; it should remain advisory. Every adaptive move by the program should be controllable by the student. This means making an index of contents available at all times to allow movement between tasks, and a menu of options allowing more exercises if the student wishes, and fewer if they prefer to move on. In a study of students' control preferences, I found that, given the option, some students did far more exercises than any teaching strategy would ever dare to suggest, whereas others would abandon an exercise as soon as they got something wrong, but return to it later (Laurillard 1984a).

Because a tutorial is a succession of explicitly designed tasks, those tasks can be interactive at the level of actions, or discursive at the level of descriptions – it is a matter of design, rather than the nature of the medium. At the level of action, it can ask students to perform exercises whose input the program can analyse in order to supply feedback. The great majority of tutorials use the mcq format to define the task set for the student, so that the input is easy to analyse. They provide only extrinsic feedback, of the form 'Yes, because . . .' where the reason is stated just in case the student made a guess and did not know the actual reason for the correct answer, or for wrong answers 'No, because . . .', or sometimes 'Try again' in case it was a trivial error. The feedback may also be given in the form of a hint, as in Figure 8.1 where the student is told how to carry out the graph reading.

This is not intrinsic feedback, but extrinsic feedback with more teaching attached. It provides information, and will assist memorisation of a procedure, and this may well be sufficient in many cases, but it will not do much to develop conceptual understanding if the student is having conceptual difficulties. For that, intrinsic feedback on action is necessary.

TUTORIAL SIMULATION

It is quite feasible for a tutorial to offer intrinsic feedback, but only if it has some kind of model of the task it sets. This defines the 'tutorial simulation', and being a combination of two complementary media, one adaptive and one interactive, it is an importantly different medium from either on their own.

Intrinsic feedback is common enough for mathematical topics, where the student's input can generate output from an equation. A better version of the above feedback would be the one shown in Figure 8.2 where the tutorial incorporates a model of the system which enables students to see the relationship between the height of the line and the comparative areas under graph and line. As they move the line, they see the area under it approximate more closely to the measure of the area under the graph.

This interaction with a model gives students an experiential sense of how the system behaves, just as a simulation does, and with this highly constrained way of experiencing the world of graphs, areas and average values, similar to the idea of 'supplantation' in learning from video, students begin to see it as the technologist would wish them to. The tutorial part of this

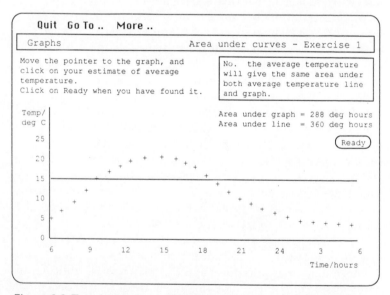

Figure 8.2 Tutorial feedback designed to help students understand the concept of average 'y' value in terms of the area under a graph.

program provides extrinsic feedback to complement the intrinsic, in the form of a canned text comment on the student's opinion that they are 'ready', having found the average temperature. The intrinsic feedback shows them how the two areas change as they move the line, but they have to be able to interpret that feedback in terms of the task. Intrinsic feedback alone will not be enough if, for example, they assume the average line just has to look right. The additional extrinsic feedback displayed in the pop-up window is the teacher's redescription, following reflection on the student's action. In fact it is canned text programmed in, in the expectation that this kind of error will occur. This does not make it fully discursive, but the program is capable of offering a redescription of the topic in the light of the student's action, tailored to that event, and therefore capable of helping the student interpret the intrinsic feedback.

The most general way of defining the aim of the program here is to help the student understand the form of representation of a real world system, i.e. the concept of average temperature as a line on a graph bearing a particular relation to the graphical representation of variation of temperature. For this kind of aim, a computer-based tutorial simulation can approximate quite closely to supporting the discursive mode, because it 'knows' about the correct interpretation of the event it is simulating via the model it uses. The interpretation has to be plugged into canned text, but it is still well-focused on the event just experienced by the student.

Another example is shown in Figure 8.3, which is essentially a tutorial, attempting to give remedial teaching on the subtraction of negative numbers. Here again, the teaching strategy is adaptive, reacting to repeated errors by assuming that the student needs conceptual help. To change their conception of subtraction of negative numbers, they need to extend their experience of how numbers behave. This is done by interpreting mathematical manipulation of numbers as actions on a number line – as they specify positive or negative numbers, the bird hops forwards or backwards along the line; as they use the operator 'add', the bird remains facing the same way, or 'subtract', and it turns round to face the other way. Again they receive both intrinsic feedback from the model in the form of the bird's behaviour in response to their mathematical formalism, and extrinsic feedback in the form of canned text interpretation of what they are doing.

The tutorial simulation is a powerful combination. Once we

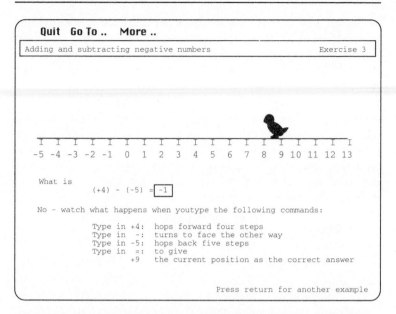

Figure 8.3 Tutorial program simulation program in basic arithmetic, showing how mathematical formalism may be mapped directly onto actions on the number line.

recognise that anything that can be modelled can be programmed as a simulation, it follows that it can also be programmed as an even more effective tutorial simulation. The model does not have to be mathematical. The economics example we looked at above, could be modelled as a series of causal relations: e.g. increase in government spending → increase in aggregate demand; increase in private investment → increase in aggregate demand; increase in aggregate demand → increase in aggregate supply; and so on. A statement by the student that supply increases as a consequence of increased government spending could then be matched to each effect in the cause–effect relations to discover its stated cause, so that the program can output the intrinsic feedback 'No, that would be caused by an increase in demand'. A more accurate model would include statements handling the crucial timescale refinements of 'in the short run' and 'in the long run', but the format of this kind of model should be clear. The difficulty lies in the complexity of producing a model that is complete enough and accurate enough to handle the range of student responses to the questions put. Designing an appropriate model requires an understanding of both the subject matter and the ways students typically conceptualise it. This is discussed further in Chapter 10. For now, it is sufficient to note that such models are possible elements of tutorial simulations for many subject areas.

Without a model of the system, tutorials are only weakly discursive, giving extrinsic feedback on students' actions. The student may be asked to carry out a task defined by the teacher (program), and their input can be matched to an expected right answer and any number of expected wrong answers, with extrinsic feedback given accordingly. 'Canned text', where the program uses pre-programmed statements as feedback in response to particular student answers, is not intrinsic feedback, as although the program reacts differently, depending on the student's action, no information in the system changes as it does if they make an input to a model. Figure 8.1, and mcq programs, do not show students what happens in the world as a result of their actions. To operate intrinsic feedback, the straightforward tutorial must be augmented with a simulation, as this is the only medium so far which has been able to offer this. Then it becomes a very powerful teaching medium, because it adds the dimension of adaptivity to the strong interactive capabilities of simulation and modelling.

TUTORING SYSTEMS

It is the explicit intention of a tutoring system (or as it is also called, an 'intelligent tutoring system' or ITS) to provide a complete individualised tutor. It sets out to address all the aspects of the learning process I identified as being essential, and in so far as it achieves this, does exactly what a tutorial can do if it is augmented by modelling and simulation components. There is an important difference in its internal structure, however. As early as 1973, Roger Hartley suggested that an adaptive tutoring system should separate out the three key components of domain knowledge, student model and teaching knowledge (Hartley 1973). Tutorial programs contain all these, but they are not separable. What makes tutoring systems distinctive is that the three components make the knowledge embedded in the program separable and therefore explicit. How important is this? A great deal of research funding has been directed at the area of 'intelligent tutoring' in the belief that it will improve the quality of teaching provision, so we need to be clear about what exactly it offers that is different from the augmented tutorial program.

It is not possible to do justice to the complexity of research in this field in a short section, but I hope to be able to explicate the kind of difference the ITS approach makes by comparing what a tutoring program and a tutoring system would do for the same teaching goal, e.g. the subtraction of negative numbers.

Let us suppose that the teaching strategy we use for wrong answers is to induce cognitive conflict by showing that the student can produce the same answer from a different expression (intrinsic feedback). Both dialogues would look the same to a student, e.g. the task 'What is X – Y?' might be instantiated as:

What is (–3) – (–5)?
–8
Well, what is (–3) + (–5) ?
–8
So (–3) – (–5) must be different. Try again.
2
Good.

but the line in italic would be generated in different ways. In the tutorial program, the teaching strategy would be embodied in a statement of the form:

A: If the student inputs $[x + y]$ then ask 'Well, what is $(x) + (y)$?'

where the values of x and y are in this case –3 and –8, respectively, and this line of program would generate the line in italic above. In the tutoring system the teaching strategy would be captured in a more general form, as a rule that can be applied to any input from the student on a range of exercises, such as:

B: If the answer to the question 'What is [expression]?' can be generated from a known bug (of the form 'expression → answer type 1'), then ask the question 'What is [answer type 1]?'

Rule B would be located in the teaching knowledge component of the system, and when invoked (i.e. in the condition that the student has made that particular type of error) would use information from the domain knowledge about the known bugs. These would be listed as something like:

	expression	→	answer type
Error type 1	$x - y$	/	$-x + y$
Error type 2	$x - y$	/	$x + y$
Error type 3	$x - y$	/	$-x - y$
etc.			

So with the student input '–8' and the knowledge that $x=-3$ and $y=-5$, which it generated itself, the system starts checking through the known bugs: does the student's answer equal 3 –5? No. Does it equal –3 + –5? Yes, so they have made error type 2, thereby invoking Rule B: ask the question 'What is $(-3) + (-5)$?', generated from the answer part of error type 2.

This would generate exactly the same italic line in the dialogue above. At each point in the running of the program, it checks the current condition of the system, and then checks through all the condition–action (if–then–) rules to see which of them correspond to the current condition, and so which of them should be invoked.

From this comparison, it should be possible to see what is meant by making the components separable. Statement A in the tutorial program has been unpacked for the tutoring system; the teaching knowledge it embodies has been decoupled from the domain knowledge it uses. Statement B could conceivably be found in a totally different topic domain. Statement A could not. In this simple fact lies much of the attraction of the ITS: the hope is that once a teaching strategy is worked out for one domain, you can bolt it onto a database of knowledge for any other domain, and so generate a new ITS. This is a logistical improvement, therefore. It makes the design of tutorial programs much more efficient. It also takes them out of the hands of programmers who cannot handle AI techniques, because these are certainly needed to cope with the complexity of decision-making in these systems. It also provides a methodological advantage, because having the teaching strategy, and indeed the domain knowledge, separable and explicit, it becomes easier to inspect them, argue with them, refine them, re-use them, etc., and this is all highly advantageous in a development area that badly needs methodological rigour.

None of this presages pedagogical improvements in design, however. In my example, I stated that the dialogue would look the same to the student, and it is a frequent complaint of ITS designers that it is difficult to demonstrate the power of their systems, precisely because they do not look very different in operation. I have shown that tutorial simulations can address most aspects of the learning process, albeit with a highly constrained discursive mode. Tutoring systems aspire to address all of them. How far do they achieve it?

The domain knowledge is explicitly defined in a tutoring system, so should be easily accessible for inspection by the student. It may exist, for example, as a set of condition–action rules, or a semantic network that could be browsed by the student. What is good for the program operation may not be so good for the student, however. Although the knowledge may be very explicit, it would not be easy to digest in this form. It has no narrative structure, only logical structure. The student would be more likely to access it not by reading it, but by asking it questions, such as 'what do you associate with x?' to a semantic network, or 'Why did you do x' to a set of condition–action rules. This is a nice solution to the problem of getting a program to simulate a reasonable dialogue with a student at the level of descriptions, except that the dialogue on offer is constrained by the form of the knowledge base – you could not ask a set of condition–action rules a question of the form 'what do you associate with X?'. So we are still a long way from the genuinely discursive program, but this is a great improvement of the mcq format, and current research programmes in the field are certainly aiming to make tutoring systems able to handle discursive activities.

Its generative teaching strategy makes a tutoring system highly adaptive, to the extent that its exact behaviour is often unpredictable by the designer. The system does not work by an algorithmic procedure, as the tutoring program does, following a recipe for action. Instead it inspects the current state of the system, checks which rule should now apply, and applies it to create the next state, and so on. The designer often cannot keep track of which rule is being invoked at any one time. The information it uses to generate the next action will come partly from the domain knowledge, which generates questions and predicts possible answers, and also from the student model, which keeps a record of everything relevant that should be known about the student. What is relevant depends on the teaching strategy built in. We may simply be interested in how fast a student can do something, in which case the student model would keep a record of response times. We may also be interested in the kind of errors they make – are they consistent? In the example above, we might design the teaching to decide that if they had made lots of type 3 errors they need tuition on the basic concepts more than further practice with the current exercise. For this to work, the student model must collect information on the type of errors as well. The more information of this kind is built in, the more individually adaptive the system becomes.

A tutoring system should be as controllable by the student as a tutoring program, giving students control over what they do and when and how long for, etc. Furthermore, some designers have argued that the student should be able to negotiate with the system, should be able, for example, to specify whether the system asks them questions or vice versa. Intriguing programming challenges are generated by ambitions of this sort, and design and hardware requirements are necessarily considerable.

To the extent that a tutoring system can call on artificial intelligence techniques to conduct a natural language dialogue, this medium comes closest to emulating a tutor by being able to support the student in reflecting on the relationship of the topic goal to the tasks they undertook. The record of student experience as far as performance on tasks is concerned is available to the system, as is the interaction at description level. It can therefore call on a great deal of information pertinent to the task of reflecting on what has been achieved in relation to the overall goal. Assuming that all this information is used by the dialogue at the end of a tutorial session, the ITS is the only medium that can be said to support genuine reflection on the particular learning experience the student has undergone.

From this analysis it is clear that the novel internal architecture of an ITS does not offer any novel pedagogical moves that could not be done some other way, except possibly in the quality of discursive, reflective dialogue it offers. Much the same effect can often be achieved by a combination of drill and practice, simulation, and concealed multiple choice questions. The novelty of ITS lies in the greater generality of the design, and therefore ultimately in greater efficiency.

It is an unfortunate feature of work on tutoring systems that it so frequently over-states the case for what they can do. The epithet 'intelligent' is used because these programs use artificial intelligence techniques and make knowledge explicit. The standard Turing test of intelligence is that the system should *appear* to exhibit intelligent behaviour. Since the behaviour of these systems is hard to distinguish from tutorial programs, however, the claim for intelligence is undermined. Similarly, the term 'student model' is misleading. It usually refers to nothing more than a data file on the student's performance to date. This sort of thing can be easily incorporated into a tutorial program without recourse to AI techniques. The fact is, however, that such features are rare in tutorial programs. The real benefit of the ITS work has been to construct a rational framework for what a tutoring system should be like, and to specify this with much greater rigour than has been the case in the design of tutorial programs.

Tutoring systems would be the acme of all the educational media, if they existed. They address all the aspects of the learning process I have defined as being necessary. They are difficult to develop, and at present contribute more to progress in AI than they do to education (see also Chapter 4). Because they are developed by people who are more interested in cognitive science than they are in improving student learning, the systems developed make little reference to learning theory or to findings in student learning research, as revealed, for example, in Wenger's comprehensive analysis of the field (Wenger 1987).

The research area is an important one, however, because it develops techniques for handling the kind of data and decision-making that learning research will find helpful if it is to implement its findings in computer-based teaching systems. Its unique contribution is in design methodology, however, rather than pedagogy. The content of these systems, the way they interact with the student, must be grounded in the kind of empirical work discussed in Chapters 2 and 3. Without that, they remain of interest only to cognitive science, not to education.

SUMMARY

This chapter has considered tutorial programs and tutoring systems in relation to the learning activities framework defined at the beginning of Part II. Those they can support are summarised in Table 8.1.

The main difference between the tutoring system and the tutorial simulation lies in the fact that the teacher's conception is expressed explicitly in the former. Neither is genuinely discursive of course, but the modelling component incorporated to allow the

Table 8.1 Summary of adaptive media characteristics

		Tprg	Tsys	Tsim
1	T can describe conception	✓	✓	✓
2	S can describe conception	✓	✓	✓
3	T can redescribe in light of S's conception or action	✓	✓	✓
4	S can redescribe in light of T's redescription or S's action	✓	✓	✓
5	T can adapt task goal in light of S's description or action	✓	✓	✓
6	T can set task goal	✓	✓	✓
7	S can act to achieve task goal	✓	✓	✓
8	T can set up world to give intrinsic feedback on actions	O	✓	✓
9	S can modify action in light of feedback on action	O	✓	✓
10	S can adapt actions in light of T's description or S's redescription	✓	✓	✓
11	S can reflect on interaction to modify redescription	O	✓	✓
12	T can reflect on S's action to *modify redescription*	✓	✓	✓

student to express their conception in some description language, makes them the only media so far to offer adaptation and redescription by the teacher, on the basis of students' actions. They are the media that come closest to covering the range of essential learning activities we defined in Chapter 4 and, especially in combination with other presentational media, are potentially effective alternatives to the one-to-one teacher–student dialogue.

Chapter 9

Discursive media

INTRODUCTION

Now we look at the media whose specific task is to bring people together to discuss. They are grouped under the generic category 'teleconferencing', i.e. conferencing at a distance. The discussion may be between tutor and student, or between students. Teleconferencing is essentially a solution to a logistical problem, rather than a pedagogical problem, normally used to overcome the problem of communicating with students who are geographically distributed. It is not usually seen as a desirable medium in its own right, unlike the other media we have considered. However, a medium that can support discussion immediately addresses two of the most difficult aspects of the learning process, namely interaction at the level of descriptions, and reflection on action, feedback and goals. Teleconferencing is built on the assumption that students can learn through discussion, even if at a distance, and moreover benefit by the access it gives to distant academic experts. As expertise in certain subject areas resides in fewer universities, it may become a lifeline for some students, so it deserves careful analysis to determine just what kind of learning it can support.

There are two forms of conferencing: synchronous (where participants use the system at the same time), using audio conferencing via a telephone, or video conferencing via cable or satellite; and asynchronous (where participants use the system at different times), using computer conferencing via a computer link. All types engage tutor and student (or student and student) in a two-way conversation. All allow an eavesdropping audience of other students to gain benefit from observing the discussion, via a telephone bridge, or a network respectively. Of course computer conferencing may also be done in real time, if the parties wish to wait the few minutes it takes for the reply to come back.

Teleconferencing appears to offer the ideal teaching situation of a tutor–student dialogue, though at a distance. It is essentially a discursive medium, not really able to offer interaction with the world, or with a simulated world, at the level of actions. Its value depends, therefore, on the quality of discussion it supports, and that is what we consider in this chapter.

We also look at another type of discursive medium, known as 'computer-supported collaborative work', which designs computer programs specifically to promote and support student discussion. Again, the quality of discussion it promotes is the central question.

AUDIO-CONFERENCING

Audio-conferencing is group discussion by telephone, and has some characteristics of face-to-face groups. The discussion needs someone to act as a 'chair', simply to do the job of making sure that everyone knows who is on-line, and that everyone who wishes to is able to speak. If there is a group of students at one site then a loudspeaker and microphone may be attached to the telephone to enable everyone to hear the conversation, and take part if they wish by taking over the microphone.

An audio-graphics system enhances the communication achieved by audio-conferencing by adding the transmission of digitised graphics between participants. As one user changes the data on their screen, for example using a light-pen to draw a new line on the graph, the data is transmitted to other users down a telephone line, to appear in the same form on their screen. At the same time the users can communicate via a second telephone line transmitting their speech. The advantage of this system is that it does not rely on *prior* shared experience, as audio-conferencing must, for the communication to work. Because participants can create diagrams on-line, the object of discussion can be dynamically changed. This gives students a little more control over the direction the discussion takes, as it gives them an additional way of expressing an idea, or asking a question. Control is relative to tutor restraint, however. The disadvantage is that the lecturer is given a presentational device via this system, and can all too easily make use of it for delivering new material, rather than allowing a student-led discussion to develop.

An evaluation of such a system at the British Open University showed that its principal educational value is that the screen can 'provide a visual focus during tutorials' and 'make it easier to assimilate information', whereas the screen input from the students can 'promote thinking, forcing students to think about what they were writing or drawing on the screen' (McConnell and Sharples 1983: 120–1). Voice communication alone will not always have the power to elicit the precision of expression that can be achieved by asking someone to draw or add to a diagram. Audio-graphics is therefore more effective at allowing the teacher, and especially students, to express their point of view, through both language and diagrams. Against that, we must balance the difficulty of communicating through voice alone, which even with a good 'chair' can be a daunting prospect for students, the medium often being judged unfavourably, for example, by Open University students. This is partly because, in reality, the time constraint on synchronous conferencing makes it difficult for the medium to be fully discursive – students rarely get the chance to 'redescribe their conception in the light of the teacher's redescription'.

Audio-conferencing is a partially discursive medium, offering no opportunity for interaction at the level of actions within a 'world'. In audio-graphics, the actions on the screens are simply ways of presenting the participants' conceptions; they would only be actions if the computers could communicate a common model on which both participants could operate and see the results. When this is possible, it makes a sufficiently significant pedagogical difference that I have classified it as a different medium – now known as 'computer-supported collaborative work' – to be discussed below.

VIDEO-CONFERENCING

Video-conferencing is a one-to-many medium, making it a sensible way to provide access for many sites to a remote academic expert.

At either end of a video-conferencing link there is a camera focused on an individual or group, which carries their picture via a video link to the screen at the other end. The video link may be high-band cable, or ISDN, or radio microwave, and over long distances may be transmitted by satellite. The lecturer is usually given control over what is transmitted via a console governing the various cameras. Cameras may also be trained on live action elsewhere, such as an operating theatre, or an experimental set-up, or on overheads, slides etc. Each local site is furnished with a microphone, or with several if the group is large, to enable individuals to communicate spontaneously. Microphones need to be equipped with a button that allows the user to signal their intention to speak to the lecturer, who then activates that line if they wish. The degree of student control over the communication is therefore similar to the situation of a large lecture, i.e. not very great, and is further diminished by the barrier of a largely unseen audience. As in a lecture, there is little opportunity for social negotiation. Video-conferencing does offer an improvement on the audio-conferencing difficulties of identifying who is talking, although the on-screen image of the individual is often small, and unless the total group is a regular one, identification can still be a problem.

Video-conferencing invites the delivery of lectures. Because of the transmission of visual information as well as audio, it is definitely a presentational medium as well as being a discursive one. Inevitably this fact is exploited by lecturers, and the potential interaction with students rarely occurs. On balance, the two-way visual link is hard to justify in an educational context. As one evaluation study found, students were reluctant to make use of the facility to ask questions themselves, and found the best use of the medium was often the traditional didactic lecture (Bollom, Emerson, Fleming and Williams 1989). The communication facility was used mainly to sort out technical failures, or to ask for more time to look at slides. Of course, the student may ask an academic question, or may be pounced on to broadcast their answer to one, but this does not make the medium truly discursive in reality. The current technology makes it an uncomfortable way to negotiate a shared conception. As a way of transmitting a didactic lecture, a video would be cheaper and easier. As a way of allowing communication with the tutor, a series of small-group audio-conferences, or audio-graphic links may be more effective.

COMPUTER-MEDIATED CONFERENCING

This is the only asynchronous teleconferencing medium.[1] It operates in a similar way to electronic mail, delivering written text in digitised form down data lines, and requiring both ends of the communication link to use a computer connected to a network, which may be local, national or international. Access to the medium therefore depends on having a computer linked into a network either via cable or via a modem.

The standard way to use the system is for the student to join the conference they are interested in, and ask the system to display all the messages sent into it that they have not already looked at. Each message is displayed in turn, and the student may either contribute comments relating to a particular message, or append a message at the end of the existing discussion. Their message will then appear on everyone else's system next time they join the conference. Computer conferencing is therefore a little like taking part in a normal conference discussion, but via text alone, and over a much longer span of time, as the discussion is asynchronous. An obvious pedagogical advantage over the normal face-to-face tutorial is that students can take time to ponder the various points made, and can make their contribution in their own time. Topic negotiation is also possible, as in face-to-face discussion, and a tutor may pursue several lines of discussion with different students within one conference, though a good moderator would probably separate them out into different 'topics' within the conference. Student control is therefore relatively high for this medium, allowing us to acknowledge the possibility of students being able to redescribe their conception in the light of the teacher's redescription. It is therefore a more fully discursive medium than the synchronous conferencing media.

The logistical advantages of computer conferencing are obvious for distance learning universities, where this can be a lifeline for students otherwise cut off from any form of discussion with tutors and fellow students. The advantages for campus-based students will only be apparent in courses with low populations, or with distant experts, or where tutors and students cannot easily arrange mutually acceptable meeting times, as is frequently the case in teaching hospitals, for example. The pedagogical benefits of the medium rest entirely on how successfully it maintains a fruitful dialogue between tutor and students, or indeed between fellow students.

The skill of conducting a fruitful dialogue via conferencing, whether one–one or one–many, is as important here for the success of the interaction as it is in face-to-face situations, perhaps more so, as there is less information from body language and facial expression to help the interlocutors. From evaluation studies of computer conferencing in many different educational contexts (Kaye, Mason and Harasim 1989), it becomes clear that the moderator (the conferencing equivalent of a chair) must, in addition to the normal duties of a chair:

• negotiate goals and timelines for the conference
• set up new branches and topics as the discussion progresses
• nurture group collaborative processes
• ensure that adequate responses and reactions are given to all relevant contributions

Keeping abreast of the conference, which can proceed apace when the moderator turns away just for a day or so, is difficult enough for a busy lecturer. The work required to play an adequate role as moderator, to ensure that the interaction will indeed be successful, is considerable, as the above list shows.

The asynchronous, text-based format of computer conferencing offers a better opportunity than the other conferencing media for reflection on participants' contributions, and improves on print by offering two-way communication, allowing students to express their own viewpoint. The success of the medium is totally dependent on a good moderator, however, and this can easily be as time-consuming as any other form of face-to-face tutoring.

The value of conferencing in all its forms is that it supports discussion between tutor and student, and theoretically, at least, allows each to express their viewpoint. In practice, the relationship is asymmetrical, as it is in any face-to-face tutorial, and the tutor is more likely to be responsible for establishing the ground rules of the interaction. Tutors generally have little trouble in articulating their own view, whatever the medium, that is their art. The more difficult trick for them is to give the student the space to express theirs, and to encourage them to elaborate it sufficiently for the tutor to make sense of any points of departure. One factor that diminishes the student's opportunity to express their view is time pressure. Analysis of audio-conferencing within a satellite television programme has shown, for example, that during the broadcast transmission, the ratio of tutor–student air-time in conferencing was 3:1, whereas once the programme was finished and the audio-conference alone continued off-air, the ratio was 2:1. This illustrates the value of an asynchronous network, which allows the student unlimited time to compose what they want to say, and also to say it. Analysis of tutor–student messages in a computer conference running during an Open University course showed that the average length of student contribution was 200 words, equivalent to over a minute of continuous speech, which would be rare indeed in the standard face-to-face tutorial.

The fact that conferencing has a one–many form, rather than one–one, reveals an expectation of the value of eavesdropping by other students. This is largely borne out by what students say about the medium, and evaluations report many expressions of delight at hearing others expressing the same worries or confusions or criticisms. In that case a dialogue between a tutor and a student can stand for many such dialogues if that student is indeed representative of many others. In the course of the dialogue, the tutor's viewpoint is also likely to be re-expressed or elaborated, which then benefits all students.

Conferencing alone does not support any task-based activity other than the description and redescription of the student's view. Certain augmented forms can do this, however. Audio-conferencing combined with television, as in 'interactive satellite broadcasting', can make use of activities set for students, much as a problem class might. Off-air versions of the same medium, where closed circuit television links off-campus students to tutors, would support the same thing. Audio-graphics allows teacher and students to pursue on-line discussion of a shared computer program, itself providing the tasks. Current experiments with computer conferencing networks are investigating ways of adding this kind of capability to an asynchronous computer conference. Thus conferencing in combination with networked video or computer programs could support defined task goals for the discussion to focus on, but conferencing alone does not do so.

By virtue of the fact that conferencing supports a discussion, it is possible for the tutor to adapt the focus of talk in the light of what the student expresses, but this requires considerable time and care on the part of the tutor, and is hardly yet commonplace in the use of the medium. The student is always able to control the interaction, however, by asking questions, and redirecting the topic, though under time constraints if it is real-time synchronous audio conferencing. The discussion is interactive at the level of descriptions, but not tasks, as I argued earlier. Moreover, discussion allows intrinsic feedback on descriptions, in the sense that every statement by the student affects what the tutor says next. It is this aspect that makes dialogue so well suited to helping students to refine their understanding at the level of description. Although it is open to tutor and student to reflect on the development of the discussion, what has been learned, and how it compares to the original intention, whether well-defined or not, I have not included this medium as one that supports reflection, as there is little enough evidence of it in practice, and the conferencing media themselves do nothing explicit to support it. Like the definition of goals, this has to be promulgated as a desirable way to conduct a conference.

The conferencing media, as we can see from this analysis, contribute more to logistics than to pedagogy. If students are necessarily at a distance from their tutor, then these media provide an extremely important lifeline to interactive discussion which is otherwise not available to them. The written form of computer conferencing offers a better opportunity for reflection on participants' contributions, and improves on print by being interactive and adaptive and allowing students to express their viewpoint. The success is totally dependent on a good moderator, however, and this is as time-consuming as any other form of face-to-face tutoring. It is not the kind of medium where students can be left to work independently. In the next section, we consider discussion between students alone.

COLLABORATION

One of the great untested assumptions of current educational practice is that students learn through discussion. In the UK the idea of 'learning through discussion' dominates many of the National Curriculum documents; it has always been acknowledged as important at university level, where seminars are a key teaching method; and now the last refuge of the software salesperson defending a third-rate program is that it 'encourages discussion' (it used to be that it 'gives them practice in using the computer'). There is increasing research on collaboration between students using computers, and this work is beginning to look at the nature of the student–student discussion that results. Student–student discussion undoubtedly has some important educational characteristics, but in comparison with the aspects of the learning process I suggested were essential, it addresses rather few. It supports the communication of the student's point of view; it is controllable by the student; it supports interaction at the level of description, although the fact that the feedback offered on a student's description is from another student, and not from a teacher is a significant difference. Argument between students about a topic can be an extremely effective way of enabling students to find out what they know, and indeed what they do not know, but it does not necessarily lead them to what they are supposed to know. As a mathematics lecturer I often found it difficult to get students to express what they had trouble with beyond 'I just don't understand it'. The most successful technique was to ask them to role-play teaching each other some small chunk of theory. After five minutes of this they were able to formulate (a) some profound questions I was unable to answer immediately, and (b) some points of such startling banality that I had assumed they were obvious after the first few minutes of the first lecture. The technique was excellent for alerting me to the deficiencies in my teaching, and for unblocking our communicative impasse, but their discussion alone was not always sufficient to sort out their problem. Discussion between students is an excellent partial method of learning that needs to be complemented by something offering the other characteristics, if students are not to flounder in mutually progressive ignorance.

Student discussion can be combined with any of the media we have looked at so far. Trigger video offers short chunks of video for group discussion. Lectures can incorporate 'buzz groups'. Role-play simulations usually use print-based materials describing case studies; some aspects of the simulation may be run on computers. Computer-supported collaborative work (CSCW) offers a computer program, usually simulations or microworlds, although some projects are now researching programs designed especially for student collaborative use, which assign specific roles to each student (see Taylor *et al*. 1991).

Studies of student–student interaction are universal in their enthusiasm for the richness of the interactions produced, and the potential they offer for learning to take place. They are all carried out as observations of what happens to take place as students interact in the pursuance of some task, whether generated by video, paper and pencil tasks, tutorial program, computer simulation, microworld or modelling task. They are equally universal in their recognition that the interactions are not always successful (see, for example, Durbridge 1984b; McMahon 1990; Hoyles, Healy and Sutherland 1991; Roschelle and Behrend, forthcoming). Studies typically identify as sources of failure those aspects of the learning process that are missing from the media combination concerned, i.e. feedback from the teacher, reflection by students on the goal–action–feedback cycle.

This is a field of research that has yet to produce a practice-oriented consensus on how student–student dialogue can best be supported to engender successful learning. From these early beginnings of recording the phenomena will eventually emerge some patterns of interactions, and some relations between these and the contextual characteristics of their occurrence. Some contexts seem to support productive interactions better than others. For example, Hoyles, Healy and Sutherland suggest that students were more likely to focus on formalization when they were required to formalize actions as code in the use of a Logo microworld than they were in a paper and pencil environment. On the other hand, although symbolic representation occurred infrequently in pencil and paper tasks, they observed that when it did, it was more likely to be done by the group, than in the Logo environment where it was often taken over by an individual 'encoder' (Hoyles *et al.* 1991). I have already pointed out in the discussion of microworlds that they support 'doing maths' less well than an environment that enforces symbolic representation. Studies like this will give us the means to develop computer and other environments that provide better support for students working together and unsupervised, both at the task level and the description level.

The medium provides interaction at task level, and allows the student to reflect on this to produce their own description, but it is neither discursive with the teacher, nor adaptive by the teacher. In tandem with adaptive media, of course, it would be quite powerful.

SUMMARY

We have considered the teleconferencing media as well as computer-oriented discussions in relation to the conversational framework defined at the beginning of Part II. They are broadly complementary to the teaching media discussed in previous

Table 9.1 Summary of discursive media characteristics

		A/C	V/C	C/C	CSCW
1	T can describe conception	✓	✓	✓	O
2	S can describe conception	✓	✓	✓	✓
3	T can redescribe in light of S's conception or action	✓	✓	✓	O
4	S can redescribe in light of T's redescription or S's action	O	O	✓	O
5	T can adapt task goal in light of S's description or action	O	O	O	O
6	T can set task goal	O	O	O	✓
7	S can act to achieve task goal	O	O	O	✓
8	T can set up world to give intrinsic feedback on actions	O	O	O	✓
9	S can modify action in light of feedback on action	O	O	O	✓
10	S can adapt actions in light of T's description or S's redescription	O	O	O	✓
11	S can reflect on interaction to modify redescription	O	O	O	✓
12	T can reflect on S's action to modify redescription	O	O	O	O

chapters as they are designed to support discussion rather than interaction. The aspects of the learning process they support are summarised in Table 9.1.

We would expect the conferencing media to be able to handle the discursive aspects of the learning process well. However, while both audio-conferencing (especially audio-graphics) and computer conferencing can support this, video-conferencing tends to approximate more to the lecture than the conversation. It is a less leisurely medium than the other two. CSCW, on the other hand, supports most aspects very well, assuming that a well-designed simulation program is being used, but cannot accommodate intrusion from the teacher on the proceedings. This may not matter if discussion between students is productive, but too often it fails to be, they may become confused, or may pursue an inappropriate path. Without the teacher's roles of redescription and adaptation, the method remains at risk of failing to support learning. That is why it is important to investigate the design of programs that can emulate aspects of the tutorial input to a simulation program for use in this way.

The conferencing media will remain important because of their logistical advantages, but this analysis also shows that they can complement other media, as the discursive aspect of the learning process is the most difficult to support via educational media. It also shows how close CSCW will come to being complete support for students, if it can be designed to incorporate the teacher's roles of adaptation and redescription.

NOTE

1 This is not quite true. We could also count the telephone answering machine as an asynchronous audio-conferencing facility. I know of no such use in education, but there is no logical or logistical or pedagogical reason why it should not be so used. If it were, it would have the same media characteristics as computer-mediated conferencing.

POSTSCRIPT

The five chapters in Part II have covered most of the technological media likely to be used in the service of education. The analysis at the end of each chapter showed the extent to which each one can support the learning process as defined by the conversational framework at the beginning of Part II. The media comparison chart in Table II.1 brings together all the media and displays the entire analysis.

We can see from the chart that only two media, tutorial simulations and tutoring systems, can claim to address the entire learning process, and that is only because I have allowed the highly constrained program–student dialogue to count as being discursive. The analysis is not fine-grained enough to differentiate all the contrasts possible, but it should serve to show where a medium needs further support, and which other media might provide it. The columns are at least additive: a combination of the two media represented by two columns will inherit the combined characteristics of both. They may even be multiplicative, as in the case of tutorial and simulation: neither on its own allows the student to 'reflect on interaction to modify description', the tutorial because there is no interaction, and the simulation because there is no facility for the student to describe their conception. In the combination, however, each provides the facility the other lacks, and so produces a multiplicative effect of better coverage of the learning process.

This kind of analysis does not determine the selection of media; it is not a prescriptive process. It should help to clarify where a particular medium fails to support the student, and to suggest which media it should be combined with. Stand-alone media-based packages will never be sufficient, because none of the media can adequately support the discursive activities that are essential for academic learning. However, the media comparison shows how to integrate a range of media in order to best exploit the strengths of each. Improvements in university teaching are less likely to come from 'multimedia' than from 'multiple media'.

It is hard to predict the optimal balance of time a student should spend in working on learning materials, participating in discussion, reading, writing, listening, practising. It will vary from one subject to another, and according to the way a course is designed by its teachers. The balance will evolve with practice.

Table II.1 Media comparison chart

	Print	Audio-vision	Television	Video	Self-assessed questions	Hypertext	Multi-media resources	Simulation	Microworld	Modelling	Tutorial program	Tutoring system	Tutorial simulation	Audio-conferencing	Video conferencing	Computer conferencing	Computer supported collaborative work
1 T can describe conception	✓	✓	✓	✓	○	✓	✓	○	○	○	✓	✓	✓	✓	✓	✓	○
2 S can describe conception	○	✓	○	○	✓	✓	✓	○	✓	✓	✓	✓	✓	✓	✓	✓	✓
3 T can redescribe in light of S's conception or action	○	○	○	○	○	○	○	○	○	○	✓	✓	✓	✓	✓	✓	○
4 S can redescribe in light of T's redescription or S's action	○	✓	○	○	✓	✓	✓	○	○	○	✓	✓	✓	○	○	✓	○
5 T can adapt task goal in light of S's description or action	○	○	○	○	○	○	○	○	○	○	✓	✓	✓	○	○	○	○
6 T can set task goal	○	✓	✓	✓	✓	○	✓	✓	✓	✓	✓	✓	✓	○	○	○	✓
7 S can act to achieve task goal	○	✓	○	○	✓	○	✓	✓	✓	✓	✓	✓	✓	○	○	○	✓
8 T can set up world to give intrinsic feedback on actions	○	✓	✓	✓	○	○	✓	✓	✓	✓	○	✓	✓	○	○	○	✓
9 S can modify action in light of intrinsic feedback on action	○	✓	○	○	○	○	✓	✓	✓	✓	○	✓	✓	○	○	○	✓
10 S can adapt actions in light of T's description or S's redescription	○	✓	○	○	✓	○	○	○	✓	✓	○	✓	✓	○	○	○	✓
11 S can reflect on interaction to modify description	○	✓	○	○	✓	○	✓	○	✓	✓	✓	✓	✓	○	○	○	✓
12 T can reflect on S's action to modify redescription	○	○	○	○	○	○	○	○	○	○	○	✓	✓	○	○	○	○

The more attentive teachers and students are to evaluating and reflecting on the practice, the more effective it will become. Given that academic knowledge is a consensual description of experience, it follows that discussion between teachers and student should play a very important part. It should be the mode of learning that drives everything else a student does, even if it is allocated only a small part of the total study time. It should not be vanishingly small, however, and there is an increasing danger that it will be. The rapid increase in student numbers in universities makes it even more unlikely that individual students will have more than the briefest conversation with their teacher during a course. Without this element of debate and discussion around academic ideas, universities will become training camps, unable to do more than expose their students to what there is to be known, and to rehearse them in the ability to reproduce it. The educational technologies will not overcome the problem of worsening staff–student ratios. Every medium has its strengths, so they can help, but each needs to be complemented by a teacher–student dialogue, and that is undeniably labour-intensive.

Part III

The design methodology

Chapter 10

Designing teaching materials

INTRODUCTION

This chapter begins the practical section of the book. Chapter 1 laid the foundations for an underlying philosophy of what academic education is trying to do, and Chapters 2 to 4 used the knowledge we have of how students learn to establish a principled approach to the selection and design of media-based methods. This formed the basis of a 'conversational framework' for the learning process, developed at the beginning of Part II as a basis for analysing the main technology-based educational media. Chapters 5 to 9 used existing examples and studies of each medium to clarify their respective capabilities, and to establish the extent to which each supports the learning process. Now there has to be a slight dislocation in the line of argument. Rather than deduce from the media capabilities the materials we should therefore offer the student, we shall put those capabilities to one side and return to a consideration of what the student needs. Then we bring the two together to see if they fit. The needs as defined will challenge the media, and clarify the extent to which they fail to deliver what pedagogy requires. We may as well know it.

This is the rational approach. In reality, this never happens. Funds are given for the development of materials using a particular medium, and the search is on for the learning objective that best fits it. While funding bodies persist in this nonsense, designers are condemned to find a *post hoc* rationalisation of what they do. But at least that much must be done. This chapter will show what a *pre hoc* rationalisation looks like.

The design of learning materials for any medium should always begin with the definition of objectives and analysis of student learning needs. Objectives will usually be given via some kind of curriculum design process that determines what students need to know or be able to do for a particular subject area. The objectives are defined in terms of the topic – the perceived priorities and values from the academic's point of view – without reference to the student, but rather thinking in terms of future learning needs, and the skills they wish to foster in their graduates. The student is considered primarily as a future expert at this stage.

In defining objectives for media-based materials, it will also be necessary to consider targeting areas of the curriculum that will clearly benefit from development. Media-based materials are too expensive to be developed by individuals, or by departments, or even by individual institutions. To be economically feasible, they must be made available, and used by larger numbers of students than any one institution could possibly muster before the materials are out of date. Distance learning universities have large student numbers, which makes it feasible for them to use media-based materials. In addition, their academic staff members teach in 'batch-processing' mode rather than 'on-line' mode, i.e. all their teaching is done through materials, so that they have uninterrupted development time. This is not true for academics in campus-based institutions. For them, the development of teaching materials takes time away from face-to-face contact with students. In the long run, there may be savings, but in the short term there is a cost. Campus-based teaching institutions cannot turn themselves overnight into media-based teaching institutions. Moreover, they do not have sufficient numbers to justify in-house production of materials, so there will always be a need for inter-institutional collaboration, a point taken up again in Chapter 12. The two key criteria for selecting specific areas of the curriculum for development are that topics must be (a) taught widely, and (b) widely acknowledged to present difficulties for students.

In addition to defining the learning objectives, it will also be necessary to address students' learning needs. Without clearly defined objectives educational design becomes mere exposition. Without having some idea of where the teacher wishes the student to be, it is impossible to bring any rational planning to the problem, or to recognise when the end has been achieved. This is not to say that with clearly defined objectives all will be well. They simply enable teachers to think more clearly about what they are doing, and provide a way of deciding whether the teaching has succeeded. Equally, without an appreciation of students' learning difficulties, the teacher risks talking over students' heads, or bypassing them completely, or at worst, creating such confusion that they are incapable of rational judgement. Students' misconceptions are typically 'pedagogenic errors', the equivalent of iatrogenic diseases (the kind that are caused by doctors' actions), born of poor teaching rather than ignorance. Students' current conceptions must be addressed by teachers if they are to guide their progression towards the teacher's conception.

This analysis of where students are and where teachers wish them to be will reveal a clear logical relation between the two. Charting the psychological means of bridging that gap is not a simple logical problem, however. We do not have a learning theory or instructional theory complete enough to perform that trick, and I even doubt that such a thing is possible. That is why this book stresses methodology more than theory. We may not be able to determine what ought to be done, but we can optimise what we are doing. A methodological approach that builds on what we know about students begins with an advantage, however, and that is why it was worth developing a principled teaching strategy. Encapsulating the complete learning process as a cyclical two-level dialogue between teacher and student, and student and world, as we did in Part II, provides a framework within which to address the construction of learning activities, and hence the design of the teaching medium. The bulk of this chapter describes what this constructive design process looks like in practice.

DEFINING LEARNING OBJECTIVES

Defining learning objectives sounds to many academics like a fearsome constraint on their creative teaching aspirations. As you delight in the intricacies and excitement of the ideas you want to promulgate, it can seem like an unwelcome intrusion to have to consider what your students will be able to do as a result. It is not about doing – the protest goes – it is about understanding, appreciating, seeing in a new way. But the point of having learning objectives is to answer the question: how will you know if the students do understand, appreciate, or see in a new way? What would count as evidence that they understand? Without knowing this, the teacher remains ignorant of the effect of their teaching. Hence the proliferation of pedagogic errors.

Academics most easily approach the definition of objectives via the definition of an aim. A teaching aim is couched in terms of what the teacher is trying to do, grounded in what the subject demands. Then, having clearly articulated what this piece of teaching is about, it is a little easier to approach the task of defining what this means for what students must be able to do. A teacher can easily produce aims such as the following diverse examples, where the teaching should help students to:

- understand Newton's Third Law of Motion
- appreciate the civic origins of architectural designs
- see gestures as having communicative value

These are not learning objectives, however, as they do not define precisely how the teacher would know whether the aim had been achieved. What would count as the student understanding the law? There is an inevitable distrust of this kind of question on the grounds that it smacks of behaviourism. How can one adequately characterise understanding as a set of behaviours? But academics think they can do this in judging examination papers. Writing an essay is a behaviour, and one that often externalises very well the content of the student's understanding. If objectives are seen in this light, as a way of backing up one's claim that the students understood as they were meant to, then the defining of objectives begins to seem less alien.

Turning an aim into a series of objectives is a challenging analytical process. The objectives have to be:

1 Precise, in the sense that a decision about whether the student can do it can be easily agreed.
2 Necessary, in the sense that without that objective the aim could not be said to have been achieved.
3 Complete, in the sense that they cover the academic ground implicit in the aim.

Anyone who has ever designed a marking scheme for an examination paper will have gone through this analysis, albeit implicitly. If it is formalised, making the implicit explicit, then it is easier to apply in situations outside those where it is essential. The procedure can be summarised as follows:

1 State the aim, x.
2 Define a behaviour, y, that would demonstrate to you that a student had achieved this aim.
3 Is y defined precisely enough that you could agree with a colleague about whether a student was exhibiting that behaviour? If not, return to 2, and refine the definition.
4 Is the aim achievable without being able to do y? If so, and if y is a useful behaviour, then define an additional aim that fits y. Otherwise return to 2 and refine or replace the definition.
5 Does the collection of ys generated so far cover everything implicit in x? If not, then return to 2 and generate an additional y.
6 List the aim and objectives so defined.

This needs fleshing out with an example, so I shall apply the procedure to the now-familiar aim of 'understanding Newton's Third Law':

1 *Aim*
   To understand Newton's Third Law.
2 *What would count?*
   Being able to name the forces acting in both static and dynamic events.
3 *Is this precise enough?*
   No. For example, does it mean all the forces, or the principal forces? Should the forces be named specifically as paired forces? What kinds of dynamic events: motion under gravity, under electrostatic forces or motive forces, or all these? Revise 2 to this effect and repeat 3.
4 *Is it possible to understand the Third Law without being able to do this?*
   No. Although a student could understand the law without being able to apply it to electrostatic forces, which may not be well understood, so exclude these.
5 *Is 2 now complete?*
   No. For example, students should be able to predict what will happen in dynamic situations using the Third Law. Add this to 2, and repeat 3 to 5.
6 *Final definition (after a few iterations):*
   Aim: to understand Newton's Third Law.
   Objectives: students should be able to:
      (a) label the principal forces acting in static situations;
      (b) label the principal forces acting in situations of motion under gravity, and under motive forces;

  (c) state which forces are paired;
  (d) predict the consequent motion in defined dynamic
      situations, that require use of the Third Law.

It should be the case that working through this kind of procedure will lead the lecturer to a more thorough analysis of what their teaching has to do. That is the point of it. It will draw mainly on their knowledge of the subject, but probably also on their experience of teaching it. For example, a physicist will automatically think of a range of types of force to which the law could apply, but a physics lecturer will also be aware that students fail to make the correct pairing of forces acting, so that refinement may come from their experience as teachers rather than from their knowledge as physicists. At the end of the analysis, there should be a sense of having elaborated and operationalised the meaning of the aim, and of the scale of the task the teaching has to accomplish. This should not be accompanied, however, by the sense of a task completed. It is most unlikely that this kind of means–end analysis will have pre-empted all the difficulties a student is likely to have in studying the topic. This analysis has stayed within the legitimate logical moves of the expert's understanding of the topic. It has not attempted to predict the illegitimate moves and prior misconceptions which a student may well bring to their study. That is why we need the further analytical step of identifying students' needs, considered in the next section.

  The same procedure will work in other subject areas as well. If we applied it to the other aims mentioned above, we might end up with the following:

Aim: To appreciate the civic origins of architectural designs.
Objectives: students should be able to:
  (a) distinguish between political and functional designs of city
      buildings;
  (b) name plausible reasons for political designs;
  (c) suggest their own examples of buildings whose
      architecture exhibits their civic origins.

Aim: to see gestures as having communicative value.
Objectives: students should be able to:
  (a) give examples of gestures which have communicative value;

    (b) distinguish communicative from non-communicative
       gestures;
    (c) interpret the communicative value of specific gestures.

Without this kind of analysis it is possible for the teaching to neglect important aspects of the exposition, for example teaching what a concept is not, as well as what it is, or neglecting the clarification of possible points of confusion such as the political/functional distinction. I could not pretend that the above analyses are the best that could be done. The procedure does not guarantee quality, because it depends too much on knowledge of the topic. I can only claim that the procedure produces a more elaborated analysis of what the teaching has to attend to than would otherwise be possible, and by operationalising the aim, begins to suggest some of the activities students will have to engage in. That kind of analysis ought be beneficial to the design of the teaching.

IDENTIFYING STUDENTS' NEEDS

It must be clear by this stage of the book that it is impossible for teaching to succeed if it does not address the current forms of students' understanding of a subject. It is always hard for academics to empathise with a learner's sense of bewilderment in encountering a new idea, for the obvious reason that they either never experienced it that way or have long since forgotten it, which is why they are where they are now. The only way subject matter experts can hope to enter into the students' world is by setting out to understand it. It used to be seen as unnecessary to try. The privilege and élitism that used to determine cultural norms in higher education allowed academics to argue that it was their job to make the knowledge available to students, and the students' job to make of it what they could; hence the uni-directional, transmission model of teaching epitomised by the lecture method. Students had to be both highly motivated and clever enough to puzzle out for themselves the obscurities of a discourse that rarely set out to be communicative, merely expository.

    As higher education becomes less élitist, and academics recognise the importance of inculcating academic knowledge in students who find the challenge too great to succeed unaided, the teaching enterprise has to aspire to something better than mere exposition. The subject matter expert must remember their own boredom and bafflement in subjects outside their chosen domain; they must ask whether their lack of motivation was essential or circumstantial. Can you recall your attention lapsing during some lesson or lecture, as you felt that this was something that held no interest for you? And was the topic essentially uninteresting? Can that really be said about anything? Or is it that the speaker failed to engage you, failed to speak your language, too quickly moved on before your basic uncertainties were addressed? That is what happens to many students every day in the thousands of lectures taking place up and down every country. But if their lecturers better understood their point of view, and addressed that, it would happen less. How feasible is that?

Is it possible for a lecturer ever to address all the concerns of a class of students? Are there not as many ways of understanding a topic as there are students? In Chapter 2 we went through a number of studies of what students bring to a subject, and from all these it was clear that in fact there are usually rather few ways of misunderstanding any one idea. In some areas, the ways are so few, and they bear such a close resemblance to the various historical conceptions of the topic, that some researchers have even suggested that misconceptions might be predictable, i.e. identical to former expert views of the subject. In physics, students appear to exhibit Aristotelian conceptions of force; in biology, they have Lamarckian views of evolution; in chemistry they have a phlogiston theory of change; in sociology they assign explanations to individual behaviour rather than social forces, and so on. It is an attractive thought that the history of ideas might be recapitulated in every student's personal development, and one that suggests that a lecturer merely has to understand the development of their own subject to know how students will conceptualise it. I do not dismiss this, but it is not the whole story, as we shall see. What students can believe about an idea is an empirically discoverable fact, and is not logically deducible from the form of the proposition that expresses it. That is why we have to rely on data to discern the forms of misconceptions. However, the data we have on the few topics researched so far suggests that for any one idea the possible misconceptions are few in number.

This empirical result reflects the experience of most teachers that the student errors they encounter in tutorials, assignments and examinations are the same every year. It is rare for a student to come up with a wholly new way of getting it wrong. So if the forms of error are relatively few in number, why are they not documented so that they can be addressed in future teaching? It has not been done because it has not been seen as a necessary or proper thing to do. Tutorials, assignments and examinations are there as feedback to the student on how they failed to learn, not to the teacher on how they failed to teach. Yet what the student produces in these encounters could easily be used as data. Through these devices, every teacher has access to extensive fieldwork data, capable of analysis into categories of misconceptions to be addressed in the design of future teaching.

This convenient solution, of teachers becoming their own educational researchers, is not quite realistic, however. As in any discipline area, good research cannot be done by untrained amateurs, and academics, in spite of their competence in their own field, have a poor record in educational fieldwork. There are now enough studies of student learning to show that the level of subject matter understanding indicated by examination results is rarely achieved by the same students put to more challenging tests. Students can achieve very good examination results and still exhibit fundamental misconceptions (see Brumby 1984, in biology, Dahlgren and Marton 1978, in economics, Bowden *et al.* 1992, in physics). The problem is that what starts out as a performance indicator soon becomes an end in itself. If students can correctly label the forces in a diagram, that is certainly an indication that they understand Newton's Third Law. But it is possible to learn how to do that without understanding the law. If that becomes the indicator, that is what they will do. Learning must be situated in the domain of the objective, as discussed in Chapter 1; here it has shifted to the domain of the performance indicator. The objective is only a necessary condition, not a sufficient one. Educational researchers look for the performance indicator that is a sufficient condition of understanding. So far, this has always been an extended interview with the student, eliciting their fullest explanation of a topic, event, or situation designed to indicate the nature of their understanding. Unfortunately, the oral examination and the one-to-one tutorial, which are the academic counterparts to the research interview, are vanishing activities.

The lecturer will find it difficult, therefore, to conduct their own educational research to produce the forms of misconception pertinent to their current teaching, but something is possible. There are two further sources of data available to them: students and the research literature.

Students

Students can sometimes make clear to a lecturer what it is they find difficult, which is why lecturers find it fruitful to ask if there are any questions, and why tutorials are supposed to be useful. The only problem is that the ones who are really struggling cannot even frame a question. Students have to be coaxed towards an awareness of what it is they fail to grasp. This is, in effect, what the research interviews frequently achieve as a by-product. By asking students to articulate and explain their perspective on a topic, the researcher is engaging them in a rhetorical dialogue that helps to disambiguate expressions, to expose and resolve internal contradictions, and to frame questions. This role does not have to be confined to researchers; it can be taken as well by other students. One of the most productive activities a teacher can suggest to students is that they engage in a kind of teacher–student role-play, where one spends, say, five minutes trying to teach the other a particular theory or concept, and the one acting as student undertakes to ask whatever questions are necessary to clarify the explanation. Five minutes is usually enough to generate some very fundamental questions from the one acting as 'teacher', who has now discovered more precisely what it is they don't know. While this technique lacks the analytical rigour and generality of the phenomenographic method, it does have the advantage of mimicking its immediate pedagogical benefits, and of defining the problem in the local students' terms, which is the principal concern of any teacher.

Critical problems in students' understanding of a subject area will often be apparent from assessment scripts and assignments. Analysis of these would give rich material for deciding what kind of learning activities students need in order to overcome their misconceptions, or to gain greater familiarity with a process, etc. It is often the case, however, that examination questions fail to tap students' deep understanding (see, for example, Dahlgren and Marton 1978, Brumby 1984), and enable them to display instrumental competence without their underlying knowledge being tested. If examination questions are designed with the benefit of a careful analysis of objectives, then they will be capable of eliciting misconceptions more clearly than if they require only the parroting of bookwork, or display of standard procedures.

Research literature

A relatively low proportion of academics read the research journals on teaching in their subject. Reading is now a luxury for academics, and the precious time there is must be for research, or at best scholarship, never teaching itself. In fact, many of the journals of subject teaching reflect this concern, being devoted entirely to informing the teacher about developments in the subject, and about teaching strategies based on experience in the classroom, rather than to an analysis of what students are likely to need. For example, a recent review of the needed research in economics education does not once mention the need to know more about students, what they know and how they think; instead the focus is on the effect of the high school curriculum, the effect of class size, the optimum curriculum sequence, the role of personal factors (Becker, Highsmith, Kennedy and Walstad 1991). The most common type of paper in these journals concerns a discussion of curriculum content: what should be taught and why. Inevitably the majority of them concern mainly the school curriculum. There are also some empirical papers addressing how topics should be taught, but most are non-comparative teaching studies, typically reporting the success of one pedagogical approach, rather than making any attempt at comparison, except by implication, with the methods that had gone before. A few of these journals also publish the kind of careful, qualitative research that illuminates what students need.

There is considerable variation across discipline areas in the quality of journals of subject teaching. Some have long and honourable research traditions; some have not even begun to support such a journal. Increasingly these journals include an educational technology section that reviews videos and software available to the teacher, and this is a vital development if the quality of materials is to improve. Because of the importance of journals as a means of articulating developments in teaching, improving quality, and disseminating ideas, Appendix 1 at the end of the book provides an annotated bibliography of some subject teaching journals that will at least alert teaching designers to what has already been done.

Because teaching has to be communication, not just exposition, the teacher must know something about their interlocutors. In social conversation we adjust our language and our arguments according to what we know about the person we are talking to, because we know that communicative success depends on it. Similarly, physics lecturers must know that when they talk about 'force', students imagine not the Newtonian action at a distance, but the kind of 'oomph' it takes to move a table, and the two are not compatible. The psychology lecturer must be aware that students naturally interpret 'short-term memory' as the kind of memory span they are aware of, not the theoretical concept of a process that spans only fractions of a second. The mathematics lecturer must remember that as students become deeply enmeshed in the intricacies of a proof, they tend to forget the meaning of the manipulations they are undertaking, so that each successive stage becomes more and more meaningless.

Many lecturers will claim that they do know their students, that they talk to them in tutorials, they take note of performance in assignments and examinations, and this informs their subsequent teaching. This is important and no doubt accounts for the many pedagogic successes that higher education can claim. But this can only be a relatively superficial analysis, and will not always reveal the psychological links that have to be made if the student is to progress to the expert view. A misconception, such as a mis-interpretation of a technical word in terms of its everyday meaning, will allow the student to build an inappropriate conceptual construction. The lecturer may be able to discern that incorrect terminological usage, but assisting the student to a correct interpretation of the technical term does not necessarily dismantle the conceptual construction they built with it. Another kind of misconception is the simplification of the internal logical structure of a concept. It will be clear to the lecturer that the student has a misconception of some kind, but its precise logical relation to the correct one may not be obvious. For example, Lybeck's analysis of the different ways of understanding the concept of 'mole' in chemistry led to a complex representation of the expert's conception that was hitherto only implicit, but within which the students' various conceptions could be placed as logical subsets (Lybeck *et al.* 1988). The naïve conception, or the lay-person's everyday model of a system, will often be the bedrock on which the academic attempts to erect a wholly new perspective, and students' attempts to reconcile the two can lead to bizarre distortions that will be difficult for the lecturer to unravel. Shifting that original conception is the first step in communicating a new idea, but it can only be done if the lecturer knows what it is.

Some knowledge of where students are conceptually, as well as where we wish to get them, is therefore essential to good pedagogic design. However the designer does it, whether through basic phenomenographic research, questions to students, teachback exercises, assignments, or via the existing literature, some initial analysis is important to motivate the design of the learning activities the student must undertake. Even if it is only guesswork based on experience of teaching, the students' supposed prior conceptual state should be articulated, as then it can be challenged and refined in the light of further experience. In Chapter 2 we considered what students bring to their learning, and this generated the following kinds of problem:

- alternative conceptions
- difficulties in generating and interpreting representational forms

Given these two known sources of learning difficulty for students, the lecturer can now augment their objectives-based analysis of what the teaching needs to address by asking, for example:

- What technical terms have everyday meanings that could lead to their misinterpretation?
- What kinds of naïve conceptions might be prevalent in this topic?
- In what ways might the internal logical structure of the main concept be distorted?
- Which forms of representation (linguistic, notational, diagrammatic, graphical, symbolic, iconic, numeric) are difficult to handle?

It is not easy to second-guess the inventiveness students can bring to their attempts at comprehension of a subject, and there is no substitute for investigation of these issues, but this kind of prior analysis may pre-empt some of the problems.

Chapter 2 also referred to the epistemology adopted by a student as being an important aspect of the way they approach learning. The epistemology appropriate to a particular course is inculcated in many ways: in the way topics are introduced, in the way the teacher invites comment, and in the ways they are assessed. This is determined more by the context of learning than by specific teaching design, and is therefore treated in Chapter 11.

DESIGNING THE LEARNING ACTIVITIES

Once both learning objectives and student needs are articulated, by whatever means, it becomes easier to think in terms of what the student must therefore do in order to attain the desired learning outcome. The first stage is analytical, the second empirical; this third stage is largely creative. From the first two stages we may well have a neat logical description of the relation between where students are and where they need to be, but this does not define the psychological pathway between the two. That is why it is a mainly creative process.

From the definition of objectives, we have an idea of what would indicate understanding by the students, but it is not straightforward to deduce from this what learning activities they therefore need to undertake. Objectives generate actions such as 'distinguish types', 'give examples', 'name parts', interpret', 'state relations', 'make predictions', but what does a student have to do in order to be able to 'distinguish types of x', 'give examples of y', etc.? What does it take to learn these things? Which mathemagenic activities will yield these objectives as outcomes? Although designing learning activities is mainly a creative process, with the analysis we have done so far, we can at least build an analytical prop to assist this process.

At this point I want to pull together all the information generated by the previous chapters, and bring it to bear on drawing up a specification for the design of teaching for some particular teaching aim. First I have set out a distillation of what we know in the form of a 'template' of decisions to be made, showing how each one relates to previous chapters. Then this analytical 'prop' for the design process is illustrated for the three different kinds of teaching aim referred to above. It may look lengthy and complex for a process that has to be gone through for each aspect of a syllabus, but the learning process itself is lengthy and complex, and this analysis amounts to a considerable simplification. Once internalised it becomes more automatic and skilled, but first it needs to be explicit.

The point of having such a template is that it should assist the process of 'pre-emptive adaptation', something akin to preventive medicine. Teaching is most effective if it can avoid creating the pits we know students are likely to fall into. In thinking through the best way to teach some topic, the academic who is already extremely knowledgeable will have great difficulty in stepping into the students' shoes to accomplish the feat of pre-emptive adaptation. The template below is meant to support that process, given what we know from preceding chapters about what students are likely to need, and is constructed using the framework developed in Part II to define how the discursive and interactive levels will be handled by the teaching.

Template for design of teaching

1 *Describe teacher's conception*
Given defined aims and objectives, and known conceptual and representational difficulties, describe main points to be made, definitions needed, relations to be drawn, structure of argument, nature of evidence, illustrative examples, processes to be demonstrated.

2 *Elicit students' conceptions*
Use evidence of students' needs from literature (if any) and from tutorials, essays, examinations, etc., as a basis for analysis of likely misconceptions and representational errors.
Define questions to student to elicit these.

3 *Pre-empt teacher's redescription of conception*
Decide on alternative forms of description, based on misconceptions identified in stage (2).
What forms of supplantation of experience might address misconceptions or representational errors?

4 *Elicit student's redescription*
Ask student to reflect on comparison between theirs and teacher's conceptions, and on goal–action–feedback loop identified in stage (5).

5 *Define form of interaction: task goal, student actions, and feedback*
Use (1), (2) and (3) to decide on:
(5.1) what new experiential interactions students are likely to need, or what prior experiences should they reflect on to appreciate the points being made;

(5.2) what mapping tasks might help to remediate represent-ational errors;

(5.3) what tasks will enable students to use the teacher's descriptions and redescriptions to adapt and modify their actions for the task goal.

The design template is meant to address every aspect of the learning process, so that we begin the detailed design with an initial understanding of what it will take for the student to learn, and how the teaching can best support this. The next three sub-sections illustrate the process by going through the template for the three types of teaching aim listed above.

Teaching aim: to understand Newton's Third Law

1 Description of teacher's conception
State the law, illustrating it with examples of its application in static and dynamic situations; show how it can be used in conjunction with the first and second laws to describe motion.

2 Elicit student's conceptions
Ask for statement of law.
To elicit alternative conceptions, ask them to: assign forces in static and dynamic events; name forces in diagram; indicate pairs of forces; indicate comparative values of forces.
To elicit their understanding of forms of representation: ask for interpretation and creation of diagrams showing arrows to represent forces, specified types of force.

3 Pre-empt teacher's redescription of conception
Offer more elaborated descriptions, contrastive descriptions to address expected confusions, justifications, e.g.:

(3.1) refer back to original statements of the law in context of specific problem given, e.g. video of skaters pushing each other;

(3.2) redefine meanings of terms, diagrammatic components etc., in context of specific problem;

(3.3) present internal inconsistencies in student's actions and descriptions.

4 Elicit student's redescription
Ask student to reflect on comparison between theirs and teacher's conceptions, and on goal–action–feedback loop identified in stage (5).

5 *Define form of interaction: task goal, student actions and feedback*

  (5.1) For new experiential interactions: the law refers to everyday experiences, but comparison of instances of paired forces acting on differing masses (e.g. boats pulling each other, skaters pushing each other) may extend that experience to situations where the application of the Law is more apparent.

Task goal: predict motion of boats, given relative masses.

Action: indicate point where they meet.

Feedback: show motion and point where they meet.

  (5.2) For mapping tasks: identify likely representational errors at stage (2).

Task: represent forces acting in a given situation.

Action: to place and name arrows to represent forces on a diagram.

Feedback: offer alternative descriptions identified in stage (3) to match misconceptions identified in stage (2).

  (5.3) To encourage reflection on actions: set up a variety of tasks as defined in 5.1 and 5.2, generating different numerical values for each one, enabling students to use the discursive and interactive feedback from earlier tasks to improve their performance on later ones.

Based on the evidence available from research, this is probably the most complete analysis we can carry out for this teaching aim. Few topics will support more. The amount of teaching devoted to this particular topic in most courses or textbooks on the subject is fairly minimal, and typically addresses no more than stages (1) and (3) at most, together with a single example from stage (5). This leaves all the rest to be carried out by the student in private study. It is a lot to ask. Perhaps this accounts for the generally poor level of achievement of this aim.

If we now consider which media to use in order to carry out the teaching we have defined as necessary, we can see that the ideal form would be a one-to-one tutorial using pencil and paper, perhaps with tutor and student in separate punts on a calm river, with a rope slung between them to allow some minimal experimentation to be done. At worst, we could use just print, and using the above analysis pre-empt what we can of the student's likely difficulties, include in-text activities to encourage the student's own description, followed by feedback addressing the predicted misconceptions, and using 'self-assessed questions' to allow the student to practise as much as possible. In between these two extremes, combinations of other media can contribute something to each stage. Video or computer animation could show the examples of boats or skaters. A computer simulation could allow experimentation with the examples. Computer-mediated communication could cope with the dialogue implicit in stages (2) and (4), but with a data link and shared screen, it would be better. Only a computer tutorial could generate and provide immediate feedback on many tasks. Video of the ideal teacher–student dialogue could offer a vicarious experience of the whole process. Several different media combinations are capable of carrying out the teaching seen to be necessary, therefore. It is not possible to say that some particular combination would be significantly better than the others without a consideration of the logistics of the teaching–learning context, which we consider in Chapter 11. It is only that, after all, that tends to rule out the ideal form of teacher and student punting on the river.

The same template can be used to generate teaching for a quite different topic.

Teaching aim: to appreciate the civic origins of architectural designs

1 *Describe teacher's conception*
   State the thesis that architectural designs have civic as opposed to functional origins, state reasons for civic origins, explain how they are recognised, and illustrate with examples of both types of design. Demonstrate the relation between styles and socio-political factors.

2 *Elicit students' conceptions*
   Alternative conceptions: ask student to state origins of given designs, classify examples of design styles, suggest further examples of each style; elicit descriptions of relations between styles and cultural context.
   Forms of representation: ask to classify design styles; interpret types of socio-political factors.

3 *Pre-empt teacher's redescription of conception*
   Offer more elaborated descriptions, contrastive descriptions to address expected confusions, justifications, e.g.:

(3.1) Refer back to original statements in context of specific example of building, showing detail on instances and non-instances of each style.

(3.2) Redefine meanings of terms, e.g. socio-political factors, in context of the specific problem.

4 *Elicit student's redescription*

Ask student to reflect on comparison between theirs and teacher's conceptions, and on goal–action–feedback loop identified in stage (5).

5 *Define form of interaction: task goal, student actions, and feedback*

(5.1) For new experiential interactions: offer access to many examples of designs and descriptions of relevant local historical factors.

Task: to explore link between designs and socio-political factors.

Actions: search for patterns in data, e.g. of co-occurrence of design types and cultural factors.

Feedback: comment on use of data, validity of findings.

(5.2) For mapping tasks: present examples of designs

Task: to classify designs.

Actions: assign classification, interpret cultural context for each type, and describe relation between the two.

Feedback: indicate any internal inconsistencies in student's relations and descriptions, or in comparison with teacher's descriptions.

(5.3) To encourage reflection on actions: set up a variety of tasks as defined in 5.1 and 5.2, generating different examples for each one, enabling students to use the discursive and interactive feedback from earlier tasks to improve their performance on later ones; ask for refinement, elaboration, disambiguation, resolution of internal contradictions.

The best kind of medium for this teaching aim would appear to be a one-to-one tutorial on a field trip to the sites where such designs can be observed. The next best would be a multimedia tutorial, using a picture database of slides of long-shots and close-ups of buildings classified by location, function, age, etc., and a historical database with information about the relevant locations, their political and economic positions over time, etc. The tutorial part would elicit descriptions, use keyword analysis to interpret the answer, together with an analysis of the selection of material from the database, and provide feedback on the basis of expected misconceptions. Asking them to suggest further examples, as in stage (2), would be impossible to handle, as it is to be expected that students would select examples from their own experience, their home town, perhaps, and the uncertain variety they could come up with cannot be predicted, and therefore could not be programmed. This aspect is clearly a valuable part of the process, as it allows students to relate their theory to their immediate experience. The only way to handle this, therefore, is through marked essays or discussion. Of course, tutors cannot be expected to know that degree of variety either, but they can make a better judgement on the basis of the case made by the student than the computer could. The refinement, disambiguation and resolution of inconsistencies in stage (5) could only be handled by a program if there were sufficient prior analysis of such tutor– student dialogues to generate standard, recognisable categories of error in the context of this topic. It is theoretically possible but very time-consuming. Against that would be balanced the priority attached to the topic, the number of students who would study it, and the likelihood of achieving the same learning outcomes via alternative methods. The other alternative method for handling computer-based dialogue, namely multiple choice questions, is not realistic here because an exhaustive list of logically-possible answers does not exist, and any mcq list would have to be constructed using plausible distractors of the kind discounted in Chapter 8.

The non-adaptive methods such as video and print would have to be designed as pre-emptively adaptive to the likely misconceptions of students. For example, presuming a difficulty in reliably distinguishing one kind of style from another, the teaching material would offer plenty of examples, together with a lot of exercises with given answers. The cost of reproducing many high quality photographs in print would suggest video or compact disc as the most economical medium, assuming other logistical considerations allow this. The complexity of the argument around the description of relevant socio-political factors, and the likely form the argument should take to pre-empt misconceptions without also inviting them, makes this difficult to handle in a non-adaptive medium. And the complexity deepens when these socio-political factors have to be linked with the architectural design styles categorisation. A tutor–student dialogue is much more likely to be effective. There are several ways of achieving this: (a) a discussion group around a video, or following a reading; (b) computer-mediated conference, which allows a small group to discuss, and many to 'lurk'; (c) a video of a tutor–student dialogue, which allows many to discuss vicariously; and (d) an audio-conference, which allows a small group to discuss and many to 'eavesdrop'. The best way depends, as always, on logistics.

The final example of application of the template relates to the third teaching aim we discussed earlier, different again from the other two.

Teaching aim: to see gestures as having communicative value

1 *Describe teacher's conception*
   State the thesis that gestures have communicative value, explain how they are recognised, and illustrate with examples of both communicative and non-communicative gestures. Demonstrate the communicative value of specific gestures.

2 *Elicit students' conceptions*
   Alternative conceptions: ask student to state function of gestures, classify examples; interpret communicative value of given gestures.
   Forms of representation: not applicable.

3 *Pre-empt teacher's redescription of conception*
   Offer more elaborated descriptions, contrastive descriptions to address expected confusions, justifications, e.g.
   (3.1) Refer back to original statements in context of specific example of gesture, showing details in instances and non-instances of each type.
   (3.2) Redefine meanings of terms, e.g. turn-taking, yielding the floor, etc., in context of the specific situation.

4 *Elicit student's redescription*
   Ask student to reflect on comparison between theirs and teacher's conceptions, and on goal–action–feedback loop identified in stage (5).

5 *Define form of interaction: task goal, student actions, and feedback*
   (5.1) For new experiential interactions: offer access to several examples of gestures in different situational contexts.

Task: to identify links between gestures and situational factors.

Actions: search for patterns in data, e.g. of co-occurrence of gesture types and situational factors.

Feedback: comment on interpretation of data, validity of findings.

(5.2) For mapping tasks: not applicable.

(5.3) To encourage reflection on actions: set up a variety of tasks as defined in 5.1, generating different examples for each one, enabling students to use the discursive and interactive feedback from earlier tasks to improve their performance on later ones; ask for refinement, elaboration, disambiguation, resolution of internal contradictions.

As before, it is possible to deliver the learning activities required here via several different media combinations. Given the minutiae of gestural behaviour it will probably be necessary to confine illustrations to video, rather than rely on photographs or animation, so text alone, or computer alone would not be sufficient. However, the interpretive problems, once the types have been defined, are unlikely to be so conceptually difficult that students need very many examples, or more than pre-emptive feedback on their own interpretations. While it is probably always the case that the tutorial dialogue is the most reliable form of teaching, there will be many examples, such as this, where the student may well be capable of refining their conceptions through unsupported reflection: by adapting their analyses in the light of the teacher's pre-emptive redescription, by reflecting on past experience, and without needing to 'act on the world' at the interactive level. Giving feedback on their interpretations via comment on a reflective essay could be sufficient for this topic.

From the earlier account of the complete learning process, we have now established some of the general forms that learning activities must take, and shown how these can be instantiated for three different kinds of teaching aim. The template has been developed to be generalisable to most topics, and provides a basic analysis of what the teaching–learning process should look like for any topic for any medium.

IMPLICATIONS FOR INTERFACE DESIGN

The most complete support from media-based materials is offered by the multimedia tutorial simulation. It has the capability, given its combined features, to support the learning process very well, but it will only do this if its features are properly exploited. The design of such a package will begin with a specification derived from the kind of analysis outlined above, which puts certain requirements on the design of the interface. The key issue here is the locus of control in the program – does it rest with student or program or both?

Control by the student is important because we cannot possibly predict the exact sequence and pacing that each individual student needs. To adapt their actions, and to reflect on the goal–action–feedback cycle students need control over what they do and when. The control features that should be available in the interface to support each type of activity are as follows:

Discursive   A structured map of the content to allow access at any time to all aspects of the teacher's description of their conception.

Concealed multiple choice questions (cmcq) with keyword analysis to allow student to express their conception.

Adaptive   Ability to sequence and select/construct their own task goal, enabling them to generate the experiences they feel they need.

Access to statement of objectives for program and for sections of content, so that they know what counts as achieving the topic goal.

Interactive   Clear task goals, so that they know when they have achieved them.

Intrinsic feedback that is meaningful, accompanied by access to extrinsic feedback (such as a 'help' option) that interprets it.

Reflective   An indication of the amount of material in each section to allow planning for self-pacing.

Requirement to test a new conception by offering a description of it for comment (e.g. via cmcq).

All the above control features should normally be available on screen throughout the tutorial, either as buttons or as pull-down menus. Given the restricted room for text on many screens, these devices often have rather cryptic labels. Iconic buttons can help. An introduction to the control devices should be an option both at the start of the program, and available throughout.

Many of the control features listed above are rarely found in educational programs, but the omission of any one impairs the student's ability to maintain control of their learning. The reflection–adaptation cycle is extremely important. It is the key to successful learning and must be supported by teaching materials, not sabotaged at every turn because the materials cannot adapt to the student's needs. None of the above features is especially difficult to program; they are the minimum requirements for good design.

The student's reflection must be focused on the content of learning, on the meaning of their interaction, not on how to operate program. This means the interface must be operationally transparent, so that time is not wasted trying to figure out how to work it. Computer environments have been the breeding ground for a new strain of learning activities, which I can only describe as 'anathemagenic' – activities that give birth to loathing. Here are some of the most common forms:

- looking for the ON button
- wondering why nothing is happening
- discovering you're unable to get back to the point you were just at
- being told you're wrong when you know you're right
- wondering how long this is going on for
- trying to guess the word the program is waiting for
- coming upon the same feeble joke for the fifteenth time
- trying to work out how to get to the point you want

You will have your own additions to the list. The considerable improvements in human–computer interface design in recent years, with the introduction of icons and mouse-clicks particularly, has brought operational transparency to many types of computer tool. Teaching programs must aspire to the same standards.

We have considered interface design from the student's point of view. How does the program *qua* 'teacher' manage the adaptation–reflection cycle? Adaptation refers to the process by which the teacher decides, on the basis of how the student describes their conception, what kind of task goal to offer. This implies that the program must be able to interpret student descriptions, must be able to generate specific types of task, and must be able to associate type of description with type of task. Reflection refers to the process by which the 'teacher' uses the student's performance in interacting with the world, to decide either how to redescribe their own conception, or what further questions to put to them. And this implies that the program must maintain a record of students' actions, must be able to interpret or categorise them, must have a questioning strategy, and must be able to associate action type with question type. To conduct the teacher's discursive activities the program will need access to either canned text (print, audio or video) or animated diagrams to express the teacher's description. To conduct the interactive process, it will need a selection of generative tasks (such as those described in Chapter 8), and either a model to provide intrinsic feedback, or a matching algorithm (i.e. one that matches student input to canned text) to provide extrinsic feedback. These necessary design features can be summarised as follows:

Discursive   Access to canned text, audio, video, diagrams.

              Keyword analysis algorithm to interpret student descriptions.

Adaptive   Associative link (e.g. matching algorithm) between type of student description and type of task goal to allow selection of appropriate task.

Interactive   Algorithm to generate specific types of task.

              Model to provide intrinsic feedback.

              Matching algorithm to provide extrinsic feedback.

Reflective   Questioning strategy to elicit student's descriptions.

              Means to interpret or categorise student's actions or descriptions to support questioning strategy.

              Record of student's actions to enable interpretation/categorisation.

These are all equally necessary if the program is to support the complete learning process, but, unlike the requirements for student control, they are much more difficult to implement. This is why multimedia designers are now promulgating the idea of the importance of student control over their learning, and there is a sudden interest in 'resource-based learning'. It has a lot more to do with the limits of computers and the complexity of learning than it does with pedagogical high-mindedness. It is a time-consuming process to address students' needs: far easier to make the material available and give them the navigation tools to find their own way through it. But beneath the rhetoric of 'giving students control over their learning' is a dereliction of duty. We never supposed students could do that with a 'real' library; why should they be able to it with an electronic one?

Until recently, it would have been unreasonable to expect that students' computers could handle a questioning strategy, and maintain and interpret a record of their actions, because of the limits of processor speed and storage capacity. These are no longer plausible excuses. The only excuse now for not providing full support to the student is the limit on design time for doing the preparatory work to discover what students need, to devise the diagnostic strategies, and to specify the generative tasks.

COMPARATIVE DEVELOPMENT COSTS

The selection of media will depend as much on the costs of development and delivery as on pedagogy and logistics. They also help to determine the balance of media within a course. A multiple media course at the British Open University, for example, might distribute student study time spent on print, video, computer, tutorial, essay in the proportions $10:1:2:1:3$. The academic development time spent for that distribution of teaching would be equivalent to the proportions $60:10:10:1:1$, assuming they get no support for writing the text, or for designing the tutorial and the essay question, but would get substantial support for the development of the video and computer material, where their input is academic design only. Thus print appears to make more efficient use of academic time in terms of study time generated, and setting essays is most efficient. If efficiency is measured in terms of student study time for learning gain, however, then it is possible that the computer or video could perform better. Several studies have been done to test the comparative efficiency of different media, but there can be no definitive result because too much depends on local circumstances and on the quality of the particular material developed. It should be clear from the complexity of the discussions in the previous five chapters that a question like 'which is the most cost-effective medium?' can only expect a silly answer – it all depends.

In order not to duck the question of costs completely, however, I think it makes sense to consider the parameters that contribute to the cost of developing a medium. Most constitute staff costs, of academics, producers, programmers, technicians, etc. Some might include development equipment not already available, and expenses such as travel, copyright, etc. Actual figures again depend so much on local circumstances that they would amount to disinformation, if I were to offer estimates.

Costs relate to the format of the development process, which will be discussed in detail in Chapter 12. Here we consider development costs only – to the point where the material is ready to be 'published' (Chapter 11 covers delivery costs, which get the materials to the student, and support costs to ensure they work successfully). The principal development cost parameters for each medium are likely to be:

- pedagogic design
- production design
- prototype production
- developmental testing
- revision of materials
- final production
- quality assurance procedures (editing, testing, etc.)
- administrative support
- technical support
- travel (for collaboration, material collection, etc.)
- project management
- copyright costs incurred

Many of these costs do not discriminate between media. The first three do. Pedagogic design is more difficult if the medium is unfamiliar, as are computer and video, for example, for most academics. On the other hand, academic time spent on development is much lower for video and computer than it is for print, because the production is done by others, either a producer and crew or a software designer. Production design is much more complex for video and computer than for print. Prototype production is more complex for computer, final production for video.

That is as far as it is reasonable to take a comparative cost analysis at a general level of description. The greatest expense is in proper design and the quality assurance mechanisms and developmental testing required to make it as good as possible, and that is the same for all media.

SUMMARY

This chapter has used the conversational framework for designing a teaching strategy developed in Part II, together with the requirements for the definition of teaching content implied by the research literature discussed throughout Part I. The teaching strategy has to:

- define aims and objectives, using the procedure outlined on p. 185
- identify students' learning needs, using the checklist on p. 193
- design the learning activities, using the template outlined on pp. 195–6

To optimise the media to be used for teaching a particular topic, the designer must decide, on the basis of the kind of analysis outlined above, which learning activities must be supported for the student. Table II.1 showed which media or media combinations can most easily support each of the activities defined in Part II as essential for learning. From this, and from the illustrative examples used in this chapter, we can see that for any topic:

- the best approach is more likely to require an integrated combination of several media, than a single medium
- several media combinations may offer adequate alternatives
- choosing the best is more likely to depend on logistics than on pedagogy

There is no simple prescriptive rule connecting the analysis of learning activities to the required medium, but the elaboration of what the teaching is trying to achieve, and how, will inform media selection by clarifying which learning activities are most likely to need support.

Throughout the chapter, the discussion has been focused at the topic level, at how to get students to think constructively about particular ideas, and how to engage with those ideas in a productive way. The understanding of an idea or concept does not in reality occur in isolation from the other aspects of a student's university life. It takes place in the context of a course, a department, and an institution, and these contextual factors will have an effect on student learning, and must be attended to if the materials are to work. As well as the pedagogical issues we have considered in this chapter, the logistics of these different institutional contexts will also affect the teacher's judgement about which are the most appropriate media to use, and how to combine them in teaching the subject. The next chapter, therefore, looks at the institutional context that envelopes the student as they learn their subject.

Chapter 11

Setting up the learning context

INTRODUCTION

There is a folk wisdom in academic circles that educational technologies come and go, and all the expensive machines end up gathering dust in cupboards. The main reason for this, when it occurs, is neglect of the learning context, not, as is often supposed, the poor quality of teaching the machines provide. There is plenty of traditional teaching on offer in universities that is poor in quality, sustained none the less by its fit with the learning context. Educational technologies, especially new ones, attract effort and ingenuity to the design and development of materials, but rarely to the embedding of those materials in their educational niche. This is one of the key reasons why they have made relatively little impact in higher education, despite their potential. That is why two chapters of this book are devoted to aspects of the learning context. In this chapter we remain with the student's perspective, and document the contextual factors that affect how they learn. In the next chapter we move to considering what this means for the institutional infrastructure and beyond.

Students are not simply learners of an academic subject: they are social beings. Like everyone else, they respond to the social, political and organisational context around them, and this directly affects what they do in their day to day work. But how, exactly?

A few years ago, in a study of students' problem solving, I was looking for evidence that students use heuristic methods of the kind advocated for problem solving, e.g. understanding the problem, doing a means–end analysis, creating sub-goals, working backwards from the solution needed, checking back, etc. An interesting finding emerged (Laurillard 1984b). On the basis of written protocols and interviews about their approach, it was difficult to credit many students with the use of these heuristics in relation to the substantive problem: in a problem about writing a device control program for a microprocessor, for example, there was no focusing on the nature of the device, or which instructions might be needed, or what form the final solution should take to do the job. But it was certainly possible to ascribe the use of these heuristics to the solving of 'a problem set by a particular teacher in a particular course' – they were solving the problem-in-context. As a consequence, the information they considered as relevant to solving the problem was: what was done in the lecture, the teacher's diagram, the wording of the question, the relation to similar examples done by the teacher, what the teacher gave high marks for. And in the checking back stage the criterion was their own level of commitment to the course, rather than the accuracy of the solution. This is all perfectly rational behaviour. But it means that in setting work for students we must think of them not so much as grappling with the intriguing ideas we have put before them, but often as trying to second-guess what we want of them. It follows from this implacable orientation to what the teacher requires, that the teacher has a great responsibility to require the sort of thing that will help them learn.

This argument does nothing to diminish the importance of students taking responsibility for their own learning. The point is that they will inevitably respond to the demands of the context, so the teacher must be sure that the demands of the context are compatible with their pedagogic intentions.

The following sections list all the contextual factors that have been found to affect the quality of student learning. In each case we consider where the teacher's responsibility lies, and how this affects the introduction of the various educational media.

STUDENT PREPARATION

As students approach each new learning session in their course they need to be oriented towards the ideas or skills they are about to encounter. This is equally true for media-based materials, whether they are part of a distance learning course, or supplementary to face-to-face teaching. Learning, when it is done within a taught course, is not a voyage of discovery with the student in control. Academics never want to spoon-feed their students, but since they generally take control of what is to be learned, and when, and how it is to be judged, students are very much at their mercy. If students are to have any control over their learning, then they need some information. The voyage of discovery may be led by the teacher, but it does not have to be a mystery tour. To be well equipped to get the most out of the learning session, they need to know:

1 Why this topic is important and interesting.
2 Its relation to other topics in the course.
3 What they need to know already.
4 The learning objectives in view.
5 How to approach it.

Whether the material is print, video, or computer program, it needs briefing notes, and a preliminary exercise, to enable students to feel some sense of ownership of what they are studying. They will watch a video on social interaction with more attention if they have already tried to list all the different forms of questioning they can think of; they will watch a simulation of the manufacture of netting with more interest if they have already tried to figure out how it might be done; if they are given access to a database resource, they will make better use of it if they are given learning objectives to aim for than if they are asked to see what they can find out.

It is the designer's responsibility to document all the points above with the exception of (2), which is most easily handled by the teacher. However, the preparation of their own briefing, covering all five points, is an ideal way for a teacher to graft externally produced materials into their own course, without too much 'tissue rejection'.

Action

Prepare briefing for the use of materials that:

1 Orients students to why this topic is important and interesting.
2 Helps them see its relation to other topics in the course.
3 Describes what they need to know in order to make best use of it.
4 Defines the learning objectives.
5 Provides preliminary exercises that alert them to what to look for.

INTEGRATION WITH THE REST OF THE COURSE

Whatever advice and guidance is provided by the course team who designed the learning materials, it is ultimately the individual academic's responsibility to determine how it should be fitted in.

New learning materials will be likely to change aspects of the existing teaching, so the possible need to revise the teaching must be kept under review. For example, computer simulations, or compact disc resources, can give students access to far more sophisticated material for doing their own analysis than was possible before. In this case they may need additional teaching on analytical procedures if they are to make good use of the new material. Access to information databases gives students a wealth of material to work from, but this is of no value to them if they are not able to make selective judgments about what to use, and critical judgments about the content of what they find. The teaching that surrounds students' use of such systems will need to address this kind of issue. This makes it essential that academics taking on new material be clear about the learning objectives it is meeting, and the prerequisite skills it entails.

In addition, the learning students achieve in relation to a package should be followed through in subsequent teaching, so that it is not isolated from the rest of the course. The work should have a natural place in the course and its role should be clear to students. Several evaluation studies of videos and computer packages have looked at retention of learning over time. But these can tell us nothing about the teaching method itself. Retention is dependent upon whether what is learned is followed up soon after by applying it in other learning sessions, or practice, or assignments. Unless students use what they learn on a package, it will soon be forgotten, no matter how good it is, or how well they learned it initially. It has to become embedded in the way they think, before retention can be expected, and that means repeated use, not just an isolated event, no matter how impressive it appears.

Action

Review new material to:

1 Check whether prerequisite knowledge and skills are covered.
2 Provide prior teaching if necessary.
3 Decide how to follow up on what students have learned.

EPISTEMOLOGICAL VALUES

Students bring their own epistemological values to studying a course, as we saw in Chapter 2. Epistemological values are not inherited, however. They are more likely to be nurtured in previous educational encounters. Every teacher plays a part in nurturing their students' epistemological values – their conception of how we come to know – and hence their conception of what learning is, and how it should be done. None of this features very much in course syllabuses, because they tend to be concerned with the content to be learned, rather than its epistemological status. It is often implicit, however, in the way academics talk about the aims of university education, and in the discussions that ensue at examination boards, as I argued in Chapter 1. So we have to consider it.

Inculcating an appropriate conception of learning, or a desirable epistemology, is not an issue peculiar to the use of educational technology. Clearly, it is fundamental to any kind of teaching. It is particularly important to confront it here, however, because the use of educational technology presupposes a diminution of teacher–student contact, and it is there, in the interstices between content-related talk, that the academic can most easily stand back from the task in hand and encourage the student to look at the nature of the academic enterprise itself. It will probably be in that kind of discussion that the student is treated to the sudden revelation that getting the right answer may not always be the most important goal. That kind of sentiment never gets written on the board, never appears in course syllabuses, or in lecture handouts, but it needs to be made explicit to students. Whatever the academic feels is an appropriate way to approach the acquisition and manipulation of knowledge in a subject should itself at some time be a topic for discussion with students. And when discussion time is reduced, as it frequently is in the implementation of educational technology, then some treatment of this issue has to be consciously included in the course.

The importance of this issue is demonstrated by Ramsden's work on students' perceptions of teaching in different departments. From questionnaire studies in a range of institutions and academic departments, he found:

> differences in students' orientations and attitudes to study which are only explicable in terms of the powerful effects of contexts of learning

and:

> associations between approaches and the perceived quality of teaching in first and second year university level study.
>
> (Ramsden 1992: 80)

Thus the quality of learning is strongly related to the quality of the academic context provided. And quality of teaching is not judged here by the clarity of the lectures given. Ramsden lists the characteristics of the learning context that are associated with a 'deep approach', among them:

> teaching that addresses the nature of the subject and its relevance;
> the lecturer's personal commitment to the subject;
> opportunities for students to choose their methods of studying.
>
> (Ibid.: 81)

The status of knowledge, one's personal commitment to it, and the appropriate ways of approaching the study of it, are all topics that should be figural in any course, if students are to take personal responsibility for their knowledge and their learning.

Action

Create an environment for students to develop their conception of learning and their own appropriate epistemology:

1 Demonstrate your own commitment to the subject, and your way of approaching it.
2 Give students opportunities to exercise choice in their method of study, and to defend their choice.
3 Provide opportunities for discussion of the status of the knowledge in the subject, how it can be known and how it may be learned.

PEDAGOGICAL SUPPORT

Since the success of new technology materials depends largely upon the way they are integrated into courses, the design team must anticipate this, and provide advice to both teachers and students on the kind of briefing students are likely to need. Research and evaluation studies of the implementation of programs in classrooms shows that they are most successful when students are properly prepared, and know what to expect when they encounter a program, what they are expected to get from it, and what to do with it. The designers may guide the teacher, and the teacher must guide the students in this. The preparation may amount to no more than reference to it in a lecture, or it may require a preparatory study by students, e.g. to collect data to compare with the output from a simulation model, to prepare a research question to be answered by using a database, etc. The work on the learning materials should be embedded into a planned learning environment such that the student is supported in the complete learning cycle with respect to some area of the curriculum.

There is a further reason for providing supporting materials. In Chapter 6 it was suggested that learning materials should address all aspects of the learning process, and where they fail to, as most do, should indicate what would count as necessary additional support. As we saw in the analysis of media characteristics in Part II, most of them fail to provide feedback on students' description of their conceptualisation of a topic, and also fail to support the reflection they need to do in order to conceptualise and describe the experiences they have had within a learning session. This aspect can be contributed via teacher–student discussion. The discussion may be mediated by networking; for example, it may involve only some students in discussion and most in observing the discussion, learning vicariously from those actively taking part. The discussion may be in small tutorial groups, or in larger seminar groups, or in lectures, or even in broadcast teleconferencing (as in interactive satellite teaching). However it is managed, it is a vital part of the learning process. Without it, students have no opportunity to stand back from their experience, articulate the academic knowledge they are acquiring, and receive feedback on how they are expressing it. This is why misconceptions persist and remain resistant to the most concerted efforts of presentational teaching. Teaching has to be interactive to overcome misconceptions; the students need individualised responses to how they express what they know. The academic has to provide the learning environment in which this kind of interaction can take place: not just interaction with the world, but interaction also with the world of ideas and descriptions.

It is the individual academic's responsibility to provide the additional support advised by the course team, and/or indicated by their own analysis of the material. Students may provide it for themselves, as they have to for much of their teaching. But equally, they often fail to, which is why university education still fails to bring all students to a desirable level of competence in their subject. The teacher who wishes to achieve a high standard of competence with their students cannot leave them to supply all the additional support for themselves. In any case, the whole point of new technology is to improve the quality of teaching and learning, not just to open up access to new information and experiences. That is not sufficient.

Action

To provide proper support for the materials used:

1 Make use of any 'teacher's guide'.
2 Review the material to decide on the additional support necessary.
3 Find ways of providing opportunities for students to discuss the topic with tutors or experts.

ASSESSMENT

New technology methods are too frequently introduced to students on an experimental, pilot basis without being properly integrated into their teaching. Students therefore see them as peripheral to the real teaching, and invest less effort in them than they otherwise would. The only real test of any learning material is its use under normal course conditions. This means it must be integrated with other methods, the teacher must build on the work done and follow it through, and most important, the work students do on the materials must be assessed. This may require new standards to be set. For example, the best way of using some programs is in small groups, or in pairs. The work produced will therefore be collaborative, and must be assessed in a different way from work produced individually. The work may best be produced as a computer print-out, or as a trace of the students' inputs to a program, or as a lab report, so the teacher may have to devise new standards for presentation of work. It may be possible for the computer to assess the work, in which case the teacher has to monitor its performance. It may be appropriate for students to assess themselves, and negotiate a mark with the teacher.

The kind of work students do using learning materials is necessarily different from what they do in learning via other methods, so the teacher has to decide what counts as a good performance, and what counts as useful feedback to students on what they did. If they have used a database package to obtain information, for example, are they to be assessed on the basis of the results they obtained, or the on imaginativeness of their exploration of it? When comprehensive and detailed biblio- graphic research is made feasible by new technology methods (see the discussion of hypermedia databases in Chapter 7), the criteria for judging this work must change. Academics ignorant of new technology are in danger of being too easily impressed by the results of a few key presses, equating it with days of hard slog among the library catalogues.

Part of the point of new teaching methods is that they change the nature of learning, and of what students are able to do. It follows that the teachers then have the task of rethinking the assessment of what they do.

Whatever changes are decided upon by the teacher, it is vital that these are communicated to students clearly. One of the greatest dissatisfactions with student performance, most commonly expressed in examiners' meetings, is that students did not appear to understand what was required of them. The greatest service teachers can do for themselves and their students is to take time to clarify assessment requirements, check that they are understood, and if not, to take steps to make them understood better. It is not unreasonable to maintain a continuing dialogue about this, so important is it for the success of any teaching method.

Action

To ensure materials are properly embedded into a course:
1 Rethink the assessment in the light of new types of learning inculcated by new teaching materials and methods.
2 Communicate these to students.
3 Defend your assessment requirements to other members of the department and institution.

ACADEMIC LOGISTICS

This is a kind of dustbin category. It includes the many decisions an academic makes that significantly affect the quality of learning the students can achieve. Many of them are scarcely decisions made by the academic, rather they are academic decisions acquiesced to by the academic. They concern amount of material covered in a course, the sequence of courses, the time allotted for contact hours, the scheduling of contact hours, the means of access students have to relevant material, or equipment, or activities, for their study, the timing of assessment, the form of assessment, the administrative and technical support given to students, etc. Most of these aspects of a student's experience are effectively out of the hands of the individual academic planning their course, and are used as constraints within which to work. But they can all have a significant effect on how students study, for example:

- amount of material covered in a course – pressure of time leads students to cut corners, cover breadth rather than depth, use superficial study methods
- scheduling of contact hours – when the contact hours are regularly interspersed with other teaching, students lose contact with the issues under discussion from one to the next, making their learning very inefficient
- access to relevant material, or equipment, or activities, for study – scarcity of library resources, media resources, space creates barriers to students being able to study as they need to
- administrative and technical support given to students – insufficient support can lead to students focusing their efforts on the superficial problem of getting the task done, rather than on the content of what the task means

These have been repeated findings in a range of evaluation studies at all levels of education. Because these aspects of student study are so often beyond the control of the individual academic planning their course, the action solutions are more likely to be found in changes to the institutional context, which we come to in Chapter 12. On the other hand, because institutional changes can sometimes occur through the action of individual academics demanding better organisational conditions for their teaching, it is worth considering them here as well.

Action

Create the conditions that allow students to study effectively and efficiently:

1 Grade the importance of material covered in a course as, for example, essential, important, optional, etc.; make sure students know what these are; encourage depth of study rather than breadth of study.
2 Arrange for students' study of your subject to be uninterrupted by the study of other subjects as far as possible; argue for block teaching rather than distributed teaching.
3 Ensure students have good access to relevant material, or equipment, or activities, for their study.
4 Ensure students have adequate administrative and technical support for their study.

RESOURCES

This chapter should have clarified the importance of the 'context of delivery', complementary to the 'context of development' we focused on in Chapter 10. The development of media-based materials is important, but delivery is paramount. The most stunning educational materials ever developed will fail to teach if the context of delivery fails. Conversely, good delivery can retrieve poor materials. The 'context of delivery' means more than a delivery system, such as lectures, or mail or broadcasting. It refers to the provision of whatever support it takes to enable students to achieve the maximum benefit from their study. It is constituted by all the factors listed in this chapter. We cannot simply send out educational materials in the pious hope that students will benefit; we must ensure that they do so, by making suitable provision for the factors that will enhance their learning. This brings us to resources.

The factors described in this chapter have all concerned the academic, and their responsibility for maintaining a 'context of delivery' that properly supports whatever educational materials are used. The full checklist of delivery factors with resourcing implications will include all the support costs that enable the materials to be used properly. Estimates of comparative costs are difficult, because local circumstances and economies of scale can have a considerable effect, but Bates' estimate for the ratio of

10:1:10–20, for production: delivery: support costs for distance teaching universities, wisely puts the latter highest (Bates 1991: 12).

Action

Ensure that resources are available to cover provision of an adequate context of delivery by costing for:

1 Academic support.
2 Administrative support.
3 Technical support.
4 Equipment provision.
5 Facilities provision (space, etc.).
6 Materials publishing.
7 Materials duplication.
8 Materials delivery (via networking, broadcasting, mail, etc.).
9 Maintenance of materials.
10 Security of equipment, materials.

SUMMARY

This chapter has outlined some of the key factors in the learning context which are likely to affect the way students learn. We began with the assertion that new teaching methods, such as educational media, depend for their success upon being properly embedded into the existing learning context. Innovation will necessarily require changes in what exists already, and if this is not acknowledged and accommodated, then the innovation will not succeed. Students respond primarily to the institutional context as they perceive it. The demands and constraints it imposes, the issues discussed in this chapter, will have a greater effect on what students know than will any ingenious pedagogic design. These are the issues every academic must attend to for their teaching, or their use of media, to succeed:

• student preparation for studying from the new materials
• integration of the new materials with the rest of the course
• discussion of epistemological values
• pedagogical support to complete the materials' coverage of the learning process

- revision of the form of assessment in line with revisions to the teaching
- logistical conditions that will allow students to study effectively
- the level of resourcing that will allow students to study effectively

Revolutionary improvements in the quality of teaching do not usually succeed in the context of one course, however. Many of the changes necessary need to occur at departmental or institutional level, or beyond. That is why, in the final chapter, we consider not just the student's learning context, but the academic's teaching context as well, to the level of their profession as a whole.

Chapter 12

Effective teaching with multimedia methods

INTRODUCTION

It is not feasible to ensure effective teaching through multimedia methods by promulgating prescriptive guidelines on how to design materials, or what to use these methods for. Our use of IT-based media over the last twenty years has been prodigious but is not matched by our understanding of it, because the emphasis has been on development and use rather than on research and evaluation. This book has used what we do know from studies of student learning and from what few evaluation studies there are to develop a methodology for the design of multimedia teaching that both builds on what is known and enables that knowledge base to continue to be developed. This chapter takes that approach to its logical conclusion by applying the methodology to the whole academic system. The implementation of new technology methods cannot take place without the system around it adjusting to the intrusion of this new organism. The biological metaphor is apt. The academic system has to learn, has to be able to respond to its environment, which is a hostile one in most countries now, and respond also to its internal changes, which again in most countries are radical ones. If academe is to preserve what is good in its traditions and also preserve its mission to develop knowledge and educate others, then the higher education system needs a more robustly adaptive mechanism that it has had to develop hitherto. This chapter postulates what that system must look like, if we are to make best use of what the new technologies can offer.

The analysis begins with five key assumptions which recall arguments developed in earlier chapters.

ESTABLISHING AN ORGANISATIONAL INFRASTRUCTURE

Quality is best established through organisational infrastructure and collaboration

It is ironic that although higher education in the UK, for example, has a worldwide reputation for quality, it is being asked to borrow the inferior mechanisms of British management, which has an unenviably poor reputation worldwide. Higher education throughout the world has developed its own mechanisms for establishing quality of teaching within an institution, through criterion-referenced selection of staff, peer review, and monitoring procedures. Academe knows better that industry how to ensure quality, because unlike industry it has always operated on the principle of individual responsibility for the standard of work, one of the cornerstones of current 'quality' theory. As the new ideology of the industrialisation of academe sweeps blindly on, it remains ignorant of the fact that 'quality assurance mechanisms' have always been in place in academe. They do not always work perfectly, and may not always be complete; academics recognise that there is still improvement to be made, which is why the introduction of 'appraisal' and 'audit' schemes have been generally accepted. But while these measures may be able to build on established mechanisms for maintaining standards, the other key mechanism for improving quality in industry, competition, is at odds with the academic enterprise. This is important because it plays a crucial part in the development of multimedia.

It is inefficient to promote quality via competition because higher education has limited public resources to provide a public service. The already meagre resources are spread even thinner as academics compete and thereby repeat. Competition allows only norm-referenced testing of 'products', not criterion-referenced testing, which is more rigorous and more suitable for the academic context. It would not be acceptable to deliver poor education to anyone, which is what competition and market forces inevitably allow. Education should always reach an agreed standard of quality, i.e. a criterion.

Competition between institutions for resources for developing educational media creates a tremendous burden on staff, necessarily to no avail for many of them, allows merely norm-referenced selection, ensures repetition of effort, encourages divisiveness between institutions and therefore disinclination to take on the products of others. Collaboration between institutions, on the other hand, is more efficient in terms of staff time, allows criterion-referenced selection by an inter-institutional discipline-based review panel, and integrates effort, expertise and experience in a difficult new area.

If institutions were encouraged to develop in competition a variety of, say, statistics packages, on the grounds that the better ones would flourish, this would be wasteful in two ways. Firstly collaborative development would pool the best ideas rather than disperse them; secondly it is time-consuming for academics to have to 'shop around' for the best package once several have been developed. In any case, it is difficult to test which is really the best without mounting costly comparative studies. If instead the experimentation is part of the process of development, then a single team can put pooled resources into producing a very good package that is known to work, at least if used in the specified way. We cannot afford textbook-style competition to improve quality. For multimedia materials, good design has to be achieved through extension of the existing quality control mechanisms already in operation in academe. As John Daniel points out in a recent analysis of the role of the British Open University, the mechanism of the course team, through the collective work of the specialists it brings together, is considered to give the content of the materials they produce a special authority (Daniel 1991: 24).

The organisational infrastructure must be cyclical to ensure improvement

High academic standards are assured partly through setting up mechanisms that are capable of monitoring, learning and changing. The 'goal–action–feedback–revise action' cycle should be evident at every point in the organisational process, and this includes management actions (Elton and Middlehurst 1992). As in any learning process, there has to be a meta-level function that reflects on the process at the next level down in order to set up improvements to it. Therefore, in thinking about how development and implementation should be organised, we must be aware that every level of operation presupposes a higher level that is monitoring and reflecting on the way the lower level carries out its tasks. The same people may be on both levels; the two levels define different aspects of their activity.

Implementation must address the context of learning and teaching

Student use of new technology does not occur in isolation from other aspects of their course as far as they are concerned. It is often developed in isolation, however, and we therefore have to take steps to explicitly re-integrate it with the remainder of the student's course. It must be embedded as a natural part of their learning, if they are to take it seriously, and to benefit from using it. In particular, teachers' attitudes, other course teaching, scheduling, logistics, administration, briefing and de-briefing, technical and academic support, and student assessment, must all be conducive to enabling students to use the new technology to the full. If they are not, it will fail, no matter how good the material.

Design must address the entire learning process

Because new technology materials are often developed in isolation from a particular course, and necessarily so, they tend to be modular in nature, and require some particular prior preparation and follow-up by the teacher. In addition, materials are usually developed for one medium, rather than a combination. Both these features have the consequence that the materials so developed cannot usually address all essential aspects of the learning process identified in Part II. In order for students to learn from these materials, they have to contribute these other aspects for themselves. Many of them will be capable of doing this, and indeed they are used to doing it for their normal university teaching, which also often fails to address all aspects of the process within any one learning session. However, many students do not find this easy; they are even more unlikely to do so when they are finding the subject matter difficult; and as learning from new technology is relatively unfamiliar, they have to develop their learning techniques differently for this in any case. It is important that the materials support them as much as possible, therefore, by addressing as many aspects of the learning process as possible. This should be considered throughout the design process.

Academic knowledge is distinct from experiential knowledge

By its nature, new technology easily supports a fragmented, informational view of knowledge, and an action-oriented approach to education, and is therefore in danger of promulgating only that. Academic knowledge has an integrative character, different from 'information', contrary to Hague's argument, which conflates the two (Hague 1991). It is an articulation of reflection on experience, rather than being synonymous with knowledge of experience *per se*. It is more than the experiential knowledge developed in skill learning: it is also knowledge of descriptions. Of course, it is possible for new technology to support the more integrative view of knowledge, and the articulation and representation of experience, but this philosophy needs to be built into the design process explicitly, from the beginning.

A BLUEPRINT FOR THE ORGANISATIONAL INFRASTRUCTURE

The remainder of the chapter is an analysis of the infrastructure necessary for ensuring that high quality teaching and learning is delivered through the use of new teaching media. It satisfies Barnett's criterion for quality maintenance in higher education – built in part on a similar analysis of student learning – that it should be a process of 'engagement' (Barnett 1992: 216). It defines the tasks to be done at each level of the organisational process and refers to specific units of academic organisation as having particular responsibilities. Each task is assigned to some type of academic unit, and these are abbreviated as follows:

AA: academic administration (departmental, institutional or national)
Ac: individual academic lecturer
CT: courseware development team (inter- or intra-institutional)
DA: discipline area (departmental, institutional or national)
RA: resource administration (departmental, institutional or national)
NFC: National Funding Council for higher education.

High academic standards are assured in the use of new media in teaching if monitoring and feedback mechanisms are established for every part of the process – design, development, implementation and student learning. Previous chapters have elaborated the design and implementation requirements for educational media, given what we know about student learning. The rest of this chapter considers the implications of this for the way the academic system must operate, in terms of the constituent tasks to be carried out by each academic unit:

Design and development
- address student's needs
- target key areas of the curriculum
- build on what is known
- use an explicit teaching design methodology
- set up a courseware development team
- institute efficient production procedures
- plan resourcing and scheduling

Implementation and student learning
- administration of hardware, software, materials
- staff development
- staff scheduling
- student assessment standards
- evaluation of implementation
- document the logistical lessons learned
- dissemination of courseware
- student briefing
- student support and de-briefing
- integration with existing course
- evaluation of pedagogical effectiveness
- document the pedagogical lessons learned

At the end of the chapter, the responsibilities and tasks are also listed under the academic unit responsible.

DESIGN AND DEVELOPMENT

Address students' needs

CT: analyse exam scripts, teachers' experience

Critical problems in students' understanding of a subject area will often be apparent from assessment scripts and assignments.

Analysis of these would give rich material for deciding what kind of learning activities students need in order to attain the defined objectives, assuming that the examination questions are well designed (see Chapter 10).

CT: elicit students' perceived problems

Students find it hard to communicate the difficulty they have with a subject, precisely because they don't know what it is they don't know. Teachers and designers have to elicit their conceptions indirectly. A method that can and should be a natural part of all teaching is 'teachback', where students role-play teaching other students an aspect of the topic. The idea is elaborated in Chapter 10.

Target key areas of the curriculum

CT: analyse course provision at universities

Teaching via new technology is only economically feasible if it is used across a wide range of institutions. Any materials developed must have a large potential market. An analysis of course prospectuses for universities would determine common topic areas. Further information from course convenors is necessary to determine the likely characteristics of the student audience, and the approach to the subject. This kind of survey is necessary to guarantee the largest possible audience for the materials developed. In order to do it, close collaboration across universities is essential.

DA: convene teachers' forum to identify key areas for development

The responsibility for developing the best uses of new technology in each subject area will rest primarily with the discipline area itself. The usual fora of academic journals, the academic conference, the professional institute, the professors' conference, etc. will enable this debate to be pursued, but each of these must recognise their responsibility to promote such debate, not once, but continually. New technology is as often a barrier to progress as it is progressive, and needs to face a political as well as a pedagogic critique (Hawkridge 1993). Academics must be aware of the politics of new technology if they are not to be misled by it, and each discipline area will have its particular challenges and vulnerabilities, which is why the debate must be reworked for each one.

NFC: promote consortia to design transferable courseware

Because of the importance of collaboration for greater efficiency of production of materials, and for the greater likelihood of widespread dissemination of them, any central funds made available for development of these materials should be given only for collaborative consortia. Central funding also makes it possible to encourage standardisation of hardware and software platforms to make materials transferable across institutions.

Inter-institutional consortia for developing multimedia materials are important for the following reasons:

- they avoid local idiosyncracies of teaching
- they pool the best ideas on teaching the subject
- they confer a consensual status on the eventual materials
- they make mutual transfer between institutions more likely
- they avoid costly and wasteful competitive developments

The NFC is in a good position to promote inter-institutional consortia. The disadvantage is in the costs of bringing people together during the design and development process. Against this must be weighed the undoubted value of an enterprise that promotes a degree of academic mobility and therefore helps to counter the dangers of stagnation evident in the current stasis.

NFC: establish links with schools and training organisations

Some schools and training organisations are already well ahead of some universities in terms of the provision of new technology for teaching. Universities must take account of this, knowing what students will be familiar with and capable of when they come from school, and knowing what they will need in later employment. Developments at university level may be separate from other developments, but they should be synergistic with them.

Build on what is known

CT: access national database of courseware, courseware reviews

If progress is to be made it is vital that courseware developers build on what has gone before. They need access to it, therefore, not just via reviews, but also in demo versions, available through networking, so that they can move forward from the best of what already exists. National and international databases already exist, for example through the Computers in Teaching Initiative (CTI) Centres and the British Universities Film and Video Council (BUFVC) for audio-visual media in the UK, but they are not used as much as they should be, and do not have funds to supply demo versions of courseware.

CT: literature search in key journals

Many subject areas have their own academic journals of research and development in teaching in that subject. These will be a valuable source of information on students' needs, and teaching design ideas. They also alert designers to where their own work might be published. Some of the main subject-based journals are listed in Appendix 1.

CT: attend key conferences

Similarly, many subject areas have conferences on teaching, increasingly with software exhibitions which allow designers to see what has gone before them. These do not always occur at the right time, but proceedings can be used to find out where relevant work is going on. Discipline areas will have to develop their own criteria for academic excellence in teaching with new technology, and it is at such conferences that these discussions will take place.

RA: promote access to national database

Access to the existing databases is already available, e.g. through the CTI and BUFVC, but is not always easy to use from every institution. This depends upon good networking provision for all departments, and information and training on how to use the network, especially for downloading software demos and articles.

An institution's IT strategy should aim to support staff members in their use of international databases such as CTI and BUFVC, to maximise their value.

RA: provide funding for journals, travel

Funding should be available for progressing quality of teaching as well as quality of research. Network access can provide for some degree of collaboration, but travel will be essential occasionally, so this has to be provided for at some level in the institution, and recognised nationally.

NFC: provide for maintenance of national database

The CTI database and information network is not yet established on a long-term basis. Such international networks will always be an essential part of the development process for new technology, and need long-term support if the expertise and experience built up so far is not to be wasted.

NFC: promote funding of research in student learning

The development of new technology materials for teaching is highly labour intensive, with the expectation that it will be worth doing because it will be used by many students for a long time. It has to be very high quality, therefore, and as close as possible to what students actually need and benefit from. It is not possible for academics to carry out this kind of research as a normal part of their teaching duties. Nor is it feasible for development teams to do it as part of the design process. Academics involved in teaching and design should be able to run longer-term research projects to develop the necessary knowledge about teaching and learning in their subject, as an alternative to research in the subject itself. However, funds are rarely available for this. It is the NFC's responsibility to recognise the need for such research, and to promote the establishment of a funding council accordingly.

NFC: provide funding for evaluation of educational multimedia

The main reason for the dearth of reliable knowledge about educational media is that funding for it over the last twenty years has been for development rather than research or evaluation. There have been several national programmes in the UK, for example, but only a tiny fraction of the funding has been earmarked for research. These programmes have paid lip-service to evaluation, but very little has been carried out, as development costs expand to usurp the entire budget. A better strategy is to mount independent evaluations, funded separately from development, but formative evaluation is still necessary as part of the development process. Either way, unless funding is earmarked for basic research prior to development, and for evalution during and following development, the knowledge base will remain inadequate.

Use an explicit teaching design methodology

CT: address critical aspects of the learning process

The learning process for academic knowledge includes learning by description as well as through experience, and like other forms of learning must be cyclical, and two-level, as discussed in Part II. The student is not a perfect learner, and given the difficulty of engaging in all aspects of the learning process oneself, the teacher offers support by taking responsibility for some of them. The essential aspects of the complete learning process are therefore:

- discussion between teacher and student at the level of descriptions of their conceptions
- adaptation of the task goal by the teacher, given the student's description
- interaction between the world and the student at the level of the task devised by the teacher
- reflection by the student on their description of their conception, given the 'goal–action–feedback' cycle

The design of any media-based materials must address all these aspects. It is very difficult for any one medium to address them all – discussion and reflection are especially difficult to manage in a mediated form where the teacher is not present. The design of any materials that do not address all aspects must assume that these will be addressed by the learning situation in which they are embedded. But this in itself should affect the design. So materials should make clear the assumptions they make about the way they should be used. This may be communicated to the teacher or to the student in the form of printed documents, videos, guides, etc.

CT: make effective use of the media

The design of any learning material should be able to give an account of how it will address all aspects of the learning process, and how the media used will contribute to this. Chapter 10 discussed the process by which a designer may decide to use a particular medium for pedagogical reasons, taking into account how the 'conversational framework' developed in Part II categorises the value of each one, and allows the designer to combine them in the most effective way. Chapter 11 discussed the logistical reasons for choosing between the media, given the conditions of a particular academic environment. It was the inconvenient conclusion of Chapter 4 that discussion between teacher and student takes precedence as the most effective way of ensuring that the student achieves the intended educational objectives. At its most pragmatic, the use of educational media can be seen as an attempt to bridge the gap between this pedagogical imperative and the worsening staff–student ratios in higher education.

NFC: establish design standards

If materials are to be used across institutions, then standards must be established so that students do not have to relearn modes of use as they move between materials produced by different organisations. Standards should be as minimal as possible so as not to stifle creativity, and should relate to ease of use, and production values, not to content or teaching style. A good model would be the standards created for the Mac environment (provision of menus, icons, etc.), or those created for textbooks (contents, page numbers, index, etc.). Whatever the standards, they have to be defined centrally.

NFC: establish copyright policy

Teaching materials created for individual teachers to use in courses must be modifiable by them, otherwise their full potential will not be exploited. Materials should make use of other materials, e.g. computer programs can be supplemented by archive video material; videos can use archive film; print can use computer program output. It is to everyone's benefit that this should be possible, but the copyright problems this creates, especially in the context of competition rather than collaboration between universities, are considerable. The use by education of privately developed material should be paid for. The use by private organisations of publicly developed material should be paid for. Educational materials developed with public money should logically be freely available within the education system. The position needs to be clarified. This has to be done at national level.

CT: address design standards

Chapter 10 outlined some design characteristics for a computer-based teaching program to ensure appropriate locus of control, operational transparency, and general features to support pedagogical requirements. Designers should be aware of current standards of good practice, established by a NFC, for making materials easy to use.

CT: consider copyright issues

The copyright issue for any existing materials planned for incorporation into the design should be investigated at the earliest opportunity to avoid problems at a later stage.

NFC: tie funding to meeting of standards

Whatever the defined standards, they have to be promulgated via recognition for adherence, and/or penalties for non-adherence.

CT: review design with peer group

If materials are to be used across institutions, they must be generally acceptable to the academic community in that discipline area. Teaching is a highly idiosyncratic enterprise. Teachers will want flexibility, and will also want to be sure that the materials they are using are compatible with the way they teach. If designs are subject to peer review at an early stage, they will benefit from the constructive criticism provided by the review process, and the eventual materials will also be relatively insulated from destructive criticism. In many subject areas there are rival schools of thought. Educational materials cannot be expected to satisfy all modes of opinion, whether they are books, videos or programs. Within a particular scholarly tradition, however, there should be consensus that this is a reasonable way to teach the subject.

DA: set up forum for discussion of academic standards

Teaching through new technology will inevitably change the way subjects are taught. In any case, new technology brings its own demands for what is to be taught even before methods of teaching are revised. Economists have to learn about spreadsheets; art historians have to learn about databases; technologists have to learn about electronic control mechanisms; designers have to learn about design tools. Curriculum changes enforce their own changes of academic standards – of what counts as a well-qualified graduate. These discussions have to take place at discipline level and will involve the professional organisations and industrial liaison staff as well.

In parallel with this, there is the debate about what counts as good teaching in a subject area. In many subject areas there are journals and conferences that act as fora for such discussions. Some of these are now dedicated to teaching through media, especially computer-based teaching; some journals and conferences have special sections or themes. There are still some areas where there is no academic forum for discussing media-based teaching, or where the debate is confined to school level, or is not quality-controlled. Every discipline should ensure that there is an academic forum for this debate, incorporating all the traditional academic procedures of reviewing, refereeing, critiquing, selecting, editing.

RA: administer refereeing process for design of courseware

All universities practise a reviewing and refereeing process for course accreditation. A similar mechanism is necessary for the development of media-based course materials. The difference is that whereas external examiners normally have extensive access to the assessment, and very limited access to the nature of the teaching, the reverse is the case with course materials. The process is more similar to the external assessor system in operation at the British Open University. Materials are reviewed and commented on against a brief description of the nature of the assessment to be used on the course. The design and development of course materials can be explicit about the teaching, but can only describe in general terms the way the material is to be used and assessed. None the less, for external assessors and reviewers to make a judgement of the quality of teaching in the prospective design, they will have to take into account the planned mode of use. This makes it important to include expectations of the way the material is to be embedded in a learning context, as outlined above.

Set up a courseware development team

CT: involve people with complementary skills and knowledge

A courseware development team should include people contributing the following skills and knowledge:

- subject matter knowledge and how it is used
- knowledge of the teaching of the subject
- knowledge of students' problems in learning the subject
- knowledge of teaching through media
- copyright knowledge
- interviewing and observation skills
- design and presentation skills for each medium
- programming skills
- production skills for each medium
- formative evaluation skills
- editorial skills and knowledge
- project management skills

The first three are not necessarily contributed by the same person. Conversely, the same person may contribute several of the above, and some points may be contributed by several people. Only one member should be the project manager, however, with sufficient authority to arbitrate the inevitable disputes successfully. As long as all the above points are covered, the team is complete. All team members need to be involved throughout the development process, although the amount of involvement will vary for the different stages.

AA: monitor composition of team

If the argument for collaborative development is accepted, then the composition of the team is the first step in the implementation of quality control. At some level of academic administration, there must be a judgement about the capability of the team to produce the planned materials. As in other types of judgement, evidence of experience and previous success will be important. This means that such evidence must be available to inspection, which in turn helps to promote the documentation of the lessons learned from educational experimentation and development that are important if the field is to move ahead. A monitoring process of this type has a key role to play, therefore.

Institute efficient production procedures

CT: use productivity tools

The production members of a course team should be familiar with all the productivity tools available for the medium they are working in: desk-top publishing for print, computer-controlled editing for video, authoring systems for programs, etc. Designers will need to make use of prototyping tools, and administrative members will need project management tools. These should be part of the baseline provision for any courseware development team.

RA: provide funding and support for productivity tools

Administrators responsible for resourcing need to be familiar with funding requirements and the criteria for selecting such tools, and aware of the need for long-term planning to provide them.

NFC: promote bulk-purchasing of productivity tools

Collaboration between universities has the additional advantage that standardisation of hardware platforms and software environments allows for more economic provision of resources. Bulk-purchasing of programs already happens for hardware and software platforms, and should be extended further into courseware support. It is most economically done at national level, where possible.

CT: use communications networks during development

Inter-university collaboration presupposes good communications between staff involved in development. Travel is inevitable, as already mentioned, but better communications networks, allowing both audio- and computer-conferencing are as productive between academics as they are between students (see Chapter 9). The JANUS project has pioneered course development in this kind of collaborative mode, and the project feasibility study emphasises the importance of good quality communications links for the enterprise to be feasible (Kaye 1991).

NFC: promote use of networks

Improved networking for academics is part of national planning for many systems of higher education. Collaboration on courseware development will be one of the key advantages of improved systems.

Plan resourcing and scheduling

CT: set up project management plans

The drafting schedule for courseware materials should reflect the following pattern: Draft 1 – Discussion – Draft 2 – Debugging – Developmental testing with target students – Discussion – Draft 3 – Piloting. The production schedule takes over from Draft 3: Handover – Final editing (of text and pictures) – Quality assurance – Duplication (of software, print, video, audio materials) – Distribution.

Thus the management tasks will include the following:

- arrange meetings, face-to-face and on-line for discussions of drafts
- keep team informed and up-to-date on schedule
- cost and keep track of resources and budget
- arrange developmental testing sites, and piloting sites and subjects
- document meetings, decisions, problems
- liaise with production staff
- investigate copyright on all material planned for use

CT: carry out developmental testing and piloting

The courseware development team is in the best position to contribute to development of the knowledge base of how to use multimedia effectively. Developmental testing (or formative evaluation) of materials with the target students should provide the opportunity for an intensive study of how students learn through such media. Designers learn more from watching a small number of students trying to learn from their materials than they ever do from questionnaire studies. By (a) targeting the weaker students, (b) observing two or three pairs working collaboratively on the materials, and (c) maintaining the belief that the materials must adjust to the students rather than vice versa, the team will be able to produce good teaching materials and document the generalisable lessons for others to learn from. All three conditions are necessary, but the third is the most important, and the most difficult to achieve.

From open-ended observation, the team could progress to more focused evaluation, using questionnaires to assign proportions of the student population to the observed behaviours, if necessary. Existing models of obtaining feedback from students at the British Open University have been documented to illustrate contrasting methods and types of outcome (Laurillard 1992b).

Piloting should allow the team to assess the success of the materials in a new environment. As discussed in Chapter 11, the context within which the materials are used help to determine their success, and each needs to adjust to the other. It is important to use the piloting phase to discover, through observation and interviewing, for example, the contextual conditions that enable the courseware to work most effectively.

DA: agree staff and student time commitment

As staff spend time on courseware development, this reduces the time they can spend on face-to-face teaching. The project plan will have its own schedule that must be prioritised if it is to be work-able. Teaching timetables have to be planned around this well in advance, therefore. At the same time, departments might be tempted to consider the use of new technology materials to increase their efficiency, and thereby release staff for development. This is a reasonable expectation, but only if it is planned for, and already has a support system in place (as outlined in the following section, 'Implementation and Student Learning').

Student time commitment will be necessary for developmental testing. This should be carried out in the context of real usage of the materials within a course, in order to study the conditions under which it can be made to work optimally. Staff teaching the course must be prepared for this and closely involved with the way the development team intend the materials to be used. They must be prepared to be involved in both developmental testing and piloting. If use of the materials is a genuine part of the course, then students will expect their work with them to be included in the assessment of the course.

RA: agree development resources

Depending on the sequence of the introduction of development and implementation of new technology methods, there will be different resource implications, as discussed at the end of Chapter 10. If development comes first, then academic staff will have to be found to replace the staff spending time on development. If implementation comes first, then support staff and support mechanisms will have to be in place so that the materials are fully exploited and can fulfil the expectation of greater efficiency. Either way, there is an initial resource outlay in the expectation of greater efficiency in the long term. This should be planned and managed at institutional level.

AA: monitor project management

The courseware development procedure is itself a form of quality assurance mechanism, so it is important that it works as well as possible. The academic administration must receive reports from the course team on project management and progress, must direct resourcing policy, and must advise on changes to the procedure as necessary, thereby ensuring the continued improvement of the development process.

CT: report on efficiency of procedure to monitoring committee

The course team will be the main source of information to the academic administration on the successes and failures of the development process. For example, local communications may be ineffective, local administrative procedures may be counter-productive, or inappropriate. With the introduction of new forms of courseware development and new academic activities, new administrative procedures or working practices may be needed. It will not be possible to predict all of these in advance, which is why a flexible and adaptive mechanism must be set up, to assist the development team, and to learn the lessons for future projects.

The project management procedures should include on-going documentation of problems encountered and apparent successes, to reduce the burden on the course team of providing this information.

IMPLEMENTATION AND STUDENT LEARNING

Administration of hardware, software, materials

RA: provide support staff for maintenance and administration

Support staff are needed for the maintenance and administration of media-based materials, just as they are for print-based materials. The analogy with library staff is close. They have to be institution-based; they have to be able to deal with a range of subjects; they have to be knowledgeable about access to the materials, rather than the details of their content; discipline-based staff are often required to manage the complexity of material and support decisions necessary; they are needed to ensure that the materials are operationally sound. Without this kind of support, students will find it too difficult and time-consuming to make proper use of the media.

RA: provide funds and locations for hardware, software, materials

Resources should be managed as centrally as possible to ensure maximum value. If an institution acquires a statistics package, for example, it should be one that several departments would feel able to use. Hardware provision has to be carefully planned and located, to ensure that best possible use is made of it. In many places there is simultaneously a demand for more hardware and under-used terminal rooms. Administrators have to monitor usage and investigate the reasons for under-use if they are to under-stand how best to provide the resources students and staff need.

NFC: promote bulk-purchasing of hardware, courseware

The capacity for this already exists in the UK, for example, in the form of CHEST and CTI. (See Appendix 2.) Such organisations need to be established long-term, to ensure that this kind of activity is carried out for the maximum benefit to the whole of higher education. Good deals for hardware and site licences will assist the moves towards standardisation.

NFC: promote transfer of courseware across institutions

It is one of the underlying assumptions of this analysis that courseware should be developed collaboratively, both to increase efficient use of resources and to improve the quality of design. The efficiency argument depends upon transfer of courseware across institutions. It is contrary to tradition for universities to use each others' teaching. At best there is great uncertainty as to how it might be done; at worst there is outright hostility to the idea. However, a recent survey in the UK showed that the majority of academics welcome the idea of collaborating in the development and sharing of courseware (Laurillard, Swift and Darby 1993). Given that the NFC recognises the importance of institutions sharing the burden of development of courseware, it must take responsibility for ensuring that academics share this viewpoint and also act on it. It should be possible to encourage transfer of materials. Three points are essential:

1 The NFC must make funds available for the costs involved in transfer.
2 The institution must make appropriately costed plans for using such materials.
3 The institution must report on its experience of transfer.

Without the first, universities will not be able to afford to do it properly in the first instance while savings benefits have not yet materialised. Without the second, it will not be clear how much the cost and therefore the ultimate saving will be, and it will not be possible to comment on the appropriateness of the plans. Without the third, the lessons will not be learned, and improvement of the way transfer is carried out will not be possible.

Staff development

AA: establish programme of staff development

Staff who are to be involved in implementing new technology methods will have an initial training requirement of a one-day subject-specific workshop, of the kind already run by CTI Centres, to raise their awareness of what is already available, and of how to gain access to continuing up-dating information. The programme should raise their awareness of current teaching practice in their field, and the debates about the uses of new technology, in order to elaborate their understanding of what they are doing, to increase their expectations of it, to develop a critical approach to the use of new technology, and to increase the likelihood that they will make their own contribution to the field.

They will also need training that (a) helps them to develop suitable ways of integrating new technology into their courses, and (b) develops their formative evaluation skills so that they can monitor and improve their use of it. This kind of course could be run locally, regionally, or nationally, but again should be subject-specific.

They also need a local one-day workshop, of the kind run by some universities' computer-based learning centres, which informs them about local terminal rooms and resource centres, management procedures, and availability of resources. Continuing access to a local management committee and technical support staff would enable these academic staff to inform the university about their experiences with implementing new technology, and to receive continuing support in their use of it. By completing the cycle of information in this way it is more likely that procedures and conditions will be improved.

AA: encourage use of materials developed elsewhere

In tandem with an NFC commitment to encouraging transfer of courseware between institutions, there should be an institutional level of commitment to acquiring courseware. Selection and acquisition should be carried out by academics, but may be encouraged by the academic administration if funds are made available for this, or if departments are favoured in other ways if they make use of materials developed elsewhere.

NFC: review policy on appraisal, quality assurance

The appraisal process addresses academics' involvement in new teaching methods, but current plans to associate this with quality in teaching do not explicitly address how the quality is to be maintained. Appraisal procedures should make use of reviews, references, evaluation reports, etc., related to courseware design, just as they do for judging the quality of research. Activity is not sufficient. It is the quality of the activity carried out that should be assessed.

If teaching excellence is the aspiration of universities, then it must become the aspiration of individual academics. This means it must be accorded both the status and rigorous judgemental procedures that research has. The procedures for design, development, evaluation and documentation laid out in this chapter provide a basis for rigorous judgement. Status is accorded via promotion and other academic rewards, and this can be promulgated to some extent via NFC policy.

AA: decide on changes to appraisal, promotion procedures

In tandem with changes in NFC policy on teaching excellence and its implications for the implementation of new teaching technologies, academic administration at institution level must debate and negotiate the appropriate changes to be made to current promotion and appraisal practice. These must then be communicated to all staff.

Staff scheduling

AA: manage administration of teaching and staff training

As academic staff begin to be more involved in the development of teaching materials, rather than face-to-face teaching, there will be considerable logistical implications for the way teaching and learning is organised within the institution. It adds to the time required for staff development, not just for staff doing the developing but also for staff who are implementing new technology methods in their courses. More importantly it changes the way space is used, and the way teaching is timetabled.

There has to be a clear understanding in all university departments of the nature of the changes being made, so that they can decide how best to organise staff and student time to achieve the best possible conditions for academic learning. New technology methods should play a part in this, but should be used as the consequence of a wider plan that encompasses the whole teaching programme. They should not drive it. Such a plan would dictate how the department would manage to use some staff for development, while the others are engaged in introducing new technology methods, and how these are best integrated with existing methods.

The new technology revolution cannot happen in one department alone. Students should have an integrated system to work in. If they attend courses offered by different departments, the work-stations they use and the software they use should be compatible. If the optimal way of managing large numbers using new technology turns out to be within a block teaching format – where students study just one subject for a few weeks, then move onto another, rather than studying several at once – then this has to be a cross-disciplinary decision. If remedial/foundational courses, such as basic maths, grammar, report writing, etc., are taught through packaged learning materials, then these should be centrally available and therefore must be acceptable to all departments. It will be the responsibility of the academic administration at both central and departmental levels to devise and monitor the optimal teaching organisation for their university.

DA: set up forum for teachers to discuss ideas, experience

In parallel with the subject-centred forum suggested above for designers to discuss ways of exploiting new technology for teaching a particular subject, there should also be a forum for teachers implementing it. It is here that the academic issues surrounding the balance of learning methods will be discussed. If teachers have been able to evaluate their experience with using the new methods, this is the forum that will receive and debate that report. It need not be separate from the one debating the design of media-based teaching in the subject, but the concerns should be widened to embrace the success and failure of ways of supporting students in their use of media, the problems of integrating learning materials with other teaching methods, and teachers' requirements for future technological development.

Student assessment standards

DA: decide on changes to assessment standards and requirements

In Chapter 11, the discussion of contextual conditions for educational technology suggested that it may be necessary to make changes to assessment standards and requirements, as the new technology changes both the curriculum and the way the content is known. If assessment is to match what students have learned, it is likely that assessment requirements and standards will change.

DA: communicate new requirements to students and academic staff

Academics introducing new technologies will have to promulgate changes to assessment requirements among other students and staff not immediately involved. Courses never exist in isolation, and others will be affected by new requirements on one course.

Evaluation of implementation

DA: provide staff time to monitor implementation

Any teaching innovation must be formatively evaluated if it is to be optimised. This takes time: to collect data, analyse it, devise improved practice, and then report on it. The data need not be extensive; it should rather be intensive. Formative evaluation is not concerned with demonstrating improved performance – which requires comparative studies, large numbers and statistical analysis – but with improving performance.

Assuming that debugging and developmental testing of the materials have already been carried out by the design team, the principal task of the teacher implementing the materials is to pilot them, and thereby determine how best to use them. The pilot study should fully integrate the materials into the course, linking them to other teaching, following up on what students did with them, and assessing their work. The study would benefit from intensive observation of a few pairs of students (pairs articulate their thinking and so expose any difficulties or successes they experience), and from pre- and post-tests on a small number of students to check the apparent learning gains. It is essential either to administer open-ended questionnaires to a small number of students, or to interview them, covering their experience of the materials in their learning context. An open-ended response either to an interview or a questionnaire enables students to express their own concerns, with little bias towards the teachers' interests. From the analysis of these responses it is possible to check the range and balance of student attitudes on each of the issues raised, by using them to devise a more structured questionnaire. Being structured, the analysis of responses from large numbers of students is straightforward.

The study carried out should enable the teacher to identify any necessary changes in how they organise the use of the materials, and any further support they need from the administration (e.g. more conveniently located work-stations, technical support to help students get started, etc.). The lessons learned by the individual teacher should also be communicated to the administration to assist their policy development.

Document the logistical lessons learned

RA: monitor logistics of implementation

The value of monitoring the implementation of teaching should be apparent for any teaching method, as this allows the resource administration to know how well the method is working and what logistical costs and perceived benefits there are. The collection of monitoring data should be routine for any university teaching system.

AA: assign committee to receive and act on evaluation reports

At either departmental or institutional level, the academic administration has the responsibility to ensure that new teaching methods are effective and properly planned and resourced. In order to develop and improve policy and procedures, they need information on how well current implementations are working. These committees will be the recipients of the reports produced by individual academics on their experience of the pedagogical value of a teaching medium, and reports from the administration documenting the data mentioned above.

NFC: use reports to revise policy on new technologies

The NFC will continue to update policy on the use of new technologies and how this is to be encouraged at university level. In order to develop policy they will need information from individual institutions on how well the new methods are working, and will therefore wish to receive reports filtered through institutional academic administrations.

Dissemination of courseware

RA: manage marketing, distribution of courseware materials

If materials are to transfer between institutions, there has to be a system of distribution. This is most economically handled on a national basis, so that there should be little burden on institutional resources. Alternatively, distribution could be handled by commercial publishers, with universities purchasing learning materials as they would books.

NFC: promote involvement of publishers

The involvement of commercial publishers in the distribution of academic courseware is negligible in most countries at present. If this is seen to be a preferable alternative to the university sector carrying out its own distribution then liaison between the NFC and the commercial publishers should be initiated.

Student briefing

CT: provide teacher's and student's guide to use of courseware

Guidelines for student briefing were discussed in Chapter 11, which suggested that academics adopting new technology materials would be likely to need help initially in how to make best use of them, for example through provision of a teacher's guide by the courseware development team. Students will need suitable preparation and support in their use of the materials, and as these will be relatively unfamiliar to the academics introducing them, they will need advice on what this should be.

Ac: review material and provide links to rest of course

Whatever advice and guidance is provided by the course team who designed the learning materials, it is ultimately the individual academic's responsibility to determine how it should be fitted in, which means they have a responsibility, as suggested in Chapter 11, to review the materials, and decide how best to prepare and follow up the students' work with them.

Student support and de-briefing

CT: use teacher's guide to suggest additional support

It was argued in the context of the design process above, that learning materials should address all aspects of the learning process, and where they fail to, as most do, should indicate what would count as necessary additional support. This may be in the form of necessary preparation, suggested written work by the students, suggested exercises for students to do using the material, suggested group work or discussion points, and possible ways of following it up.

Ac: provide additional support

It is the individual academic's responsibility to provide the additional support advised by the course team, and/or indicated by their own analysis of the material. It was argued in Part II that teaching has to be discursive to overcome students' misconceptions; the students need individualised responses to how they expresss what they know. The academic has to provide the learning environment in which this kind of interaction can take place: not just interaction with the world, but interaction also with the world of ideas and descriptions.

Ac: plan provision of additional support

In taking on new learning materials, the academic has to be aware that this is not something that students can be sent to, and there is nothing more to be done. There will be an integrative task to do, at the very least, and there may be resourcing implications for the additional support resulting from the above analysis, the most likely being academic staff time. This must be planned by the individual academic, and communicated to any departmental planning.

Integration with existing course

Ac: review other teaching to see how it might be modified

New learning materials will be likely to change aspects of the existing teaching, so possible changes to this must be kept under review, as suggested in Chapter 11.

DA: set up forum to promote collaboration across courses

The point was made earlier that the new technology revolution cannot take place in one department alone. The same point applies to courses. Students will take several courses within a department and will expect some carry-over of use of technology from one to another. In addition, with increasingly modular courses, students will find themselves moving between departments several times during their undergraduate course. If their learning is not to become too fragmented, the departments must collaborate in their use of the new learning materials, as they do when they run inter-departmental courses. Collaboration among staff both within and between departments will be necessary for all teaching, not just that involving new technology.

Evaluation of pedagogical effectiveness

CT: provide materials to aid evaluation

As part of the formative evaluation carried out by the course team they will have developed pre- and post-tests, feedback sheets, tracing capabilities in the computer program, questionnaires, observation sheets, etc. and these can be made available to the teacher as part of the teacher's guide to the courseware. This will enable the teacher to continue the evaluation begun by the development team.

Ac: monitor student use of courseware materials

The teacher's interest will probably be in using the media in the context of other teaching, but they will also want to know what learning benefits students derive from the material *per se*. Each case will be different as the material will be embedded in different course contexts, so there is a considerable role for the teacher to play in discovering what kind of learning accrues from their own students' use of it.

Ac: analyse assignments

The best source of information on the pedagogical value of the learning materials used will come from the way students carry out assignments based on them. If these require some kind of descriptive report of what they learned, rather than simply an operational account of what they did, it will be possible for the teacher to obtain a clearer idea of how their thinking and conceptualisation of the topic has developed. This requirement of the assignment should made clear to students, who will easily assume they are only meant to report on what they did, and not on how they think.

Ac: change format of briefing, de-briefing, support as necessary

From analysis of students' use of the materials, and their assigned work, the academic will have some idea of what worked well, what students still fail to understand, what they failed to exploit, etc., and will be able to decide on this basis what, if anything, should change in the way the material is used.

Document the pedagogical lessons learned

Ac: report on lessons learned

The academic's experience of using new technology materials is the best source of information about the value of this kind of learning method. Our collective knowledge of how to use it and how to design it can only progress on the basis of such information, so it is essential that it be documented. The various academic fora already alluded to above should be in receipt of

such reports, and academics should receive as much encourage-
ment and inducement as possible to document and publish their
experience. Unless more academics contribute to building this
knowledge, the new technologies will be no more than costly
failures.

CT: receive and act on reports

The particular course teams responsible for developing a set of
materials should be in receipt of any evaluation report concerning
it. Even if they disband as a team, the individuals need to complete
their own learning cycle and find out what ultimately happened
to the various implementations of what they created. They as
individuals will be likely to contribute to further developments,
and will take their experience with them. It is important that this
experience should be informed by feedback on how successful
it was.

DA: receive and publish reports

Each discipline area should take responsibility for developing
knowledge about how to teach using new technology in their
particular field. The fora created for academic debate and
discussion of these issues will need to receive reports on the
experience of teachers using the new methods. The wide
promulgation of the lessons learned will inform that debate. The
evaluation reports from individual academics should find a place
for discussion and debate outside the institution, and within the
subject field itself. Individual departments may wish to contribute
to this development of knowledge, and will therefore ensure that
their staff are enabled and encouraged to make such a
contribution.

SUMMARY

An organisational infrastructure for educational technology in
higher education must enable the system to learn about itself. The
decision-making hierarchy must be in a position to receive
feedback on the effects of its decisions at each level in exactly the
same way as the student needs feedback on their interactions with
the world in order to learn. Among the tasks defined for each unit

254 The design methodology

of organisation, in addition to guidelines for how they should act, this chapter has suggested how each unit might receive reports on the effects of their actions, primarily through evaluation. The tasks are collected together for each unit in the lists below.

National Funding Council for Higher Education

- promote consortia to design transferable courseware
- establish links with schools and training organisations
- provide for maintenance of national database
- promote funding of research in student learning
- provide funding for evaluation of educational multimedia
- establish copyright policy
- establish design standards
- tie funding to meeting of standards
- promote bulk-purchasing of productivity tools
- promote use of communications networks
- promote bulk-purchasing of hardware, software
- promote transfer of courseware across institutions
- review policy on appraisal, quality assurance
- use reports to revise policy on new technologies
- promote involvement of publishers

Discipline area

- convene teachers' forum to identify key areas for development
- set up forum for discussion of academic standards
- set up forum for teachers to discuss ideas, experience
- decide on changes to assessment standards and requirements
- communicate new requirements to students and academic staff
- provide staff time to monitor implementation
- monitor logistics of implementation
- set up forum to promote collaboration across courses
- receive and publish reports

Academic administration

- monitor composition of team
- agree staff and student time commitment
- monitor project management
- establish programme of staff development

- encourage use of materials developed elsewhere
- decide on changes to appraisal, promotion procedures
- manage administration of teaching and staff training
- assign committee to receive and act on evaluation reports

Resource administration

- promote access to national database
- provide funding for journals, travel
- administer refereeing process for design of courseware
- provide funding and support for productivity tools
- agree development resources
- provide support staff for maintenance and administration
- provide funds and locations for hardware, software, materials
- manage marketing, distribution of courseware materials

Courseware development team

- analyse exam scripts, teachers' experience
- elicit students' perceived problems
- analyse course provision at universities
- access national database of software, reviews
- literature search in key journals
- attend key conferences
- address critical aspects of the learning process
- make effective use of the media
- address design standards
- consider copyright issues
- review design with peer group
- involve people with complementary skills and knowledge
- use productivity tools
- use communications networks during development
- set up project management plans
- carry out developmental testing and piloting
- report on efficiency of procedure to monitoring committee
- provide teacher's and student's guide to use of courseware
- use teacher's guide to suggest additional support
- provide materials to aid evaluation
- receive and act on reports

Academic lecturer

- review material and provide links to rest of course
- review material to decide additional support
- plan provision of additional support
- review other teaching to see how it might be modified
- monitor student use of courseware materials
- analyse assignments
- change format of briefing, de-briefing, support as necessary
- report on lessons learned

This blueprint for an organisational infrastructure capable of ensuring a continual improvement in student learning is applicable to any teaching method, but is essential for the use of educational technology because of its innovative character. Educational technology entails a departure from the traditional modes of teaching at university level, which have always provided adequate opportunities for the teacher–student discussion that has been identified as so important for learning at this level. To continually improve, the development of educational technology must have the cyclical character of any learning process, and this has been built into the list of tasks. To be successful, the implementation must address the full context of the teaching–learning process. To be effective, the design must address all the activities essential for learning. To be applicable to higher education, the design process must acknowledge the special nature of academic learning. All these requirements have been built into the organisational infrastructure identified in this chapter. Some of it may seem like a blue skies blueprint, but much of it is already in place in many countries. In any case, it is important to clarify what to aim for.

Higher education must be able to evolve and adapt to new conditions while preserving the traditional high standards of an academic education. Academics must take responsiblity for what and how their students learn – that is the premise I began with. If universities are to maintain that responsibility, and not allow their standards to be undermined by the diminution of resources, then we must also take responsibility for enabling the system itself to be reflective and adaptive.

Appendix 1

Journals on subject-matter teaching

This appendix lists a selection of journals, both general and subject-oriented, that are likely to publish articles on the use of educational technology for teaching and learning at tertiary level. Many will also publish software and courseware reviews of interest to subject teachers.

General

British Journal of Educational Technology, National Council of Educational Technology, UK (see Appendix 2).

Computers and Education, Pergamon Journals Ltd, Oxford, UK.

Educational Researcher, American Educational Research Association, USA (see Appendix 2).

Educational Technology, Educational Technology Publications Inc, New Jersey, USA.

Educational Technology Abstracts, Carfax Publishing Company, an abstracting journal for research and development in education and training technology.

Educational Technology Research and Development, Association for Educational Communications and Technology, Washington, USA.

Instructional Science, Kluwer Academic Publishers, The Netherlands.

Journal of Computer Assisted Learning, Blackwell Scientific Publications Ltd, Oxford, UK.

Journal of Educational Television, Carfax Publishing Company, Oxford, UK.

Learning and Instruction, the journal of EARLI (see Appendix 2), Pergamon Journals Ltd, Oxford, UK.

Resources in Education, Educational Resources Information Center,

National Institute of Education, Washington DC, USA, an abstracting journal for papers on educational research.

Biology

Biochemical Education, Pergamon Journals Ltd, Oxford, UK.
Journal of Biological Education, Institute of Biology, London, UK.

Chemistry

Journal of Chemical Education, American Chemical Society, Easton, PA 18042, USA.
Software Reviews, published by CTI Centre for Chemistry, University of Liverpool (see Appendix 2).

Economics

Computers in Higher Education Economics Review, published by the CTI Centre for Economics, University of Bristol (see Appendix 2).
Economics, Economics Association, UK.

Engineering

European Journal of Engineering Education, Carfax Publishing Company, UK.
International Journal of Applied Engineering Education, Pergamon Journals Ltd, Oxford, UK.

Geography

Journal of Geography in Higher Education, Carfax Publishing Company, Oxford, UK.

Humanities

Computers and the Humanities, Kluwer Academic Publishers, The Netherlands.
Literary and Linguistic Computing, Oxford Journals, UK.
History and Computing, Oxford University Press, UK.
Computers and Texts, published by the CTI Centre for Textual Studies (see Appendix 2).

Information Studies

Journal of Education for Library and Information Science, Association for Library and Information Science Education, Kent State University, USA.
Education for Information, IOS Press, The Netherlands.

Languages

System, an international journal of educational technology and applied linguistics, Pergamon Press Inc, Elmsford, New York, USA.
Computer Assisted Language Learning, Intellect Books, UK.
ReCALL, published by the CTI Centre for Modern Languages, University of Hull (see Appendix 2).

Law

Journal of Legal Education, Association of American Law Schools, University of Iowa, USA.
The Law Technology Journal, published by the CTI Law Technology Centre, University of Warwick (see Appendix 2).

Management and Accounting

Accounting Education, Chapman and Hall, UK.
ACCOUNT, published by the CTI Centre for Accounting, Finance and Management, University of East Anglia (see Appendix 2).
Management Education and Development, University of Lancaster, UK.

Mathematics

Journal for Research in Mathematics Education, National Council of Teachers of Mathematics, Reston, VA 22091 USA.
International Journal of Mathematics Education in Science and Technology, Taylor & Francis Ltd, Basingstoke, UK.

Medicine

Academic Medicine, Hanley and Melfus, Philadephia, USA.

Journal of Audio-Visual Media in Medicine, Butterworth Scientific Ltd, Guildford, UK.
Medical Education, Blackwell Scientific Publications, Oxford, UK.

Physics

American Journal of Physics, American Association of Physics Teachers.
Physics Education, 5112 Berwyn Rd, College Park, MD20740, USA, Tel: 301 345–4200.

Psychology

Psychology Teaching Review, British Psychological Society.
Psychology Software News, an international newsletter, published by the CTI Centre for Psychology, University of York (see Appendix 2).

Social Studies

Computers in the Human Services, Haworth Press, Binghampton, NY 13904-1580, USA.
New Technology in the Human Services, published by CTI Centre for Human Services, University of Southampton (see Appendix 2).

Useful addresses

This appendix lists addresses of selected organisations that can provide information on aspects of educational technology at tertiary level. For subject-oriented information see the CTI Centres listed at the end.

Australia

Educational Research and Development Unit (ERADU) Royal Melbourne Institute of Technology, PO Box 2476V, Melbourne, Vic 3001.
Tertiary Education Institute (TEDI) University of Queensland, Brisbane, Qld 4072.

Canada

Instructional Development Centre, McMaster University, General Sciences Building, Hamilton, Ontario L8S 4K1.
Open Learning Agency, 300–475 West Georgia Street, Vancouver V6B 4M9.
Educational Technology Department, Concordia University, 1455 De Maisonneuve Blvd W, Montreal, Quebec H3G 1M8.

Europe

European Association for Research on Learning and Instruction, Center for Instructional Psychology and Technology, University of Leuven, Vesaliusstraat 2, B-3000 Leuven, Belgium.
GOLEM (Technology and Education), Istituto di Psicolgoia del CNR, Viale Marx 15, 00137 Roma, Italy.

DELTA (Development of European Learning through Technological Advance) DGXIII Rue de la Loi 200, B-1049 Brussels, Belgium.

UK

British Universities Film and Video Council (BUFVC), 55 Greek Street, London W1V 5LR. Tel: (71) 734 3687, fax: (71) 287 3914. Aims to promote the use of audio-visual media for higher education and research.

CHEST, Bath University Computing Services, Claverton Down, Bath, BA2 7AY. Produces a software directory and arranges deals on software products for the academic community.

Computers in Teaching Initiative Support Service (CTISS), University of Oxford Computing Service, 13 Banbury Road, Oxford, OX2 6NN. Co-ordinates and disseminates the work of the CTI Centres listed below.

Institute of Educational Technology (IET), Open University, Milton Keynes, MK7 6AA. Carries out research, development and evaluation of educational technology methods for distance learning in higher education.

National Council for Educational Technology (NCET), University of Warwick Science Park, Sir William Lyons Road, Coventry CV4 7EZ. Aims to promote the use of educational technology at all levels of education and training.

Information Technology Training Initiative (ITTI), CVCP University Staff Development Training Unit, Level 6 University House, Sheffield, S10 2TN. Promotes awareness of and competence in information technology methods among university staff.

USA

American Educational Research Association (AERA), 12340 17th St NW, Washington, DC 20036. Publishes a journal and organises an annual international conference on research at all levels of education.

Learning Research and Development Center (LRDC), University of Pittsburgh, Pittsburgh, PA 15260. Carries out research on learning and instruction; publications list available.

Rutgers Centre for Electronic Texts in the Humanities, 169 College Avenue, New Brunswick, NJ 08903. Tel: (908) 932 1384, email: ceth@zodiac.rutgers.edu. International inventory of electronic texts, acquiring and disseminating text files to the academic community.

Educational Technology Center, University of California, Irvine, CA 92717. Research and development projects, especially in computer-based learning.

Computers in Teaching Initiative (CTI) Centres

These centres were set up by the Universities Funding Council to promote and evaluate the use of computers for teaching and learning in UK universities. The centres are subject-focused and provide newsletters, journals, resource guides and expert support for each discipline represented. Membership is also available for academics outside the UK.

CTI Centre for Accountancy, School of Information Systems, University of East Anglia, Norwich NR4 7TJ. Tel: 0603 592312, email: ctiac@uk.ac.uea

CTI Centre for Biology, Donnan Laboratories, University of Liverpool, PO Box 147, Liverpool, L69 3BX. Tel: 051 794 3586, email: ctibiol@uk.ac.liv.ibm

CTI Centre for Chemistry, Donnan Laboratories, University of Liverpool, PO Box 147, Liverpool, L69 3BX. Tel: 051 794 3576, email: ctichem@uk.ac.liv.ibm

CTI Centre for Computing, Faculty of Informatics, University of Ulster at Jordanstown, Newtownabbey, County Antrim, N. Ireland, BT37 0QB. Tel: 0232 365131 x3020, email: cticomp@uk.ac.ulster.ujvax

CTI Centre for Computing in Economics, University of Bristol, Social Science Buildings, 8 Woodland Road, Bristol, BS8 1TN. Tel: 0272 288476, email: cticce@uk.ac.bristol

CTI Centre for Engineering, c/o CATU, Dept. of Mechanical Engineering, Queen Mary and Westfield College, Mile End Road, London E1 4NS. Tel: 071 975 5528, email: ctieng@uk.ac.qmw

CTI Centre for Geography (with Geology), Dept. of Geography, University of Leicester, University Road, Leicester, LE1 7RH. Tel: 0533 523827, email: cti@uk.ac.le

CTI Centre for History, University of Glasgow, 1 University Gardens, Glasgow G12 8QQ. Tel: 041 339 8855 x6336, email: ctich@uk.ac.glasgow

CTI Centre for Human Services, Dept. of Social Work Studies,

University of Southampton, Southampton, SO9 5NH. Tel: 0703 592779, email: ctihumserv@uk.ac.soton.ibm

CTI Centre for Land Use Studies, Dept. of Agriculture, University of Aberdeen, 581 King Street, Aberdeen, AB9 1UD. Tel: 0224 480291, email: ctiland@uk.ac.aberdeen

CTI Centre for Law, Faculty of Law, University of Warwick, Coventry, CV4 7AL. Tel: 0203 523294, email: ctilaw@uk.ac.warwick

CTI Centre for Library and Information Studies, Dept. of Library and Information Studies, Loughborough University of Technology, Loughborough, LE11 3TU. Tel: 0509 223057, email: ctilis@uk.ac.lut

CTI Centre for Mathematics and Statistics, c/o Faculty of Education, University of Birmingham, Birmingham, B15 2TT. Tel: 021 414 4800, email: ctimath@uk.ac.bham
also at
Dept. of Statistics, University of Glasgow, University Gardens, Glasgow, G12 8QW. Tel: 041 339 8855 x4046, email: ctistat@uk.ac.glasgow

CTI Centre for Medicine, Royal Fort Annexe, Bristol University, Tyndall Avenue, Bristol, BS8 1UJ. Tel: 0272 303137, email: cticm@uk.ac.bristol

CTI Centre for Modern Languages (with Classics), School of European Languages and Cultures, University of Hull, Cottingham Road, Hull, HU6 7RX. Tel: 0482 466373, email: cti.lang@uk.ac.hull

CTI Centre for Music, Dept. of Music, Lancaster University, Lancaster, LA1 4YW. Tel: 0524 593776, email: ctimusic@uk.ac.lancaster

CTI Centre for Physics, Dept. of Physics, University of Surrey, Guildford, Surrey, GU2 5XH. Tel: 0483 509329, email: ctiphys@uk.ac.surrey.ph

CTI Centre for Psychology, Dept. of Psychology, University of York, Heslington, York, YO1 5DD. Tel: 0904 433156, email: ctipsych@uk.ac.york

CTI Centre for Sociology & the Policy Sciences, Dept. of Applied Social Science, University of Stirling, Stirling, FK9 4LA. Tel: 0786 67703, email: ctisoc@uk.ac.stirling

CTI Centre for Textual Studies, Oxford University Computing Services, 13 Banbury Road, Oxford, OX2 6NN. Tel: 0865 273221, email: ctitext@uk.ac.ox.vax
also at

Office for Humanities Communication, The Library, University
of Bath, Claverton Down, Bath, BA2 7AY. Tel: 0225 826344,
email: c.mullings@uk.ac.swurcc

Glossary

Adaptive
Describes computer programs or teachers capable of using information about a student's performance on a task, or series of tasks, to determine the form of the subsequent teaching, or the exercises set for that student.

Anathemagenic
Coined by the author to contrast with 'mathemagenic' (qv), to describe learning activities that 'give birth to loathing'.

Approach to learning
The umbrella term used to describe what a student brings to learning, including both how they handle the information, and their personal learning intentions.

Asynchronous
Contrasts with 'synchronous' (qv) to mean 'not at the same time'; applied to forms of communication where interlocutors are not both present at the same time, such as electronic mail.

Atomistic
Coined by Svensson, the term contrasts with 'holistic' (qv) to describe, for example, a fragmented knowledge structure, or an approach to learning that fails to recognise that knowledge needs to be integrated.

Audio-graphics
Not in widespread use, but a handy way of referring to a form of communication where the audio channel, e.g. a telephone line, allows normal conversation, and a data channel allows the interlocutors to exchange data for display on a computer screen at the same time.

Audio-vision
A term in common use at the Open University to describe a combination of audio and visuals, e.g. an audio-cassette talking the student through the visual component displayed in a diagram.

Automaticity
Not having to think about what you are doing – normally used for motor skills, such as changing gear while driving, but used also in education in a metaphorical sense to apply to familiar concepts, or standard moves in an argument.

Collaborative learning
Means what it says, but is acquiring a special meaning as it is used mostly now to refer to students working on a computer-based learning program that requires them to collaborate by, for example, taking different roles, operating different controls, etc.

Concealed multiple-choice question (CMCQ)
Describes a version of MCQ (qv) that conceals the choices. The program invites open-ended input from the student and compares it, using a matching algorithm of some kind, with each choice programmed in. The closest match is taken to be the student's choice, thereby communicated to the program without the disadvantage of suggesting answers the student may not have thought of.

Courseware
Course material produced for any medium – print, audio, video, computer program, etc.

Discursive
Describes a medium that supports discussion between students, or between student and teacher. Each interlocutor should be able to articulate a view, re-articulate in the light of the other's utterance, ask and reply to questions, though not necessarily synchronously. Thus letter-writing is discursive, whereas lecturing is not.

Evaluation
Refers to ways of testing the quality or value of something: in the educational context usually course materials, or teaching methods, but sometimes also students. However, evaluation of students is more usefully referred to as 'assessment'. Evaluation methods for course materials include, for example, pre- and post-testing of students' knowledge, observation, interviewing.

Experiential knowledge/learning
Describes knowledge gained through experience / learning

through experience. Contrasts, and moreover often conflicts, with academic knowledge and learning through instruction.

Extrinsic feedback
Contrasts with 'intrinsic feedback' (qv) to describe someone's evaluation of an action (e.g. applause as a comment on a kick of a ball), where the feedback is generated from a context external to the action itself.

Formative evaluation
Contrasts with 'summative evaluation' (qv). Describes the evaluation of course materials that provides information for improvement of those materials.

Holistic
Coined by Svensson and others, the term contrasts with 'atomistic' (qv) to describe, for example, an integrated knowledge structure, or an approach to learning that recognises that knowledge needs to be integrated.

Hypertext/hypermedia
The term 'hypertext' is attributed to Ted Nelson, and refers to text whose interconnectedness is made explicit and navigable. The interconnections are defined by the author (or even by the user), in the form of links between words or phrases or chunks of the document. They are made navigable by defining those chunks as 'buttons', such that when the user interrogates that button (e.g. by clicking on it with a mouse) the connected word or phrase or chunk appears. The chunks can also be audio or video material, hence the extension of the idea to 'hypermedia'.

Interactive
Used to differentiate computer-based learning from other methods by virtue of the computer's capability to be programmed to change its behaviour according to the learner's input.

Intrinsic feedback
Contrasts with 'extrinsic feedback' (qv) to describe the result of an action (e.g. a goal as the result of a kick of a ball), where the feedback is generated from the same context as the action itself.

Mathemagenic
Coined by Rothkopf to describe activities that 'give birth to learning', from the Greek *mathema* meaning 'something learned' and -*genus* meaning 'given birth to'.

Microworld
A computer program that embodies rules governing the behaviour of defined objects and their interaction with each other, thus evoking the impression of 'a little world' in which the user can manipulate the objects to build something in that world, via a language understood by the program.

Modelling program
A program that takes as input descriptions of a system, allowing the learner to create their own model of its behaviour. The program determines the form the description takes, and the form of the output (numerical, graphical or text), but uses the learner's definition to generate the system's behaviour.

Modem
An add-on box connected between the computer's communication slot and a telephone line to allow data transfer between computers over a distance.

Multimedia
Originally used by distance learning institutions in particular to describe their courses delivered via text, television, radio, telephone, etc. Now used to refer to workstations that support not just alpha-numeric/graphic displays, but also audio-visual material stored on CD-ROM or hard disk.

Multiple-choice question (MCQ)
The most common form of interaction offered by computer-based learning programs: the question is put, and is followed by some possible answers, including the correct answer and some plausible distractors, or common incorrect answers. The student selects one, and this is meant to represent their answer.

Pedagogenic error
Coined by the author to mean 'teacher-induced error' (from the Greek *paedagogos* meaning 'teacher', and *-genus* meaning 'given birth to'): the teaching profession's equivalent of 'iatrogenic disease', meaning 'disease induced by the physician'.

Phenomenography
Coined by Marton to mean 'descriptions of the phenomena', specifically, the alternative ways students conceptualise key phenomena; contrasts with the philosophical method of 'phenomenology', which 'studies the phenomena' to develop a fully justified and unitary knowledge of what is.

Reflective
Refers to those teaching methods or learning activities that encourage the student to reflect on what they know, or on what they have experienced.

Self-assessed question (SAQ)
Used in distance teaching texts to enable the student to check their answer to the question against a model answer. The answer is usually given at the end of the text.

Simulation
A computer program that runs a model of the behaviour of a system, and displays that behaviour in text, numerical or graphical form, for example, a spreadsheet simulating the cash-flow of a business. The user can usually control the initial values of parameters in the model.

Summative evaluation
Contrasts with 'formative evaluation' (qv). Describes the evaluation of course materials that provides information on the success or otherwise of the implementation of those materials, possibly in comparison with alternative teaching methods.

Supplantation
Coined by Salomon to describe the way a medium, particularly television, can use special techniques to do certain kinds of cognitive processing for the viewer, for example, a zoom to 'supplant' selective attention to part of a scene.

Synchronous
Contrasts with 'asynchronous' (qv) to mean 'at the same time'; applied to forms of communication where interlocutors are both present at the same time, such as the telephone.

Teachback
Coined by Pask to describe the teaching technique where students 'teach back' to the teacher what they have just learned. Also used by the author as an interviewing technique.

Teleconferencing
Any form of interactive person(s)-to-person(s) communciation at a distance, from the Greek *tele-*, meaning 'far off'.

Tutorial program
A computer program that presents information, sets exercises for the student, accepts answers in some specified format, and gives feedback on those answers.

Tutoring system
Performs the same tasks as a tutorial program but in a different way: generating the information from a database, generating exercises from rules using information already collected about the student, and generating feedback from both the database and the student record.

References

Anderson, J.R. (1981) 'Tuning of search of the problem space for geometry', Proceedings of the Seventh International Joint Conference on Artificial Intelligence, 165–70, Vancouver, Canada: University of British Columbia.

Barnett, R. (1990) *The Idea of Higher Education*, Milton Keynes, Open University Press.

Barnett, R. (1992) *Improving Higher Education: Total Quality Care*, Milton Keynes, Open University Press.

Bates, A. (1991) 'Third generation distance education: The challenge of new technology', *Research in Distance Education*, 3 (2) 10–15.

Beaty, E., Dall'Alba, G., and Marton, F. (in press) 'Conceptions of learning', *International Journal of Educational Research*.

Becker, W., Highsmith, R., Kennedy, P., and Walstad, W. (1991) 'An agenda for research on economic education in colleges and universities', *Journal of Economic Education*, 22 (3) 241–50.

Bollom, C.E., Emerson, P.A., Fleming, P.R., and Williams, A.R. (1989) 'The Charing Cross and Westminster Interactive Television Network', *Journal of Educational Television*, 15 (1) 5–15.

Bowden, J., Dall'Alba, G., Martin, E., Laurillard, D., Marton, F., Masters, G., Ramsden, P., Stephanou, A., and Walsh, E. (1992) 'Displacement, velocity and frames of reference: Phenomenographic studies of students' understanding and some implications for teaching and asessment', *American Journal of Physics*, 60 (3) 262–9.

Brna, P. (1989) 'Programmed rockets: an analysis of students' strategies', *British Journal of Educational Technology*, 20 (1) 27–40.

Brown, G. and Atkins, M. (1991) *Effective Teaching in Higher Education*, London: Routledge.

Brown, J.S., Collins, A., and Duguid, P. (1989a) 'Situated cognition and the culture of learning', *Educational Researcher*, 18 (1) 32–42.

Brown, J.S., Collins, A., and Duguid, P. (1989b) 'Debating the situation: A rejoinder to Palincsar and Wineburg', *Educational Researcher*, 18 (4) 10–12.

Brown, J.S. and Van Lehn, K. (1980) 'Repair theory: A generative theory of bugs in procedural skills', *Cognitive Science*, 4 379–426.

Brumby, M. (1984) 'Misconceptions about the concept of natural selection by medical biology students', *Science Education, 68* (4) 493–503.

Champagne, A.B., Klopfer L.E., and Gunstone, R.F. (1982) 'Cognitive research and the design of science instruction', *Educational Psychology, 17* (1) 31–53.

Clark David, R. (1991) 'The demise of multimedia', *Computers and Graphics* July 1991, 75–80.

Crane, G. (1991) 'Hypermedia and the study of ancient culture', *Computers and Graphics, 11* (4) 45–51.

Dahlgren, L.O. and Marton, F. (1978) 'Students' conceptions of subject matter: an aspect of learning and teaching in higher education', *Studies in Higher Education, 3* (1) 25–35.

Daniel, J.S. (1991) 'The international role of the Open University', *Reflections on Higher Education, 3* 15–25.

Davies, M.M. (1989) 'Why can people jump higher on the moon? A study of what children learn from *Corners*, a children's TV programme', *Journal of Educational Television, 15* (1) 25–36.

Durbridge, N. (1984a) 'Using audio-vision to teach mathematics', in E. Henderson and M. Nathenson (eds) *Independent Learning in Higher Education*, Educational Technology Publications, Englewood Cliffs, New Jersey.

Durbridge, N. (1984b) 'Developing the use of video cassettes in the Open University', in O. Zuber-Skerritt (ed.) *Video in Higher Education*, London: Kogan Page.

Elton, L. and Middlehurst, R. (1992) 'Leadership and management in higher education', *Studies in Higher Education, 17* (3) 251–64.

Entwistle, N.J. (1981) *Styles of Learning and Teaching: An Integrated Outline of Educational Psychology*, Chichester: John Wiley.

Entwistle, N.J. and Ramsden, P. (1983) *Understanding Student Learning*, London: Croom Helm.

Eysenck, M.W. and Warren Piper, D. (1987) 'A word is worth a thousand pictures', in, J.T.E. Richardson, M.W. Eysenck, and D. Warren Piper (eds) *Student Learning: Research in Education and Cognitive Psychology*, Milton Keynes: SRHE and Open University Press.

Gagné, R.M. (1977) *The Conditions of Learning*, New York: Holt Rhinehart and Winston.

Gagné, R.M. and Merrill, M.D. (1990) 'Integrative goals for instructional design', *Educational Technology Research and Development, 38* (1) 23–30.

Glaser, R. (ed.) (1987) *Advances in Instructional Psychology Volume 3*, Hillsdale NJ: Lawrence Erlbaum Associates.

Golden, A. (1990) 'The effects of quality and clarity on the recall of photographic illustrations', *British Journal of Educational Technology, 21* (1) 21–30.

Golluscio, R.A., Paruelo, J.M., and Aguiar, M.R. (1990) 'Simulation models for educational purposes: An example of the coexistence of plant populations', *Journal of Biological Education, 24* (2) 81–6.

Hague, Sir Douglas (1991) *Beyond Universities. A New Republic of the Intellect*, Hobart Paper, Institute of Economic Affairs, 2 Lord North Street, London SW1P 3LB.

Hamilton, W. (1951) *Plato: The Symposium*, translated by W. Hamilton, London: Penguin.

Hartley, J.R. (1973) 'The design and evaluation of an adaptive teaching system', *International Journal of Man–Machine Studies, 5* (3) 421–36.

Hawkridge, D. (1993) *Challenging Educational Technology*, London: Athlone Press.

Hodgson, V. (1984) 'Learning from lectures', in F. Marton, D.J. Hounsell, and N.J. Entwistle (eds) *The Experience of Learning*, Edinburgh: Scottish Academic Press.

Holland, S. (1987) 'New cognitive theories of harmony applied to direct manipulation tools for novices', CITE Technical Report No. 17, IET, Open University, Milton Keynes MK7 6AA.

Hoyles, C., Healy, L., and Sutherland, R. (1991) 'Patterns of discussion between pupil pairs in computer and non-computer environments', *Journal of Computer Assisted Learning, 7* 210–28.

Jonassen, D. (1991) 'Hypertext as instructional design', *Educational Technology Research and Development, 39* (1) 83–92.

Kaye, A. (1991) 'Computer networking for development of distance education courses', CITE Technical Report No. 146, IET, Open University, MK7 6AA.

Kaye, A., Mason, R., and Harasim, L. (1989) 'Computer conferencing in the academic environment', CITE Report No. 91, IET, Open University, MK7 6AA.

Kelley, P., Gunter, B., and Buckle, L. (1987) ' "Reading" television in the classroom: More results from the television literacy project', *Journal of Educational Television, 13* (1) 7–19.

Laurillard, D. (1978) 'Evolution and evaluation', in J. McKenzie, L. Elton, and R. Lewis (eds) *Interactive Computer Graphics in Science Teaching*, Chichester: Ellis Horwood.

Laurillard, Diana (1979) 'The processes of student learning', *Higher Education, 8* 395–409.

Laurillard, D.M. (1982) 'D102 Audio-visual media evaluation: Interim Report Blocks 2 and 3', IET, Open University, Milton Keynes MK7 6AA.

Laurillard, D.M. (1984a) 'Interactive video and the control of learning', *Educational Technology, 24* (6) 7–15.

Laurillard, D.M. (1984b) 'Learning from problem-solving', in F. Marton, D.J. Hounsell, and N.J. Entwistle (eds) *The Experience of Learning*, Edinburgh: Scottish Academic Press.

Laurillard, D.M. (1987a) 'The different forms of learning in psychology and education', in J.T.E. Richardson, M.W. Eysenck, and D. Warren Piper (eds) *Student Learning: Research in Education and Cognitive Psychology*, Milton Keynes: SRHE and Open University Press.

Laurillard, D. (1987b) 'Evaluation report on the CADED project', Queen Mary and Westfield College, Mile End Road, London E1 4NS, UK.

Laurillard, Diana (1991) 'Mediating the message: television programme design and students' understanding', *Instructional Science, 20* 3–23.

Laurillard, Diana (1992a) 'Phenomenographic research and the design of diagnostic strategies for adaptive tutoring systems', in M. Jones and

P. Winne (eds) *Adaptive Learning Environments*, Berlin: Springer-Verlag.

Laurillard, D. (1992b) 'Closing the feedback loop', PLUM Report No. 22, IET, Open University, Milton Keynes, MK7 6AA.

Laurillard, D., Lindström, B., Marton, F., and Ottosson, T. (1991) 'Computer simulation as a tool for developing intuitive and conceptual understanding', Report No. 1991:03, Department of Education and Educational Research, University of Göteborg, ISSN 0282-2156.

Laurillard, D., Swift, B., and Darby, J. (1993) 'Academics' use of courseware materials: A survey', *Association of Learning Technology Journal, 1* (1), University of Wales Press.

Lockwood, F. (1992) *Activities in Self-Instructional Texts*, London: Kogan Page.

Lybeck, L., Marton, F., Strömdahl, H., and Tullberg, A. (1988) 'The phenomenography of the "mole concept" in chemistry', in P. Ramsden (ed.) *Improving Learning: New Perspectives*, London: Kogan Page.

McConnell, D. and Sharples, M. (1983) 'Distance teaching by Cyclops: an educational evaluation of the OU's telewriting system', *British Journal of Educational Technology, 14* (2) 109-26.

McDermott, L.C. (1991) 'Millikan Lecture 1990: What we teach and what is learned – Closing the gap', *American Journal of Physics, 59* (4) 301-15.

McMahon, H. (1990) 'Collaborating with computers', *Journal of Computer Assisted Learning, 6* 149-67.

Marton, F. (1981) 'Phenomenography – describing conceptions of the world around us', *Instructional Science, 10* 177-200.

Marton, F. (1988) 'Describing and improving learning', in, R.R. Schmeck, *Learning Strategies and Learning Styles*, New York: Plenum.

Marton, F., Hounsell, D.J., and Entwistle, N.J. (eds) (1984) *The Experience of Learning*, Edinburgh: Scottish Academic Press.

Marton F. and Ramsden, P. (1988) 'What does it take to improve learning?' in P. Ramsden (ed.) *Improving Learning: New Perspectives*, London: Kogan Page.

Marton, F. and Säljö, R. (1976a) 'On qualitative differences in learning I: Outcome and process', *British Journal of Educational Psychology, 46* 4-11.

Marton, F. and Säljö, R. (1976b) 'On qualitative differences in learning II: Outcome as a function of the learner's conception of the task', *British Journal of Educational Psychology, 46* 115-27.

Marton, F. and Wenestam, C.-G. (1979) 'Qualitative differences in the understanding and retention of the main point in some texts based on the principle–example structure', in M.M. Gruneberg, P.E. Morris, and R.N. Sykes (eds) *Practical Aspects of Memory*, London: Academic Press.

Moyse, R. (1991) 'Multiple viewpoints imply knowledge negotiation', *Interactive Learning International, 7* 21-37.

Moyse, R. (1992) 'A structure and design method for multiple viewpoints', *Journal of Artificial Intelligence in Education, 3* 207-33.

Neuman, D. (1987) 'The origin of arithmetic skills', *Göteborg Studies in Educational Sciences, 62*, University of Gothenburg.

OECD (1987) 'Universities under scrutiny', Office of Economic
  Co-operation and Development, Paris, ISBN 92–62–129227.
Ogborn, J. (1990) 'A future for modelling in science education', *Journal
  of Computer Assisted Learning*, 6 103–12.
Ohlsson, S. (1991) 'System hacking meets learning theory: Reflections on
  the goals and standards of research in artificial intelligence and
  education', *Journal of Artificial Intelligence in Education*, 2 (3) 5–18.
Panofsky, C.P., John-Steiner, V., and Blackwell, P.J. (1990) 'The
  development of scientific concepts and discourse', in Luis C Moll (ed.)
  *Vygotsky and Education: Instructional Implications and Applications of
  Sociohistorical Psychology*, Cambridge: Cambridge University Press.
Papert, S. (1980) *Mindstorms: Children, Computers, and Powerful Ideas*,
  Brighton, Sussex: Harvester Press.
Pask, G. (1976) 'Conversational techniques in the study and practice of
  education', *British Journal of Educational Psychology*, 46 12–25.
Perry, W.G. (1970) *Forms of Intellectual and Ethical Development in the College
  Years*, NY: Holt Rhinehart and Winston.
Perry, W.G. (1988) 'Different worlds in the same classroom', in P.
  Ramsden (ed.) *Improving Learning: New Perspectives*, London: Kogan
  Page.
Ramsden, Paul (1988) (ed.) *Improving Learning: New Perspectives*, London:
  Kogan Page.
Ramsden, Paul (1992) *Learning to Teach in Higher Education*, London:
  Routledge.
Ramsden, P., Marton, F., Laurillard, D.M., Martin, E., Masters, G.N.,
  Stephanou, A., and Walsh, E. (in press) 'Phenomenographic research
  and the measurement of understanding: An investigation of students'
  conceptions of speed, distance and time', *International Journal of
  Educational Research*.
Resnick, L. and Omanson, S. (1987) 'Learning to understand arithmetic',
  in R. Glaser (ed.) *Advances in Instructional Psychology Volume 3*, Hillsdale,
  NJ: Lawrence Erlbaum Associates.
Reusser, K. (1992) 'Tutoring systems and pedagogical theory:
  representational tools for understanding', planning, and reflection in
  problem-solving', in S. Lajoie and S. Derry (eds) *Computers as Cognitive
  Tools*, Hillsdale NJ: Lawrence Erlbaum.
Robbins, L. (1963) 'Higher Education: Report of the Committee', Cmnd
  2154, London: HMSO.
Romiszowski, A. (1988) *The Selection and Use of Instructional Media*, NY:
  Kogan Page.
Roschelle, J. and Behrend, S.D. (forthcoming) 'The construction of
  shared knowledge in collaborative problem solving', in C. O'Malley
  (ed.) *Computer Supported Collaborative Learning*, London: Paul
  Chapman Publishing Ltd.
Rothkopf, E.Z. (1970) 'The concept of mathemagenic activities', *Review of
  Educational Research*, 40 325–36.
Rowntree, D. (1992) *Exploring Open and Distance Learning*, London: Kogan
  Page.
Säljö, R. (1979) 'Learning in the learner's perspective: Some

common-sense conceptions', Internal Report, Department of Education, University of Göteborg No. 76.

Säljö, R. (1984) 'Learning from reading', in F. Marton, D.J. Hounsell, and N.J. Entwistle (eds) *The Experience of Learning*, Edinburgh: Scottish Academic Press.

Säljö, R. (1988) 'Learning in educational settings: Methods of enquiry', in P. Ramsden (ed.) *Improving Learning: New Perspectives*, London: Kogan Page.

Salomon, G. (1979) *Interaction of Media, Cognition and Learning*, San Francisco: Jossey-Bass.

Saunders, P. (1991) 'The third edition of the test of understanding in college economics', *Journal of Economic Education, 22* (3) 255–72.

Self, J. (1989) 'The case for formalising student models (and intelligent tutoring systems generally)', Paper at the 4th International Conference on AI in Education, Amsterdam.

Sellman, R. (1991) 'Hooks for tutorial agents: A note on the design of discovery learning environments', CITE Technical Report No. 145, IET, Open University, MK7 6AA.

Schneider, W. (1985) 'Training high performance skills', *Human Factors, 27* (3) 285–300.

Slack, S. and Stewart, J. (1989) 'Improving student problem solving in genetics', *Journal of Biological Education, 23* (4) 308–12.

Stevens, A., Collins A., and Goldin, S.E. (1979) 'Misconceptions in students' understanding', *International Journal of Man-Machine Studies, 11* 145–56.

Svensson, L. (1977) 'On qualitative differences in learning III: Study skill and learning', *British Journal of Educational Psychology, 47* 233–43.

Taylor, J., O'Shea, T., Scanlon, E., O'Malley, C., and Smith, R. (1991) 'Discourse and harmony: Preliminary findings in a case-study of multimedia collaborative problem solving', PLUM Paper No. 7, IET, Open University, Milton Keynes, MK7 6AA.

Vygotsky, L. (1962) *Thought and Language*, Cambridge, Mass: MIT Press.

Warren Piper, D. (1992) 'Are professors professional?' *Higher Education Quarterly, 46* (2) 145–56.

Wenger, E. (1987) *Artificial Intelligence and Tutoring Systems: Computational and Cognitive Approaches to the Communication of Knowledge*, Los Altos, California: Morgan Kaufman.

Wertsch, J.V., Minick, N., and Arns, F.J. (1984) 'The creation of context in joint problem-solving', in B. Rogoff and J. Lave (eds) *Everyday Cognition: Its Development in Social Context*, Cambridge, Mass: Harvard University Press.

Whalley, P. (in press) 'An alternative rhetoric for hypertext', in C. McKnight, A. Dillon, and J. Richardson (eds) *Hypertext: A Psychological Perspective*, Chichester: Ellis Horwood.

Whelan, G. (1988) 'Improving medical students' clinical problem-solving', in P. Ramsden (ed.) *Improving Learning: New Perspectives*, London: Kogan Page.

Index